Unity through Division

Indonesia, like many other countries around the world, is currently experiencing a process of democratic backsliding, marked by a toxic mix of religious sectarianism, polarization and executive overreach. Despite this trend, Indonesians have become more, rather than less, satisfied with their country's democratic practice. What accounts for this puzzle? *Unity through Division* examines an overlooked aspect of democracy in Indonesia: political representation. In this country, an ideological cleavage between pluralism and Islamism has long characterized political competition. This cleavage, while divisive, has been a strength of Indonesia's democracy, giving meaning to political participation and allowing a degree of representation not often observed in young democracies. While the recent resurgence of radical Islam and political polarization in Indonesian politics may have contributed to democratic erosion, these factors have simultaneously clarified political alternatives and improved perceptions of representation, in turn bolstering democratic participation and satisfaction. This compelling book effectively challenges the wisdom on the role of Islam in Indonesian political life and provides a fresh analysis for debates on democratic backsliding in Indonesia and beyond.

DIEGO FOSSATI is Assistant Professor in the Department of Public and International Affairs at City University of Hong Kong. He studies political behavior, accountability and representation, especially in the context of Southeast Asia.

Unity through Division

Political Islam, Representation and Democracy in Indonesia

DIEGO FOSSATI
City University of Hong Kong

Shaftesbury Road, Cambridge CB2 8EA, United Kingdom

One Liberty Plaza, 20th Floor, New York, NY 10006, USA

477 Williamstown Road, Port Melbourne, VIC 3207, Australia

314–321, 3rd Floor, Plot 3, Splendor Forum, Jasola District Centre, New Delhi – 110025, India

103 Penang Road, #05-06/07, Visioncrest Commercial, Singapore 238467

Cambridge University Press is part of Cambridge University Press & Assessment, a department of the University of Cambridge.

We share the University's mission to contribute to society through the pursuit of education, learning and research at the highest international levels of excellence.

www.cambridge.org
Information on this title: www.cambridge.org/9781009203036

DOI: 10.1017/9781009203074

© Diego Fossati 2022

This publication is in copyright. Subject to statutory exception and to the provisions of relevant collective licensing agreements, no reproduction of any part may take place without the written permission of Cambridge University Press & Assessment.

First published 2022

A catalogue record for this publication is available from the British Library

Library of Congress Cataloging-in-Publication Data
NAMES: Fossati, Diego, author.
TITLE: Unity through division : political Islam, representation and democracy in Indonesia / Diego Fossati.
DESCRIPTION: New York, NY : Cambridge University Press, 2022. | Includes bibliographical references and index.
IDENTIFIERS: LCCN 2022016956 (print) | LCCN 2022016957 (ebook) | ISBN 9781009203036 (hardback) | ISBN 9781009203067 (paperback) | ISBN 9781009203074 (epub)
SUBJECTS: LCSH: Political participation–Indonesia. | Representative government and representation–Indonesia. | Democracy–Indonesia. | Islam and politics–Indonesia. | Indonesia–Politics and government–21st century. | BISAC: POLITICAL SCIENCE / World / General
CLASSIFICATION: LCC JQ776 .F67 2022 (print) | LCC JQ776 (ebook) | DDC 320.9598–DC23/eng/20220511
LC record available at https://lccn.loc.gov/2022016956
LC ebook record available at https://lccn.loc.gov/2022016957

ISBN 978-1-009-20303-6   Hardback

Cambridge University Press & Assessment has no responsibility for the persistence or accuracy of URLs for external or third-party internet websites referred to in this publication and does not guarantee that any content on such websites is, or will remain, accurate or appropriate.

A Rita

Contents

List of Figures		*page* xi
List of Tables		xiii
Acknowledgments		xv
1	Introduction	1
	1.1 Puzzle	1
	1.2 Argument	4
	1.3 Contribution	10
	1.4 Method	13
	1.5 Structure of the Book	15
2	Explaining Democratic Survival in Indonesia	19
	2.1 An Unlikely Democracy	19
	2.2 Ordinary People and Democracy: An Analytical Framework	23
	2.2.1 Evaluating Democratic Performance	24
	2.2.2 Representation, Participation and Legitimacy	27
	2.2.3 Representation, Polarization and Populism	31
	2.3 Representation and Participation in Indonesian Politics	33
	2.3.1 An Ideological Cleavage about Islam	33
	2.3.2 Formal and Informal Participation	37
	2.4 Conclusion	42
3	The Ideological Roots of Electoral Politics	43
	3.1 A Clientelistic Democracy?	43
	3.2 District-Level Analysis	45
	3.2.1 Data and Measures	47
	3.2.2 Electoral Geography	50
	3.3 Examining Macro-Level Electoral Patterns	54
	3.3.1 Dealignment or a Resurgence of Ideology?	55

viii   *Contents*

	3.3.2 Regional Variation and Clientelism	63
	3.3.3 Resurgent Islamism and Electoral Participation	67
	3.4 Conclusion	72
4	**Political Elites and Ideological Competition**	**73**
	4.1 Ideological Competition in Young Democracies	73
	4.2 Surveying Elites	75
	4.2.1 Indonesia's Political Elites at a Glance	77
	4.3 Policy Attitudes of Indonesian Politicians	79
	4.3.1 Measuring Political Islam	79
	4.3.2 The Economic Dimension	83
	4.4 Islam and Other Attitudes	86
	4.4.1 Anti-Chinese Prejudice	86
	4.4.2 Democracy	89
	4.5 Political Parties	93
	4.5.1 How Much Do Political Parties Differ from Each Other?	93
	4.5.2 Party Positions	96
	4.6 Conclusion	103
5	**Public Opinion on Political Islam**	**104**
	5.1 Studying Political Islam in Mass Attitudes	104
	5.2 A Deep-Rooted Cleavage	107
	5.2.1 A Profile of Political Islam in Indonesia	107
	5.2.2 Political Participation	110
	5.2.3 Party Choice	113
	5.3 Islam and National Identity	117
	5.3.1 Political Islam and the Structure of Indonesian National Identity	118
	5.4 Political Islam and Political Preferences	122
	5.4.1 Democracy	122
	5.4.2 Populism	124
	5.4.3 Economic Issues	128
	5.4.4 Decentralization	132
	5.5 Conclusion	134
6	**Ideological Representation**	**135**
	6.1 Studying Substantive Representation	135
	6.2 Ideological Congruence in Indonesia	137
	6.2.1 Political Islam	138
	6.2.2 Economic Issues	140
	6.2.3 Inequalities of Representation	142
	6.3 Political Parties and Representation	146
	6.3.1 Party–Voter Ideological Linkages	146
	6.3.2 Variation in Representation across Parties	150
	6.3.3 Ideological Linkages and Clientelism	153

Contents ix

6.4 Ideological Representation and Partisanship: An Experiment 154
    6.4.1 Experimental Design 155
    6.4.2 Data 157
    6.4.3 The Effect of Elite Cues on Preferences Regarding
        Political Islam 159
6.5 Conclusion 163

7 Meaning and Evaluation of Democracy 165
7.1 Democratic Attitudes in Indonesia 165
    7.1.1 The Meaning of Democracy: Measures and Data 169
    7.1.2 The Structure of Public Conceptions of Democracy 174
7.2 Political Islam and Conceptions of Democracy 176
7.3 The Meaning of Democracy and Evaluations of
    Democratic Performance 181
7.4 Conclusion 185

8 Conclusions 187
8.1 A Resilient Democracy 187
8.2 Indonesia: A Democracy in Decline? 190
    8.2.1 Representation and Participation 191
    8.2.2 Accountability 195
8.3 Practical Implications 199

References 203
Index 219

Figures

1.1	Public satisfaction with democracy in Indonesia, 2004–2020	*page* 2
1.2	Perceptions of representation and satisfaction with democracy	7
2.1	Electoral turnout in Indonesia, 1955–2019	41
3.1	Map of electoral support for the PNI (1955) by district	51
3.2	Map of electoral support for NU (1955) by district	51
3.3	Map of electoral support for Masyumi (1955) by district	52
3.4	Historical and contemporary electoral returns in 1999 and 2019	57
3.5	Estimated effects of historical electoral returns on contemporary elections, 1999–2019	58
3.6	Religious fractionalization and support for pluralist, traditional Islamic and modernist Islamic parties	60
3.7	Marginal effects of historical electoral returns by ethnolinguistic fractionalization	67
3.8	Differences in electoral turnout, 2014–2019	69
4.1	Elite survey respondents by political party	78
4.2	Ideological groups among Indonesia's political elite	81
4.3	Ideological profile of Islamic organizations	82
4.4	Economic policy preferences of Indonesia's political elite	84
4.5	Policy priorities of Indonesia's political elite	85
4.6	Political Islam and support for liberalism among Indonesia's political elite	92
4.7	Voter party choice as seen by Indonesian politicians	96
4.8	Party ideology: A smaller or larger role for Islam in politics?	101
4.9	Party ideology and internal ideological cohesion	102

List of Figures

5.1	Ideology groups in the Indonesian electorate	107
5.2	Political and civic engagement by different ideological groups	113
5.3	Estimated probability of informal participation by ideological group	114
5.4	Ideological groups and party choice	115
5.5	Ethnic understandings of national identity for two ideological groups	120
5.6	Political Islam and attachment to national identity	121
5.7	Preference for a "strong leader" by ideological group	123
5.8	Populism and pride in Indonesia's achievements	127
5.9	Policy priorities among three ideological groups	130
5.10	Political Islam and support for redistribution	131
5.11	Support for and satisfaction with regional autonomy by ideological group	133
6.1	PII distributions for politicians and voters	139
6.2	Distribution of economic policy preferences of politicians and voters	141
6.3	(a) Politicians' and (b) voters' preferences regarding political Islam and economic redistribution	143
6.4	Ideological overlap between politicians and voters by (a) education and (b) income quintile	145
6.5	Average PII values of politicians and voters by party	147
6.6	PII distributions for voters and legislators of nine parties	148
6.7	Politicians' and voters' average support for redistribution by party	149
6.8	Party features and ideological distance between politicians and voters	152
6.9	Average treatment effects for party and leader cues	160
6.10	Estimated support for Islamic bylaws by experimental treatment group	162
7.1	Predicted probability of satisfaction with and support for democracy by conception of democracy	185

Tables

3.1	Ideological groups and political parties: Past and present	*page* 49
3.2	Correlation coefficients for three ideological streams	53
3.3	Historical and contemporary district-level electoral outcomes for three ideological groups	56
3.4	Determinants of electoral support for Gerindra, 2019	62
3.5	Historical partisan legacies and ethnolinguistic fractionalization for three ideological groups	66
3.6	Support for ideology-based parties and electoral turnout	70
4.1	Views on political Islam among Indonesia's political elite	80
4.2	Support for stereotypes about Chinese Indonesians among politicians	88
4.3	Support for liberal principles among Indonesian politicians	91
4.4	Factor analysis of self-assessed party positions	98
4.5	Party positions: Measurements and descriptive statistics	100
5.1	Political Islam and sociodemographic factors among Indonesian Muslims	109
5.2	Factor analysis of dimensions of national identity in Indonesia	119
5.3	Measurement scale for populist attitudes	125
6.1	Correlation coefficients between centrism on political Islam and party features	151
6.2	Support for religious bylaws across partisan groups	158
7.1	Five dimensions of democracy: Measurement and structure	171
7.2	Determinants of conceptions of democracy	178
7.3	Conceptions of democracy, evaluations of democratic performance and support for democracy	183

Acknowledgments

This book is the product of several years of research on Indonesian politics, and I have many to thank for their support. I owe my first debt of gratitude to the Department of Government at Cornell University, whose nurturing and supportive environment enabled me to develop as a scholar with a strong egalitarian ethos and a drive to produce meaningful social research. I am especially thankful to my advisor, Tom Pepinsky, for teaching me how to write and for his years of guidance and patience with my unsophisticated ideas. Ken Roberts and Nicolas Van de Walle were also exceptionally supportive and helpful, ensuring that I had the best possible experience as a graduate student. I feel immensely privileged to have been part of this community.

I started working on this book at the ISEAS–Yusof Ishak Institute in Singapore, where I was appointed as a visiting fellow shortly after graduating from Cornell. I am deeply grateful to ISEAS for generously funding the Indonesian National Survey Project and for trusting a young scholar like me to supervise the project's implementation. It was a pleasure to work alongside my colleagues in the Indonesia Study Group, especially Hui Yew-Foong and Siwage Dharma Negara, in designing the survey and drafting a report of its findings.

After leaving ISEAS, I found another welcoming community at the Centre for Governance and Public Policy (CGPP) at Griffith University, which provided crucial support for a number of survey projects, on which part of this book is based. At the CGPP, I was able to rely on a strong research culture and support from an outstanding group of like-minded colleagues, which made my time there a rewarding intellectual experience. Ferran Martinez i Coma, Duncan McDonnell, Lee Morgenbesser and

Annika Werner provided insightful guidance for my early analysis of substantive representation in Indonesia. My supervisor, Haig Patapan, gently but persistently encouraged me to write a book based on my research, something I wasn't sure I could ever accomplish.

During my time in Australia, I also had an opportunity to network and work with some exceptional scholars of Indonesian politics. Collaborating with Edward Aspinall, Marcus Mietzner, Burhan Muhtadi and Eve Warburton helped me develop a new research agenda based on political Islam and voting behavior. I am especially thankful to Eve for reading the introductory chapter of what would have otherwise been a very different book and for letting me know that it was terrible, and to Ed, without whose generosity this book would not exist.

I wrote the book while serving as an assistant professor in the Department of Asian and International Studies (AIS) at City University of Hong Kong. These last few years have been challenging for all, but I found that my department was the perfect place to write this book, thanks to colleagues and friends such as Toby Carroll, Renaud Egreteau, Claudia Kim, Dan Lynch, Tom Patton, Jaemin Shim, Mark Thompson, Linda Tjia, Brad Williams and Jun Zhang. This project was also supported by Hong Kong's University Grant Committee's Early Career Scheme (ECS) grant 21603520. I am grateful to Jenika Huang for her research assistance, which was funded by this ECS grant.

At Cambridge University Press, Sara Doskow recognized the potential of my project, and John Haslam, Rachel Blaifeder and Jadyn Fauconier-Herry helped to ensure its smooth implementation. I am very grateful to each of them. In addition, feedback from two anonymous reviewers was instrumental in improving my book.

It is difficult to overstate the importance of the support that I received from my family while completing this project and throughout my academic career. I am most grateful to my wife, Junxiu, for filling my life with endless love and joy. She gave me the focus I needed to write this book, and her support and grace kept me motivated and sane during difficult times.

Lastly, I owe a long-standing debt of gratitude to Rita, Mariantonia and Eugenia, the women who raised me. They made sacrifices to enable me to grow and thrive, and it is only thanks to their support that I have been able to fulfill my professional aspirations. Above all, I am grateful to my mother, who taught me the value of education, the nobility of persevering despite adversity and the importance of being honest and kind. This book is for her.

I

Introduction

1.1 PUZZLE

Democracy is in decline in Indonesia. After the breakdown of authoritarianism in the late 1990s, this large and diverse country defied expectations by establishing democratic institutions and implementing several waves of free and fair national and local elections. For many years, Indonesia was hailed as a model for other young democracies, and its politics were praised for their stability, inclusiveness and ideological moderation. Recently, however, Indonesia's democratic trajectory has taken a darker turn, marked by a toxic mix of rising illiberalism, creeping polarization and executive overreach. Given this trend, which is widely acknowledged by observers of Indonesian politics, it would be reasonable to assume that ordinary Indonesians have become increasingly disillusioned with the country's democratic institutions. In theory, as the limitations of Indonesia's democracy become clearer, public dissatisfaction with democracy should increase.

However, public opinion data present a sharply contrasting picture. As shown in Figure 1.1, satisfaction with democracy in Indonesia has oscillated substantially among the Indonesian public since the mid-2000s, when the country's second democratic election was held and Indonesia completed its transition to democracy.[1] Crucially, the recent erosion of democracy has not been accompanied by a rise in public dissatisfaction with democracy. On the contrary, Indonesians have become more

---

[1] These data are from surveys implemented by Lembaga Survei Indonesia. I am grateful to Burhan Muhtadi for graciously sharing these data.

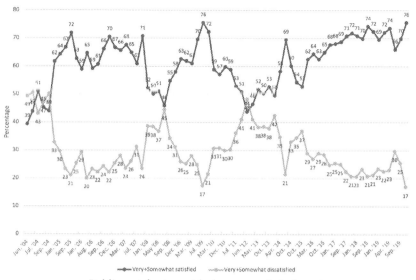

FIGURE 1.1. Public satisfaction with democracy in Indonesia, 2004–2020

satisfied with how democracy is practiced in their country, to the extent that in February 2020, satisfaction with democracy reached an all-time high of about 76%, with only 17% of the Indonesian public expressing dissatisfaction with democracy. Interestingly, this strong trend appears to have started in the mid-2010s, at about the same time that observers of Indonesian politics began to argue that the country's democracy was deteriorating.

This intriguing pattern points to substantial dissonance between experts and the public in evaluations of democratic performance in Indonesia. For example, while political scientists consider Indonesia's democracy to have been largely stable from its establishment to the mid-2010s (Aspinall, Mietzner and Tomsa 2015), in the eyes of ordinary Indonesians, its performance varied greatly during that period. Most importantly, the Indonesian public appears to be far less troubled by the recent erosion of Indonesia's democracy than are scholars of Indonesian politics.

This puzzle is not readily explained by either of the two prevailing approaches to analyzing democratic attitudes. The first approach is rooted in studies of political culture, which show that public understanding of democracy varies substantially by country and region (Dalton, Sin and Jou 2007; Norris 2011). From this perspective, it may simply be that political scholars' concerns about rising illiberalism in Indonesia do not resonate much with large segments of the Indonesian electorate. In Indonesia, as in many other Asian countries, liberal values are poorly consolidated in public opinion, because many people understand democracy in terms of policy outcomes rather than adherence to democratic principles (Aspinall et al. 2020). Consequently, the public may not perceive declining levels of liberalism as a reason for dissatisfaction with democratic governance. However, this explanation overlooks the fact that Indonesians are indeed aware of and concerned about democratic backsliding in their country. In a public opinion poll conducted in 2019, for example, a record number of Indonesian citizens reported being worried about discussing political issues in public, joining social organizations and practicing their religion freely; they even expressed fear of being arrested arbitrarily (Mujani and Liddle 2021, 77). While liberal values in Indonesia may be less consolidated than those in other political cultures, Indonesians are cognizant of democratic backsliding and anxious about its implications for civil freedoms.

The second approach to analyzing democratic attitudes views satisfaction with democracy, as with other political regimes, as resulting from evaluations of government performance (Gilley 2006; Ferrín and Kriesi 2016; Magalhães 2016). From this perspective, support for and satisfaction with democracy are tied to a democracy's ability to provide desirable public goods such as economic growth, security and broad-based social services. In addition, procedural issues related to democratic governance, such as curbing corruption and ensuring fairness and the rule of law, may play a crucial role in ensuring democratic legitimacy and support for democratic institutions. From this perspective, we should not expect to observe dramatic changes in public satisfaction with Indonesia's democracy over the last several years. Although Indonesia has made progress in reducing economic inequality, its economic performance, as captured by macroeconomic indicators such as growth, unemployment, inflation and exchange rates, has generally remained stable. Furthermore, the unpopular and controversial reform of Indonesia's anti-corruption agency, implemented in 2019, has been seen as a setback in the country's fight against notoriously widespread corruption. The trends displayed in Figure 1.1 thus reveal an interesting and as yet unaccounted for empirical anomaly.

In the Indonesian case and beyond, as I discuss later, focusing on mass democratic attitudes is a fruitful and valuable analytical approach, given the trend of democratic backsliding observed in many countries (Bermeo 2016; Mechkova, Lührmann and Lindberg 2017). While democratic regimes are characterized by checks and balances, the degree to which institutional boundaries and limitations are respected ultimately depends on the existence of entrenched social norms (Levitsky and Ziblatt 2018). In the absence of voters who are willing to sanction incumbent politicians who engage in antidemocratic behavior, democratically elected politicians may gradually hollow out democratic institutions. Successful democracies therefore require engaged publics that are willing to defend democratic principles and institutions from the authoritarian ambitions of incumbent politicians. When ordinary citizens do not value democracy as a form of governance or when they are dissatisfied with how democracy is practiced in their country, they may be more receptive to authoritarian messages that undermine the legitimacy of democratic institutions. Understanding the drivers of public satisfaction or dissatisfaction with democracy is thus vital for research on democracy.

1.2 ARGUMENT

Why have Indonesians become increasingly satisfied with democracy despite their country's democratic decline in recent years? I answer this question by focusing on an overlooked aspect of democratic practice in Indonesia, namely political representation.

Although democracy in Indonesia has in many respects fallen short of expectations, the deep-rooted ideological division regarding the role of Islam in politics has provided Indonesian citizens with meaningful political choices, pitting pluralist understandings of society and politics against more exclusionary Islamist ideologies. This has given significance to political participation and allowed a degree of ideological representation that is not often observed in young democracies. Indonesians may be unhappy about some of Indonesia's democratic institutions and the slow pace of political reform, but they may still value their democracy's ability to provide political goods such as meaningful representation and avenues for participation. Studying democratic attitudes through this framework enables us to account for the puzzle presented above.

The recent trends of increasing polarization and Islamism may well be injurious to democracy in Indonesia, but in terms of their implications for political representation, they may help to explain why Indonesians have recently become more satisfied with the country's democracy. First, increasing partisan polarization may have further consolidated ideological division over the role of Islam in politics in the minds of the Indonesian public, thereby clarifying political alternatives and strengthening partisan

1.2 *Argument*

affiliations. Second, the increasing influence of radical Islam may have bolstered perceptions of fair representation, especially among Islamist Indonesians, a conspicuous minority in the electorate who have long been underrepresented in political institutions. Aggregate levels of public satisfaction with democracy may thus have risen because of the very developments that have prompted fears about democratic decline.

Individuals and countries may differ substantially in their attachment to democratic values and satisfaction with democracy, yet a recurring assumption in the literature, following seminal work by Easton (1975), is that a political regime must deliver valuable policy outcomes to be perceived as legitimate by the public. As mentioned above, several studies find that support for democracy is related to macroeconomic performance, whereas others focus on how the provision of public goods such as public safety and bureaucratic efficiency strengthens support for democracy. Certainly, the ability of a political regime to deliver such desirable outcomes is not the sole determinant of the degree of support that the regime enjoys from its citizens, as the perceived legitimacy of political regimes may also be rooted in ideological and historical factors. Yet empirical research indicates that a regime's performance, broadly understood as its ability to provide a wide range of public goods, is crucial to determining whether citizens support its principles and institutions (Gilley 2006). Democracies need to "deliver"; otherwise, public disaffection may jeopardize their legitimacy. Indeed, a lack of public support may threaten a democracy's very survival (Claassen 2020).

This insight is not lost on experts of Indonesian politics. In a recent monograph, three leading scholars of voting behavior in Indonesia argue that Indonesian voters can be described as "critical democrats" (Mujani, Liddle and Ambardi 2018): While they are overwhelmingly supportive of democracy as a system of governance, this support is not unconditional.[2] Instead, as these scholars show empirically, Indonesians' support for democracy is shaped by their evaluation of democratic performance, which in turn "is apparently strongly influenced by the degree to which the citizen evaluates governmental performance in overcoming major problems confronted by the society, particularly involving the economy, corruption, security and order" (p. 18). In Indonesia, as elsewhere, democracy is therefore a garden that requires tending. Public support for and satisfaction with democracy are strengthened when democracy performs

---

[2] See also Mujani and Liddle (2015).

well in key governance areas, and they are eroded when policy outcomes fall short of expectations.

These explanations help to contextualize the Indonesian case, as they reveal a link between government performance and democratic support that political scientists have observed in other countries. However, the literature on public opinion and voting behavior in Indonesia suffers from a major deficiency in its treatment of democratic attitudes: It overlooks the fact that citizens may have different expectations of democracy. As democracy is a complex, multidimensional construct (Lindberg et al. 2014), citizens may have different yet overlapping interpretations of what democracy means. These different interpretations may generate different expectations of democratic governance, such that citizens judge democratic performance by different standards. More broadly, whereas some citizens may evaluate democracy in terms of the "outputs" that the government produces, such as economic performance, others may focus more on "inputs," specifically a democracy's ability to provide avenues for meaningful representation and participation (Norris 1999; Dahlberg, Linde and Holmberg 2015). However, research on public opinion in Indonesia focuses on government outputs, leaving the equally important dimension of democratic inputs largely unexplored.

The argument that intangible democratic qualities such as opportunities for representation and participation are crucial to evaluations of democratic performance is controversial in the Indonesian context. Although Indonesia is widely considered an electoral democracy, prevailing approaches to the study of Indonesian politics do not paint a flattering picture of the status of substantive representation in this country. Some scholars argue that clientelistic factors, not programmatic ones, shape citizen–politician linkages (Aspinall and Berenschot 2019). Others emphasize that Indonesia's political parties all have the same economic policy platforms, which are designed to protect and consolidate the interests of predatory elites (Robison and Hadiz 2017). Still others note that political parties collude in large, heterogeneous coalitions that compromise accountability (Slater 2018). Research on voting behavior has long contended that evaluations of economic performance and candidate traits trump ideological considerations (Mujani, Liddle and Ambardi 2018). Given such negative assessments of the status of political representation in Indonesia, it is perhaps no surprise that substantive representation, understood as ideological congruence between citizens and their representatives, is not systematically studied in the Indonesian context.

1.2 Argument

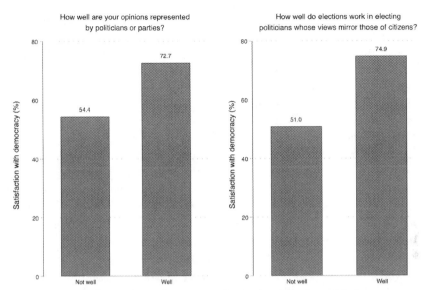

FIGURE 1.2. Perceptions of representation and satisfaction with democracy

Yet perceptions of representation matter for satisfaction with democracy in Indonesia. Consider, for instance, the data reported in Figure 1.2, which shows the association between evaluations of representation and satisfaction with democracy in Indonesia based on a nationally representative survey conducted in August 2020.[3] The survey asked two questions that are commonly found in public opinion and elite surveys of attitudes toward representation:[4]

1. In general, how well do you think your opinions are represented by Indonesian politicians and political parties? (Very well, quite well, not very well or not well at all)
2. In your view, focusing on Indonesia's current electoral system, how well do elections work in appointing members of parliament whose views mirror what voters want? (Very well, quite well, not very well or not well at all)

Figure 1.2 shows a strong association between the answers to each of these questions and satisfaction with democracy. Specifically, satisfaction

---

[3] This was a telephone survey conducted by Lembaga Survei Indonesia with a sample of 1,220 participants. The respondents were drawn at random from a list of about 207,000 individuals who had previously participated in face-to-face surveys conducted by the polling institute between March 2018 and March 2020.
[4] See, for instance, Dahlberg, Linde and Holmberg (2015).

with democracy was 18.3% higher among respondents who felt that their opinions were well or very well represented by politicians and 23.9% higher among respondents who felt that Indonesia's elections work well or very well (versus not very well or not well at all) in selecting a political class whose views are congruent with those of the citizens. These results from Indonesian public opinion echo findings of comparative research demonstrating that substantive representation and evaluations of democratic performance are closely intertwined (Reher 2015; Stecker and Tausendpfund 2016).

Popular views of representation are therefore consequential, and their omission from public opinion research hinders the study of democracy in contemporary Indonesia in three ways. First, our understanding of the relationship between democratic performance and satisfaction with – or support for – democracy among ordinary Indonesians is incomplete. When we focus primarily on the quality of governance in our analyses of satisfaction with democracy, we neglect the fact that a substantial proportion of the public may evaluate democracy according to other benchmarks, as they may hold alternative or more complex understandings of what a democracy is supposed to deliver. This perspective is explored in multiple comparative studies in other contexts (Canache, Mondak and Seligson 2001; Norris 2011; Dahlberg, Linde and Holmberg 2015) but overlooked in the literature on Indonesian politics. As a result, our ability to accurately identify public expectations of and pockets of discontent with democratic performance that may lead to questioning regarding the legitimacy of democratic institutions is limited. Studying substantive representation is therefore essential to explore the various paths that connect evaluations of democratic performance to public support for democracy and, ultimately, to democratic durability.

Second, this theoretical omission limits our ability to account for major political developments in contemporary Indonesia. The seemingly anomalous trends presented in Figure 1.1 offer a case in point. Indonesians' increasing satisfaction with democracy is difficult to explain for experts who see democracy from a liberal perspective, as Indonesian politics have become less rather than more liberal in recent years. It is equally problematic to see this surge in satisfaction as a result of improved economic–bureaucratic performance, as Indonesia has recently experienced only stable macroeconomic growth and has made no discernible progress in its fight against corruption. More broadly, a focus on economic performance is a blunt analytical tool in an era of increasing polarization and the resurgence of more radical forms of political Islam. By expanding our

1.2 *Argument*

conceptualization of democracy, we can develop new explanations for these apparent anomalies.

Finally, by failing to acknowledge the complexity of the public's conceptions and expectations of democracy, we overlook an important dimension of democratic practice in Indonesia, namely that this country displays exceptionally high levels of civic and political engagement. Associational life in Indonesia is among the most vibrant in the world, thanks to a historical legacy of mutual help associations, charities, religious organizations and cooperatives, and electoral participation is similarly very high. However, although some scholars acknowledge the benefits of civic engagement in the Indonesian context (Lussier and Fish 2012), the implications of participatory politics for voting behavior and public opinion remain largely unexplored. By studying representation and participation more comprehensively, we can uncover whether and to what extent Indonesians understand democracy as being about inputs as well as outputs, and we can investigate how participatory conceptions of democracy in Indonesia are associated with support for and satisfaction with democracy. Doing so may provide new insight into an important strength of Indonesian democracy.

In this book, I build on theoretical and empirical research that conceptualizes representation as an essential feature of democratic politics (Pitkin 1967). As mentioned earlier, by "representation" I primarily mean substantive representation, which, following most empirical research on the subject, I understand as congruence in opinions between citizens and politicians (Dalton 1985; Powell 2004; Luna and Zechmeister 2005; Costello, Thomassen, and Rosema 2012). I first argue that Indonesia has performed well in this domain relative to other countries. Since the first democratic elections after the New Order in 1999, Indonesian democracy has offered something to ordinary citizens that many other fledgling democracies have not, as a deep-rooted ideological cleavage has structured political competition. This division is essentially religious in nature. While some Indonesians favor a greater role for Islam in social and political affairs, others support a clearer demarcation between the state and Islam and reject the idea that Islam should be prioritized over other religions. I refer to this axis of ideological competition as "political Islam," and I devote the first part of the book to documenting its meanings and empirical manifestations among Indonesian citizens and politicians.

Second, I argue that the division over political Islam has been instrumental in ensuring public satisfaction with democracy in Indonesia and has thus contributed to the country's remarkably high levels of political participation and, more broadly, to the resilience of its democratic institutions. I build on the idea outlined previously that democratic performance can be assessed from various points of view, some of which cannot be reduced to measures of economic and bureaucratic performance. From this perspective, enabling meaningful representation is a key goal for a democracy. Citizens are more engaged when they know that they have real political choices, as they are more likely to believe that their participation matters, to develop a sense of ownership of democratic institutions, to be willing to contribute to make these institutions work, and to defend them from authoritarian threats.

Advancing this argument in the Indonesian context requires evidence of the enduring relevance of political Islam in structuring Indonesian politics. Throughout this book, I show that this historical division still has profound implications for public opinion, electoral behavior, substantive representation, partisanship and public understandings of democracy. In short, the cleavage over political Islam has enabled ideological representation on an important issue that continues to resonate in society. In so doing, it has helped to give meaning to political participation, consolidate the legitimacy of democratic institutions in the minds of Indonesian citizens and ultimately sustain democracy in Indonesia.

1.3 CONTRIBUTION

The analysis presented in this book makes three main contributions to the study of Indonesian politics. First, I contribute to research on democracy in Indonesia by providing a novel perspective on why democracy, despite recent setbacks, has proven resilient in this country. Indonesia is often described as a harsh environment for democracy given its history of failed democratic experiments, military involvement in politics and poorly consolidated liberal values. In contrast with existing explanations of democratic success in Indonesia, which focus on structural and institutional factors such as patronage, inclusive power-sharing arrangements and legacies of state capacity (Aspinall 2010; Horowitz 2013; Slater 2020), I highlight the role of a major historical cultural–social cleavage in giving structure, depth and meaning to Indonesian politics. By shifting the analytical focus to concepts such as representation, legitimacy and participation, I bring ordinary citizens to the fore and emphasize their role in sustaining democratic practice. In this respect, I follow studies that similarly identify citizen engagement as crucial to explaining democratic survival in Indonesia (Lussier 2016; Dibley and Ford 2019). However,

1.3 Contribution

rather than focusing on associational life, I am interested primarily in representation as allowed by formal electoral institutions and in the implications of representation patterns for democratic legitimacy. I thus propose a novel pathway through which civic engagement in politics may strengthen democratic institutions.

Second, this book contributes to research on political representation in Indonesia by identifying political Islam, understood as an ideological spectrum that structures political competition, as a key dimension of citizen–politician linkages. The predominant approach in qualitative studies is to study citizen–politician linkages as being driven primarily by clientelism (Aspinall and Berenschot 2019). In a notable exception, Mietzner (2013) questions the consensus on the "end of ideology" in post-Suharto Indonesia and suggests that ideological differentiation on religious issues is an important feature of Indonesia's party system. Yet the implications of this insight for substantive representation remain largely unexplored, as studies on voting behavior rarely focus on ideology as a driver of electoral choices. I document the importance of political Islam in Indonesian politics in two ways. First, following studies of Islam in public opinion (Pepinsky, Liddle, and Mujani 2018), I conceptualize political Islam as an ideological dimension that varies across individuals. I extend the empirical reach of this literature by examining how political Islam is associated with policy positions, partisan allegiances, social identities, national identity, ethnic prejudices and democratic attitudes among ordinary Indonesians and politicians. Second, I analyze how this ideological division functions as a dimension of representation by studying party ideological differentiation and citizen–politician ideological congruence using surveys of elites and ordinary citizens specifically designed for this purpose. I therefore advance understanding of the meanings and implications of political Islam for democratic legitimacy, and I study representation using methods that have not previously been applied to the Indonesian context.

Third, I contribute to the recent debate on democratic backsliding in Indonesia. The issue of rising illiberalism, coupled with increasing ideological–partisan polarization, has been an especially consequential development in recent years, as it has marked a clear discontinuity with the early years of democracy (Davidson 2018). Research on polarization in this country predominantly focuses on political elites, especially by exploring their ability to polarize the electorate using populist appeals based on national or Islamic identity (Hadiz and Robison 2017). With only a few exceptions (Muhtadi and Warburton 2020), studies rarely consider ideological and partisan polarization from the perspective of ordinary citizens, as research on Indonesian public opinion is still influenced by the traditional portrayal of the Indonesian electorate as ideologically moderate (Mujani and Liddle 2009). More broadly, we do not know much about the process of democratic erosion as perceived and evaluated by Indonesian citizens, which hinders our ability to fully grasp the implications of the country's increasingly illiberal and polarized politics. By studying public perceptions of democratic backsliding, I shed new light on the concerning trends that characterize modern Indonesian politics and analyze the full range of implications of increasing polarization and illiberalism. Although there is little doubt that such developments have negative repercussions for democracy in Indonesia, they may also help to explain why public satisfaction with democracy is on the rise. Polarization may have a positive side, as it may help to clarify that citizens have meaningful choices when participating in elections and strengthen their attachment to political parties. The increasing influence of Islamist ideas, while troubling for pluralist Indonesians, may be welcomed by citizens who favor a larger role for Islam in politics, especially given that this ideological group has been traditionally marginalized in Indonesian politics. My analysis thus helps to build a more complete empirical and theoretical picture of the implications of increasing political polarization and illiberalism for democratic regression in Indonesia.

In short, this book enhances understanding of the nature of democracy in Indonesia through the three contributions outlined in the previous paragraphs. Although my primary focus is on the Indonesian case, the analysis also has implications for a broader set of countries that have experienced some degree of democratic backsliding. Interestingly, the recent wave of autocratization appears to be unfolding in a novel way (Bermeo 2016; Curato and Fossati 2020). While authoritarian transitions in the past were usually abrupt and led by military actors, democratic backsliding today tends to be initiated by elected incumbents who use executive powers to gradually but relentlessly erode democratic institutions. Authoritarian actors seek to increase support for their agendas using the language of democracy, such as by invoking the "will of the people" or the rights of the majority. The very idea of democracy is becoming increasingly contentious, as multiple actors articulate competing visions of democratic accountability and fight for supremacy. The question of what it means to be a democracy has thus become a crucial battleground for democratic survival.

These new patterns of democratic backsliding have important implications for research on democracy. As authoritarian actors increasingly aim

1.4 Method

to rule by consensus rather than by coercion alone, and as their initiatives to erode democratic institutions are often supported by voters, the role of ordinary citizens in preserving democratic institutions is becoming more crucial than ever. Studying ordinary citizens' opinion formation and voting behavior is therefore key to understanding the conditions under which democracy may falter and die. With a focus on public opinion, I analyze how the public understands and evaluates democracy. Shedding new light on these processes may improve our understanding of why citizens choose to submit to or fight against incumbent politicians' attempts to erode democratic institutions.

Finally, this book contributes to the literature by proposing a new approach to measuring and analyzing public conceptions of democracy. First, this novel method acknowledges the multidimensional nature of views on democracy, thereby improving on existing measures of conceptions of democracy, which typically exclude participatory and deliberative understandings of democracy. Second, this new approach captures the complexity of each dimension of democracy. Rather than using a very limited number of questions to measure people's understandings of democracy, as in prior research, each dimension is disaggregated into a large number of easy-to-understand attributes that can be individually evaluated by survey respondents and analyzed by researchers using a range of quantitative tools. Finally, this method acknowledges that ordinary citizens may have multiple and possibly conflicting or conflated conceptions of democracy. This approach thus expands the conceptual map of meanings of democracy and provides a more flexible tool for analysts to investigate the complex structures of public conceptions of democracy.

1.4 METHOD

The argument developed in this book is based on survey data collected in Indonesia via various methods and at different times between 2017 and 2020. The data analyzed all come from original surveys that I designed either individually or in collaboration with other researchers to investigate the themes covered in this book.[5] A prominent data source is the Indonesia National Survey Project (INSP), a survey that I designed with a

---

[5] While the argument outlined in this book is entirely novel and I am solely responsible for it, these datasets are also used in single-authored and collaborative journal articles published in various academic outlets. References to these sources are provided throughout the book.

team of Indonesia-focused researchers at the ISEAS–Yusof Ishak Institute in Singapore. This survey, implemented in May 2017 through face-to-face interviews conducted by enumerators trained by Lembaga Survei Indonesia, was based on a multistage cluster sampling method in which villages or their urban equivalents (*kelurahan*) were the primary sampling unit. A system of quotas and various sampling stages ensured that the final sample of 1,620 respondents was highly representative of the Indonesian population in terms of a wide range of sociodemographic factors. Data obtained from this broad survey of how ordinary Indonesians perceive various political, economic and social issues are used throughout this book.[6]

In other cases, the surveys that I designed were administered to online samples for which respondents were recruited through various incentives. This method presents substantial advantages over surveys conducted by personal interviews in terms of costs and scheduling. It enabled me to implement two surveys in 2018 and 2019 on specific issues analyzed in this book (religious and national identity and conceptions of democracy). However, surveys that are not based on random samples may be limited in terms of representativeness. To ensure that the collected samples mirrored the Indonesian population as closely as possible, I applied to each of these surveys quotas for gender, age, education, place of residence (urban/rural) and religion. This resulted in highly diverse samples, including Indonesians from all walks of life. In addition, generous sample sizes, ranging from 1,300 to 2,000 respondents, allowed a large volume of data to be collected on various subgroups of the population. Although the use of non-probability samples may not be suitable to draw descriptive inferences about a given population, these samples are usually considered as a reliable tool for analyzing relationships between variables (Baker et al. 2013), which is my purpose in the context of this book.

To complement the public opinion surveys, I draw data from an original survey of Indonesian political elites that I designed with Edward Aspinall, Burhan Muhtadi and Eve Warburton. This survey was conducted in early 2018 with a sample of 508 Indonesian politicians on provincial legislative councils (*Dewan Perwakilan Rakyat Daerah*, or DPRD). As in the INSP, the survey was conducted via face-to-face interviews with a randomly selected sample. The total population of 2,073 politicians at the time was first stratified into three main regions (Sumatra,

---

[6] The survey experiment analyzed in Chapter 6, which I designed with Burhan Muhtadi and Eve Warburton and implemented in December 2018, was based on the same methodology.

1.5 Structure of the Book

Java and other islands). Provinces, the primary sampling unit, were selected in each region according to each province's proportion of the area population. This data collection project was unprecedented in the context of Indonesia and involved one of the largest samples to date of political elites collected in a single country. These novel data shed new light on how Indonesian politicians conceptualize various economic and social issues, and they enable a more thorough investigation of variations in policy attitudes across political parties. Furthermore, by matching this dataset to public opinion data, we can study representation and ideological congruence between citizens and politicians in depth.

I thus rely on a diverse array of survey sources for the analysis carried out in this book. I apply a wide range of data analysis techniques that are commonly used in survey and public opinion research. In some sections of the book, when my goal is primarily descriptive (such as when I identify ideological divisions within the Indonesian electorate or among political elites), I analyze simple descriptive statistics and bivariate correlations. In other sections, I apply quantitative regression techniques to simultaneously analyze how various factors are related to an outcome of interest, such as policy preferences, or to explore more systematically the interactions between different variables. In still other sections, when my aim is to account for complex multidimensional concepts such as national identity and the meaning of democracy, I use factor analysis to disaggregate and analyze the components. Finally, my analysis of polarization relies on experimental methods to identify the implications of this trend for opinion formation, satisfaction with democracy and partisan affiliations.

1.5 STRUCTURE OF THE BOOK

In Chapter 2, I elaborate on the theoretical framework that guides the analysis and briefly discuss the trajectory of Indonesia's democracy over the last twenty years. I start by presenting Indonesia as a difficult place for democracy to take root and by noting that substantive representation is an issue that is largely overlooked in research on democracy in this country, as prior studies focus on describing the pathologies of citizen–politician linkages. I then develop the argument, first by reviewing research on the roles of ordinary people and public opinion in democracy, then by discussing the relationship between representation and satisfaction with democracy and finally by exploring the roles of polarization and populism in evaluations of democratic performance. I then return to the Indonesian case to engage more closely with the literature on political

Islam, participation and democratic erosion and discuss in greater detail the contributions of my analysis.

My empirical analysis begins in Chapter 3, where I examine aggregate electoral returns to measure the influence of the division over political Islam on voting behavior in modern Indonesia. As mentioned earlier, studies suggest that electoral behavior is driven primarily by patronage, candidate traits and evaluations of government performance rather than by ideological and partisan considerations, and the weakness of political parties and mass partisan affiliations are recurring themes in the literature. However, no studies analyze the full spectrum of available electoral returns (both over time and across districts) to reach such conclusions. As a result, our understanding of how deep-seated partisan affiliations rooted in political Islam have shaped voting behavior since Indonesia's democratization is incomplete. A quantitative analysis of district-level electoral returns from five legislative elections indicates that electoral geography today shows important continuities with the first Indonesian general election of 1955. Furthermore, a longitudinal analysis demonstrates the importance of historical partisan affiliations as a driver of voting behavior, as voter turnout plummeted in the 2009 elections but has increased significantly in recent years. Finally, I leverage the aggregate electoral data to show that electoral participation today is higher in districts with deep-rooted historical partisan identities, which suggests an important and overlooked association between mass partisanship and political engagement.

Following this macro-level analysis, I turn my attention to micro-level data to ascertain whether and to what extent political Islam functions as an ideological division that structures political competition in Indonesia. Specifically, I explore using a series of original surveys how political Islam is perceived by Indonesian politicians and voters and whether it shapes linkages between citizens and their representatives. In Chapter 4, I analyze the legislator survey. Scholars of Indonesian politics acknowledge that ideological competition is grounded in the cleavage over political Islam; the degree to which politicians and political parties differ on the issue of state-Islam relations is an open question. This study is the first attempt to systematically measure party positions on political Islam with a survey of political elites, and it enables me to show that although Indonesian parties differ little on fiscal and economic policy, they are clearly differentiated in their views of the role of Islam in public affairs.

Chapter 5 considers public opinion with an analysis of various surveys specifically designed to investigate ordinary citizens' perceptions of

1.5 *Structure of the Book*

political Islam. First, I leverage the INSP dataset to show that ordinary people, like politicians, are divided in their views on political Islam, and I investigate various sociodemographic factors that are associated with this cleavage. Drawing from the same data, I further show that political Islam is associated with participation and partisanship. I then analyze a more focused survey conducted using an online sample to explore the relationships between political Islam and national identity and between Islam and populism, a key feature of contemporary Indonesian politics. The data analyzed in this chapter enable me to portray a comprehensive picture of political Islam as perceived by the mass public and to show that the cleavage over political Islam is associated with a specific conception of national identity. To a certain extent, political Islam is also associated with policy preferences in important domains such as fiscal policy and decentralization, and with populist understandings of politics.

After establishing that political Islam is a deep-rooted and meaningful ideological dimension for both politicians and ordinary citizens, I probe whether political Islam indeed functions as the main avenue for representation in Indonesia. To address this question, in Chapter 6, I study elite and mass survey data to offer an exhaustive picture of ideological representation in Indonesia. After introducing the method, I analyze patterns of substantive representation on economic, social and religious issues, first by considering how the preferences of the political elite correspond with those of the public, and then by examining the role played by political parties as avenues of democratic representation. The findings are consistent with the analysis performed in Chapter 4, as they show large differences across the two areas: While a substantial degree of ideological congruence between politicians and voters can be observed for political Islam, the opposite is true for economic policy, where politicians and voters are tightly clustered in a narrow ideological space. Finally, by leveraging a survey experiment, I further show how partisan and leader cues can affect ideological positions on political Islam for various groups of voters. This chapter thus documents that democracy in Indonesia has provided a substantial degree of ideological participation and that political parties, while deficient in other respects, have performed an essential (if imperfect) democratic function in this domain.

In Chapter 7, I analyze the relationship between political Islam and democratic attitudes. I start by showing that the cleavage over political Islam is related to satisfaction with democracy, as on average, Islamist individuals tend to be more satisfied with democracy than pluralists. To investigate the sources of this link, in the remainder of the chapter, I focus on conceptions of democracy and their implications. After discussing the methodological approach, I conduct data analysis that reveals that the structure of conceptions of democracy is more complex than assumed. Although most Indonesians think of democracy in liberal–egalitarian terms, others appear to subscribe to a participatory view. I further demonstrate that such conceptions of democracy are related to both political Islam and evaluations of democratic performance. Specifically, Islamists are systematically less likely to endorse a liberal understanding of democracy, and those who hold a liberal–egalitarian view of democracy are more likely to be dissatisfied with democracy. Conversely, respondents who understand participation as being an essential aspect of democracy are more, not less, satisfied with democracy in Indonesia. This chapter thus shows that political Islam informs how ordinary people understand democracy and evaluate its performance in Indonesia. Again, these findings underscore the importance of this ideological division, and they indicate that public satisfaction with democracy is linked to opportunities for political representation and participation.

The book concludes with Chapter 8, in which I summarize the findings and discuss their implications for democracy and representation in Indonesia and elsewhere. I also discuss some open questions that intersect with the arguments proposed in this book, most importantly those pertaining to issues of public opinion formation, responsiveness, accountability and democratic consolidation.

2

Explaining Democratic Survival in Indonesia

2.1 AN UNLIKELY DEMOCRACY

Since the end of the National Revolution and the establishment of an independent republic in 1949, observers have often been skeptical about the prospects for democracy in Indonesia. When democracy finally did collapse in the late 1950s and a debate emerged in academia over what caused this collapse, many scholars highlighted the unavoidability of the turn toward authoritarianism. According to Harry Benda, for example, the demise of liberal democracy should not have been surprising, as liberal values were largely absent from Indonesia's political culture. Even those who disagree with such a culturalist view, such as Herbert Feith, stress that the odds were clearly stacked against democracy because of persistent revolutionary mobilization and the need to integrate various social groups into inclusionary power-sharing arrangements.[1]

When the New Order regime broke down in 1998, the consensus outlook for democracy in Indonesia was once again grim. After thirty years of stable authoritarian rule, the country faced extensive social unrest amid a devastating economic crisis that had thrown millions into a precarious state and left Indonesia at the mercy of international donors. Widespread crime and thug harassment as well as numerous episodes of large-scale violent ethnic conflict plunged the country into a state of turbulent anxiety. A full-fledged military challenge in Aceh and secessionist tensions in Papua and East Timor called into question Indonesia's ability to survive as a united nation. After thirty years of authoritarianism,

---

[1] See Feith (1962) and Benda (1964).

liberal values were rooted no more deeply in Indonesian political culture than when Benda lamented their absence. Against this background, many feared a tragic repetition of the mass murders that spearheaded Suharto's ascent to power or simply that the still-powerful military would step in and seize power.

Yet none of this happened. Suharto's successor, B. J. Habibie, surprised many by proving himself as the illuminated leader who would shepherd the country into full democracy. The economy stabilized, violence subsided, the military did not intervene and Indonesia entered a new normal. Today, Indonesia is the world's third largest democracy, the most successful example of democratic consolidation in Southeast Asia and an increasingly assertive actor in the international arena. Despite persistent flaws in its democratic institutions, Indonesia has successfully held five cycles of largely peaceful, free and fair national legislative elections and countless local elections. Its citizens enjoy substantial civil and political rights, its economy has grown without interruption for twenty years and poverty has abated significantly.

Certainly, as mentioned in the Introduction chapter, Indonesia's democracy is far from ideal. A particularly influential view portrays it as a mere vehicle for economic elites to assert their exploitative power, stressing the continuities between contemporary Indonesia and the authoritarian New Order (Hadiz and Robison 2013). Other scholars focus more closely on political and social institutions to offer a fine-grained picture of the pitfalls of democratic practice in Indonesia (Aspinall and Mietzner 2010). For example, a widely shared opinion is that political parties tend to behave like cartels, monopolizing political power and forming large, ideologically heterogeneous coalitions that compromise accountability (Slater 2018). Many scholars highlight major deficiencies such as pervasive corruption and a weak rule of law, and several scholars argue that Indonesian politics are primarily driven by clientelistic networks rather than by programmatic considerations (Aspinall and Berenschot 2019; Muhtadi 2019).

Acknowledging these shortcomings only partially detracts from the overall positive record of Indonesia's democracy since the breakdown of authoritarianism. Over the last twenty years, Indonesia's democratic trajectory has appeared more stable and successful than any other regime in the region. However, scholars of Indonesian politics observe an erosion of democracy in recent years, which could be attributed to a mix of structural factors, strategic behavior by political elites and acquiescence by ordinary citizens (Warburton and Aspinall 2019). The rise of a new

2.1 An Unlikely Democracy

brand of populism reminiscent of the right-wing nativist movements that have spread in many countries worldwide has been a key feature of Indonesian politics since 2014, when Prabowo Subianto competed against Joko Widodo in a close presidential election. Many people engaged in scholarly research and public debates consider Prabowo's rise and his exclusionary rhetoric to be a direct challenge to democratic institutions (Aspinall 2015; Hadiz and Robison 2017). A related phenomenon has been a turn toward increasingly illiberal politics on a range of social and political issues. This trend, particularly visible in the growing political clout and mobilizational capacity of radical Islamist groups, has threatened the poorly consolidated rights of groups such as religious minorities and LGBT communities and has hindered meaningful progress on human rights issues (Diprose, McRae, and Hadiz 2019). An additional dynamic in Indonesia's democratic backsliding relates to the incumbent government's continued manipulation of the state apparatus for partisan gains and use of executive powers to curb freedom of association (Mietzner 2018; Power 2018). In short, democratic institutions in Indonesia have visibly deteriorated since the mid-2010s.

This body of literature is instrumental in denouncing the erosion of democracy in contemporary Indonesia and in exposing how political elites are both driving and capitalizing on it for their own gain. Yet the predominant focus on elite politics impedes the study of democratic backsliding from a public opinion perspective, and an important trend is overlooked. While in many contexts, democratic backsliding has been coupled with rising levels of public disaffection with democratic institutions (Foa and Mounk 2017), satisfaction with democracy is rising in Indonesia. After falling to a low level of 53% in October 2015, the share of ordinary Indonesians who were "somewhat" or "very" satisfied with how democracy works in their country rose substantially; by mid-2017, it was around 70%.[2] Given the multidimensionality of Indonesia's democratic decline, we should be careful not to attribute excessive importance to any specific source of data, and it should be stressed that analyzing public opinion alone cannot provide a comprehensive picture of democratic backsliding in Indonesia or elsewhere. Yet dismissing this trend would be equally problematic, as a clear pattern has unfolded and persisted over several years. Increasing levels of satisfaction with democracy in the wake of an erosion of democratic institutions suggest that there

---

[2] These data are from the *Lembaga Survei Indonesia* surveys used to generate Figure 1.1.

may be aspects of democratic backsliding in Indonesia that are not fully acknowledged or understood. If Indonesia's democracy is getting worse, why are Indonesians more satisfied with it?

Prior studies do not offer satisfactory explanations of this anomaly. As studies of democratic backsliding overwhelmingly focus on elite dynamics to describe democratic regression, they struggle to account for developments in public opinion, such as rising levels of public satisfaction with democracy. Research on public opinion suffers from some important limitations. For example, longitudinal variation in democratic satisfaction has yet to be studied systematically, as studies either rely on cross-sectional research designs or do not exhaustively consider variation over time. Most importantly, however, studies exclusively analyze democratic performance as a function of policy outputs, rather than examining the full range of expectations and demands that citizens may have of democracy and its institutions. For example, Mujani and Liddle (2015) analyze various measures of satisfaction with democracy and find that they are positively and significantly correlated with evaluations of macroeconomic performance and an index of perceptions of government performance.[3] While satisfaction with democracy in Indonesia, as in other countries, may well rest at least in part on assessments of economic and bureaucratic performance, this focus on outcomes cannot explain the recent surge in satisfaction with democracy. As mentioned earlier, the quality of democracy in Indonesia has declined in many respects since the mid-2010s, and performance in other areas has been largely stable: Economic growth rates and unemployment have barely changed over the last few years, poverty has continued to decrease at a very slow pace, political reform has stalled and the fight against corruption is facing new challenges after a new law curbed the autonomy of the country's top anti-corruption agency.

Broadly understood, Indonesia's record in terms of government "outputs" for the recent past is mixed at best. It is therefore problematic to rely primarily on this approach to study how ordinary citizens evaluate Indonesia's democracy at a time of democratic backsliding. I suggest in this book that a more fruitful avenue could be to focus on the *inputs* rather than the outputs of democracy, specifically on the dynamics of political representation, a factor that has long been identified as being crucial in other contexts, in shaping public satisfaction with democracy

---

[3] See also Mujani, Liddle and Ambardi (2018).

2.2 Ordinary People and Democracy

(Norris 1997; Stecker and Tausendpfund 2016). Section 2.2 outlines the theoretical framework that orients my analysis, first by discussing the role of ordinary people in democratic practice and then by engaging with prior research on the relationship between representation and satisfaction with democracy. I then return to the Indonesian case for an introductory discussion of patterns of political representation and participation in this country.

2.2 ORDINARY PEOPLE AND DEMOCRACY: AN ANALYTICAL FRAMEWORK

Few would doubt that democracies need democrats to function. While many empirical studies on democracy focus on political elites and institutions, public attitudes and the engagement of ordinary citizens have long been considered crucial for establishing and maintaining a functioning democratic system. For instance, many scholars observe that democratization is linked with the emergence of specific values among the public that are closely related to socioeconomic change (Inglehart 1997). The increasing availability of material resources and the transition to postindustrial societies has produced important cultural changes, as citizens have gradually embraced values of self-expression that are foundational to a liberal democracy. Together with these new values, rising education levels have enabled citizens to articulate and fight for democratic demands, thereby increasing the likelihood of democratization (Welzel and Inglehart 2008). Beyond democratic transitions, ordinary citizens have an important role to play in preserving democratic institutions once they are established. While democratic regimes provide formal checks and balances to constrain executive powers, such institutional arrangements ultimately rest on the informal social norms that underpin them, as their survival is contingent on whether such norms are shared and upheld in everyday democratic practice (Helmke and Levitsky 2006). To constrain potentially authoritarian elites, citizens must be willing to act to preserve democratic institutions and punish incumbents for antidemocratic behavior (Graham and Svolik 2020). In the absence of such checks by ordinary citizens, democratic institutions can be hollowed out and bent to serve authoritarian purposes. The presence of deep-rooted democratic values and an engaged public willing to defend them are thus essential for the healthy functioning and the very survival of a democracy.

The pivotal role of ordinary citizens in defending democratic institutions is especially evident in light of the recent wave of democratic backsliding (Bermeo 2016). Over the past decade, democratic institutions and practices have deteriorated substantially in many regions of the world, and this new wave of autocratization appears to be unfolding in a novel way (Glasius 2018; Lührmann and Lindberg 2019; Curato and Fossati 2020). Although the authoritarian transitions of the past were often abrupt and commonly led by military actors, contemporary democratic backsliding has tended to be initiated by elected incumbents, who have used their executive powers to pursue a strategy of gradual but relentless erosion of democratic institutions. Rather than experiencing outright collapse, some democracies have undergone a subtle process of deterioration in which the avenues for political participation and contestation have shrunk substantially.

These developments require new analytical approaches to determine how and why democracies falter, deteriorate or die. The opaque, complex and fluid nature of contemporary democratic backsliding indicates that general theories based on structural, cultural or institutional factors may provide only limited analytical traction (Waldner and Lust 2018). As Bermeo suggests (2016, 5), a promising alternative approach is to unpack the multiple processes through which democracies regress. In this vein, a recurring feature of contemporary democratic backsliding is that authoritarian actors appear to invest considerable resources to obtain consensus rather than ruling primarily by coercion (He and Wagenaar 2018; Morgenbesser 2020). As the normative power of democratic discourse remains strong, authoritarian agents try to increase support for their agendas by using the language of democracy, such as by invoking the "will of the people or by building a democratic façade to repressive practices" (Mechkova, Lührmann, and Lindberg 2017, 168). An implication for empirical research on democracy is that more attention should be devoted to studying how ordinary citizens understand democracy, evaluate its performance and respond to attempts by political elites to undermine democratic institutions. With a focus on public opinion and voting behavior, this analysis focuses on the interactions between political elites and ordinary citizens as a key domain to understand and account for the current wave of democratic backsliding.

2.2.1 Evaluating Democratic Performance

As support for democracy among ordinary citizens is vital for democratic institutions to survive and thrive, many political science studies investigate the determinants of support for democracy. As mentioned in Section 2.2,

2.2 *Ordinary People and Democracy* 25

a first important driver of support for democracy is socioeconomic modernization, which is intertwined with the emergence of liberal values that are closely identified with democratic political regimes. However, sociocultural change alone does not fully explain why some citizens support democratic institutions while others do not. Political scientists have thus focused on other factors as drivers of democratic support. A particularly interesting avenue of research studies support for democracy as resulting, at least to an extent, from evaluations of democratic performance. The premise guiding these analyses is that public support for any political regime depends on its performance, that is, its ability to deliver outcomes that are valued by ordinary citizens (Easton 1975). This implies that support for democracy is closely intertwined with the ability of democratic regimes to provide a wide range of public goods such as security, satisfactory economic performance and a wide range of civil, political and social rights. When democracies fail to deliver on their promises, public dissatisfaction may result in declining support for the institutions, practices and even the principles that underpin democracy (Rohrschneider 2002).

The insight that government performance shapes support for democracy has been widely studied in empirical research. However, the concept of "support" for democracy is complex and multidimensional (Norris 1999, 2011), and such dimensions may vary independently from one another. For example, citizens may be supportive of the principles of democracy while also being disillusioned with how it is practiced in their country or highly critical of specific political actors or institutions. In general, support for the "political community," understood as "a basic attachment to the nation beyond the institutions of government" (Norris 1999, 10), tends to be quite stable and high over time, as does support for the regime principles that represent the values of democratic government. In contrast, satisfaction with democracy can vary greatly between individuals, across countries and over time. Studies focus on both levels of analysis and identify a significant relationship between support for or satisfaction with democracy and government performance. For instance, support for democracy has been found to be influenced by government performance in both developed and young democracies (Mattes and Bratton 2007; Magalhães 2014). Various studies find that satisfaction with democracy is affected by factors such as economic performance (Cordero and Simón 2016; Kriesi 2018), procedural fairness (Magalhães 2016), provision of public safety (Fernandez and Kuenzi 2010), the effectiveness of bureaucrats and officials (Ariely 2013) and

26   *Explaining Democratic Survival in Indonesia*

the delivery of "political" goods such as freedom and accountability (Huang, Chang, and Chu 2008).

Government performance and democratic attitudes are thus intimately connected. This link is significant for the debate on contemporary democratic backsliding, as it points to the possible vulnerability of democratic regimes that fail to meet citizens' expectations regarding democratic performance. A disconnect between public expectations and performance may produce political instability and compromise the legitimacy of democracy as a form of government in the eyes of the public, and in this respect, declining rates of public satisfaction with democracy may be considered an initial sign of democratic deconsolidation (Foa and Mounk 2017). This idea resonates with research on legitimacy, which has long identified government performance as one of the most important determinants of whether citizens perceive a political regime as legitimate (Gilley 2006). In established democracies, a lack of legitimacy may pave the way for the emergence of populist or authoritarian actors who may seek to impair democratic institutions. In young democracies, low levels of legitimacy may hinder significant progress toward full democratic consolidations. Certainly, the link between satisfaction with democracy and regime durability is complex, and some studies fail to find a positive association between support for democracy and democracy itself (Welzel 2007; Fails and Pierce 2010). Nevertheless, recent research suggests that democratic institutions are more resilient when citizens are supportive of democracy (Claassen 2020). Focusing on democratic performance is therefore a fruitful avenue for understanding satisfaction with and support for democracy; in turn, healthy levels of democratic support may have positive implications for the durability of democratic regimes.

However, this scholarship often overlooks the fact that ordinary citizens may hold different conceptions of what it means to be a democracy (Huber, Rueschemeyer and Stephens 1997; Lindberg et al. 2014). At the least, as suggested by proponents of a "minimalist" definition of democracy (Przeworski et al. 2000), a democracy must be an *electoral* democracy, with free and fair elections and adequate levels of political competition. For some, a democracy is also supposed to be *liberal*, a political regime that limits the power of electoral majorities with checks and balances to protect individual and minority rights (Fawcett 2018). From a different perspective, in a *deliberative* democracy, government should be guided by reason, and its decisions should be reached through a process of dialogue and compromise rather than by appealing to emotions and identities (Fishkin 1991; Cohen 1997). Other scholars articulate a

2.2 Ordinary People and Democracy

participatory notion of democracy, stressing the importance of citizen involvement in democratic politics beyond the formal channels provided by delegation to elected representatives (Barber 2003). Finally, an *egalitarian* conception of democracy acknowledges the importance of material and immaterial inequalities and asks whether all citizens are equally empowered to participate in and benefit from democratic politics (Young 2002). Such a multidimensional conceptualization of democracy has implications for satisfaction with democracy. As individuals may harbor different views and expectations of what democracy is, they may hold democratic practice to different standards and formulate diverging evaluations of whether democracy is "delivering" (Canache, Mondak, and Seligson 2001; Norris 2011).

More broadly, while most research focuses on *outputs* as measures of democratic performance, it is important to underscore that the *inputs* of the democratic process are an equally important dimension of democratic performance (Dahlberg, Linde, and Holmberg 2015). For some citizens, democracy may have instrumental value, as they may directly benefit from good governance, economic growth or otherwise tangible public goods such as security and functional infrastructure. Yet for others, support for democracy may be understood as being more intrinsic, as it depends on intangible features inherent to democratic political systems, such as opportunities for participation, accountable government and representation (Evans and Whitefield 1995). Empirical research indicates that intrinsic considerations are at least as powerful as instrumental ones as determinants of democratic support (Rose, Mishler, and Haerpfer 1998; Mattes and Bratton 2007). Thus, studying the dynamics of representation, citizen–politician linkages and participation, whether formal or informal, may generate valuable insights into democratic legitimacy and durability.

2.2.2 Representation, Participation and Legitimacy

In her analysis of the concept of representation, Hanna Pitkin notes that representation can assume various meanings in political and social life (Pitkin 1967). From a formalistic point of view, representation results from contractual arrangements that grant authority to an agent (the government) to act for a principal (the citizenry) and specify if, how and to what degree the agent is accountable for their actions. From a different point of view, which is adopted by most empirical research, representation can be understood as the practice of standing or acting for others rather than a mere legal arrangement. Descriptive representation entails a representative who "stands for" their constituency by virtue of their similarity to them, such as based on their class, ethnic or gender identity. Substantive representation regards a representative as acting for the represented rather than standing for them. What matters in this case, which is most relevant for the analysis carried out in this book, is not what representatives look like, but what they think and do, such as whether they hold policy priorities and positions that are congruent with those held by their constituents (Luna and Zechmeister 2005; Costello, Thomassen, and Rosema 2012; Dalton 2017). Issues of descriptive and substantive representation are pivotal to modern democracy, and they have been contentious in academia and beyond. In public discussion on representation, key recurring themes include debates on who should be represented, how representatives should be chosen and how they should behave vis-à-vis their constituents. Many scholars criticize representative democracy for the lack of involvement of ordinary people in decision-making processes (Urbinati 2006; Alonso, Keane, and Merkel 2011).

For better or worse, representation is typically considered essential to contemporary democracy given the size, complexity and heterogeneity of modern societies. Indeed, representation performs two essential functions in democratic governance. The first is that the institutions established for representation provide key mechanisms for citizens to control government. Elections to choose representatives provide opportunities to select capable leaders and discuss policy alternatives, and they include powerful incentives for representatives to be responsive and accountable to their constituents. Second, representation strengthens the role of the government in the eyes of ordinary citizens (Birch 2007, 141–143). The legitimacy of a political regime is consolidated when power holders are elected representatives. As laws are formulated and implemented by representatives selected through free and fair elections, citizens are more likely to see representatives as having the right to rule, to comply with what is required from them and to contribute to the functioning of the political community. Furthermore, representation provides a channel through which the government can mobilize consensus. Representative government creates a two-way channel for communication between the representative and the represented in which government officials can inform citizens about their initiatives and justify them and citizens can express their grievances and criticisms through institutional channels. Representation thus has the dual function of allowing for popular control while at the same time providing tools for political elites to perpetuate their rule. Both of these functions

2.2 Ordinary People and Democracy

have repercussions for legitimacy, and they are thus closely connected to evaluations of democratic performance.

Empirical studies find a significant association between representation and satisfaction with democracy. Some studies analyze public opinion data and find that satisfaction with democracy is higher in individuals who believe that elections produce parliaments with representatives whose opinions mirror those of their constituents (Dahlberg, Linde, and Holmberg 2015). Others leverage a combination of surveys of politicians and the public to analyze patterns of representation directly rather than relying on views reported by citizens. With this approach, the quality of substantive representation is measured as congruence in policy priorities or policy positions on salient issues between politicians and voters: The closer the match between politician and citizen attitudes, the higher the quality of representation. Comparative research indicates that indeed, patterns of citizen–politician attitudinal congruence are closely tied to satisfaction with democracy, perceptions of democratic legitimacy and participation. Reher (2014, 2015, 2016), for instance, shows that both congruence in policy priorities and policy positions affect satisfaction with democracy and electoral turnout. Stecker and Tausenpfund (2016) investigate the connection between substantive representation and satisfaction with democracy in various policy areas and find similar results. Bakker et al. (2020) find that incongruence is linked with lower levels of democratic satisfaction and support for antiestablishment parties. While these studies focus overwhelmingly on European cases, evidence suggests that, as posited by theoretical work on representation, there is a close link between substantive representation and satisfaction with democracy, which has implications for democratic durability.

While substantive representation is crucial for democracies to work and to be perceived as legitimate political regimes by their citizens, its practice in many democratic regimes and in young democracies especially is far from ideal. First, substantive representation is often undermined because elected representative bodies overrepresent males, members of ethnic majorities and affluent social classes (Wängnerud 2009; Carnes 2012). Second, regardless of the patterns of descriptive representation, a lack of congruence regarding policy priorities or positions is common. For instance, political elites may be divided on issues on which citizens hold homogeneous positions, or they may fail to deliver policies on which a high degree of voter consensus exists. Most notably, for the purposes of this analysis, substantive representation is considered compromised when elections fail to provide meaningful choices to voters, as political parties lack differentiated programmatic platforms on important political and social issues. Such is the case in many young non-Western democracies, in which politics is structured around valence issues and clientelism rather than ideological competition between alternative party platforms (Hicken 2011; Bleck and Van de Walle 2013).

Certainly, the absence of interparty ideological divisions does not imply a lack of representation. A politician in a clientelistic political system, for example, may dutifully represent their constituents' interests in the national legislature and help secure policies that benefit them. Yet when political parties fail to articulate alternative views of and policy options about key social, cultural and economic issues, an important dimension of democratic deliberation and representation is missing. For this reason, scholars of democracy often maintain that a party system with stable patterns of ideological competition is crucial for democratic representation and accountability (Mainwaring and Torcal 2006). Without meaningful ideological division rooted in society and political parties that consistently represent various positions associated with it, representation is compromised and democratic legitimacy is consequently impaired.

A final point worth noting is the relationship between representation and political participation. In political theory, participatory understandings of democracy are often considered as alternatives to representative democracy (Cunningham 2002, 123–141). Representative democracy only requires modest levels of participation by ordinary citizens, mainly in the form of voting, and many scholars highlight the various maladies that follow from this feature of modern democracy. These include general apathy about political issues, ordinary people's lack of power in setting the political agenda and the direction of government, enduring patterns of political exclusion and disenfranchisement, and persistent inequalities in political skills between elites and citizens. In democratic practice, however, representation and electoral participation are two sides of the same coin. Several studies show that higher levels of descriptive representation increase participation by ethnic and gender minorities, as they foster feelings of empowerment and trust in political institutions (Banducci, Donovan, and Karp 2004; Rocha et al. 2010). In a similar vein, low levels of ideological congruence between citizens and politicians discourage electoral participation (Lefkofridi, Giger, and Gallego 2014; Schäfer and Debus 2018). Substantive representation, democratic satisfaction, ideological competition and political participation are therefore intimately linked in democratic practice. Studying them jointly, as this book does,

2.2 Ordinary People and Democracy

may contribute to our understanding of how certain democracies can maintain resilience during hard times.

2.2.3 Representation, Polarization and Populism

Conceptualizing representation as a key factor affecting support for and satisfaction with democracy has implications for two important developments that have characterized democracy in recent years. The first is rising partisan polarization, which can be described as a tendency to divide the world into "us" versus "them" along partisan lines (Robison and Moskowitz 2019). Polarization is widely understood to have deleterious effects on democracy. When political elites seek to polarize voters for political gain, they create an ideological and affective divide that may severely weaken democratic institutions. Specifically, partisan polarization may help legitimize incumbents' attempts to use their dominant positions to curtail civil liberties and impair checks and balances or the efforts of opposition forces to systematically undermine the legitimacy of democratic institutions (Svolik 2018; Graham and Svolik 2020). Several scholars thus identify partisan polarization as a serious danger to the stability of democratic regimes (McCoy, Rahman, and Somer 2018; Svolik 2019; Arbatli and Rosenberg 2021), and polarization is typically discussed in public debates as one of the more pervasive ailments of contemporary democracy (Klein 2020).

The experiences of countries such as Egypt, Venezuela and Hungary provide a powerful warning about the perils of polarized politics. However, assuming that representation and participation are essential to the survival of democratic politics, partisan polarization may also have positive implications for democracy (Wang 2014; Lupu 2015; LeBas 2018). First, more polarized political debates increase the salience of political divisions. As such, they may strengthen perceptions that representative politics offers meaningful political alternatives, and they may clarify the various options available to ordinary citizens. This in turn may increase public satisfaction with democracy by suggesting that the range of political views held by common citizens are mirrored by political elites. Second, when political alternatives become clearer and more salient in public debates, citizens may be more likely to acknowledge meaningful differences between political parties and thus be more inclined to develop partisan affiliations. In turn, mass partisan affiliations are often considered crucial for democratic consolidation, as they contribute to the stabilization of party systems (Dalton and Weldon 2007). The effect of partisan polarization on democratic institutions is thus more complex than commonly assumed.

The second feature of contemporary democratic politics is that the dynamics of representation and satisfaction with democracy are closely connected with populism, which most studies, following Mudde (2004) and others, understand as a "thin ideology," or as a malleable world-view that pits virtuous ordinary citizens against corrupt political elites. Like polarization, populism articulates an "us versus them" narrative, often including an ethnic component in which elites and foreigners collude against "the masses." Populism has thus developed an unflattering reputation in both research and public debate. Especially with the remarkable rise of populist parties and political actors in Europe and the United States in recent years, populism is seen as a threat to democracy because of its contempt for deliberation, debate and compromise, its hyper-majoritarian understanding of democracy, its illiberal character, its use of corrosive rhetoric that undermines the legitimacy of democratic institutions and the way it oversimplifies complex social issues. Populism is thus often perceived as a pathology of liberal democracy, as it poses a serious challenge both to individual rights and to representative institutions.

Again, while it would be counterproductive to overlook the potentially negative implications of populism for democracy, a more complex picture emerges when we assess the implications of the rise of populism in terms of representation, participation and satisfaction with democracy. As much as populism is a threat to democracy, it could also be considered as a "corrective" for a number of deficiencies in contemporary democratic practice (Kaltwasser 2012). In attacking the institutions of representative democracy, populism denounces the limitations of representation, especially the lack of congruence between citizens and elites on important policy issues such as immigration and the exclusion of substantial segments of the population from democratic politics. The rise of populism may thus strengthen representation by giving a voice to citizens who do not feel represented and by forcing political elites to listen to their voice when setting the political agenda and future policy directions. Indeed, some studies find that populism is closely related to satisfaction with democracy and participation (Webb 2013; Pauwels 2014). Populism can also arise from disillusionment with democratic institutions, as dissatisfied democrats are more likely to espouse populist narratives and vote for populist parties (Bowler et al. 2017). However, holding populist political views may bolster political mobilization; some empirical studies

2.3 Representation and Participation in Indonesian Politics

report high rates of engagement among populists (Huber and Ruth 2017; Anduiza, Guinjoan, and Rico 2019).

In short, both polarization and populism may have negative as well as positive ramifications for how ordinary citizens evaluate democratic institutions. As both phenomena are common in modern Indonesian politics, their relationships with representation, participation and satisfaction with democracy in Indonesia are worth investigating.

2.3 REPRESENTATION AND PARTICIPATION IN INDONESIAN POLITICS

Indonesia is often described as a democracy in which patronage is a key factor shaping the relationship between politicians and citizens (Aspinall and Sukmajati 2016; Aspinall and Berenschot 2019). For many Indonesians, political behavior is primarily transactional, as political support is offered in exchange for the promise of various material benefits. This interpretation of political competition in Indonesia is well documented, and it reflects many Indonesians' experience of political engagement (or lack thereof). However, this view does not imply that citizen–politician linkages in this country should be understood as being primarily clientelistic. While we may assume that the behavior of a small segment of the electorate may be driven primarily, if not exclusively, by transactional considerations, it would be inaccurate and unfair to reduce the political engagement experiences of many others to the pursuit of material gains. To provide a more nuanced and complete overview of political competition and voting behavior in Indonesia, we must allow for the possibility that for most Indonesian citizens, political participation also involves expressing views on important social issues and long-standing political debates.

2.3.1 An Ideological Cleavage about Islam

Political scientists have long identified an association between voting behavior and deep-rooted social, economic and cultural divisions. In their landmark study of electoral politics in Western Europe, Lipset and Rokkan (1967) observe that European party systems in the 1960s appeared to be "frozen," as their structures echoed political divisions that were already well defined in the 1920s. The researchers argue that this continuity arose from deep-seated differences in economic interests, ethnicity, religion and geography that structured political competition at the time. In the context of democratic consolidation, a party system rooted in social cleavages is typically considered as being more institutionalized (Croissant and Völkel 2012), which in turn may have positive repercussions for democratic development. When political parties are closely linked to social groups and their preferences, their ability to function as platforms for political representation is strengthened, which further increases the legitimacy of democracy and ordinary citizens' propensity to develop partisan affiliations.

The most prominent ideological dimension of Indonesian politics concerns the role of Islam in state affairs; we thus need to focus on this ideological cleavage to account for patterns of substantive representation in Indonesia. Since Indonesia's early years as an independent state, and perhaps even since the colonial era, Indonesians have been divided on the issue of state-Islam relations. At one end of the ideological spectrum, some prominent figures in Indonesian nationalism, such as Mohammad Natsir, have promulgated Islam as a force for mobilization and envisioned an independent Indonesia as a state that would follow Islamic principles and laws. At the opposite end, leaders inspired by communism and socialism have advocated for a secularist state and have sometimes seen Islamic institutions and traditions as obstacles to the construction of a more modern and equal society. Between these two extremes, other nationalist figures, such as Sukarno and Mohammad Hatta, have pursued a pluralistic synthesis of the various ideological strands of the nationalist movement, allowing a role for Islam in public affairs while stressing the character of the nation as a multireligious community and rejecting more radical incarnations of Islamist political thought.

These cultural–ideological differences on the issue of state-Islam relations have had important implications for political behavior in Indonesia. During the period of liberal democracy (1950–1957), when Indonesian politics was shaped primarily by Sukarno, Indonesian political elites and the voting public were divided into two main ideological camps. Those with a secularist or pluralist ideological orientation were represented primarily by the Nationalist Party (PNI) and the Communist Party (PKI), which were particularly influential in Central Java, Bali and North Sumatra. Indonesians with more Islamist political leanings were split between two forms of political Islam, namely "traditionalist" or traditional Islam, propagated especially in rural Java by Nahdlatul Ulama (NU), a religious organization that also acted as a political party in the 1950s, and "modernist" or modern Islam, most common in regions outside Java and cities, which was represented by the Muhammadiyah

2.3 Representation and Participation in Indonesian Politics   35

(another religious organization) and the Masyumi party. The division over political Islam thus had important ramifications for political organization and voting behavior in the highly polarized political climate of the 1950s.

The central role of ideology in politics ended abruptly with the Tragedy of 1965–66, when the political left was annihilated by a military-led campaign of mass murder. The New Order regime established thereafter aggressively suppressed ideological debate in the pursuit of technocratic governance and implemented an agenda of depoliticization of the public. Despite three decades of authoritarianism, however, the division over political Islam survived beneath the surface of apparent ideological consensus, remaining a latent political–cultural reference point for many Indonesians. In his analysis of the 1999 elections, King documents the resilience of this ideological division by showing that the results of the first post-Suharto election were significantly correlated with electoral results in the mid-1950s (King 2003). Modernist and traditionalist Islamic parties were substantially stronger than their predecessors forty years prior, and support for the Indonesian Democratic Party of Struggle (PDI-P), led by Sukarno's daughter Megawati Sukarnoputri, was highly correlated with previous nationalist support. The sociocultural divisions that were prominent at the inception of independent Indonesian politics and were then constrained for thirty years by the ideological straitjacket of the New Order again became a powerful force orienting political competition and voting behavior shortly after democratization.

Since the foundational election of 1999, the importance of political Islam in shaping political competition in Indonesia has varied. Starting with the 2004 elections, a trend of "dealignment" with historical partisan affiliations became visible in Indonesian politics, as ideological considerations appeared to become increasingly marginal for political elites and ordinary citizens alike (Ufen 2008b). This trend intensified with the 2009 elections, when the country's electoral laws were reformed to create an open-list proportional representation system that provided strong incentives for candidates to stress personal appeals rather than party affiliations. Over the last two electoral cycles (2014–2019), however, the salience of ideological–religious issues in political debate has increased. This ideological resurgence has been intertwined with the process of democratic erosion described in the Introduction chapter. First, the resurgence of ideological debate has been coupled with the illiberal turn in Indonesian politics. As radical Islamist actors who were previously at the fringes of the political arena have gained new influence and advanced

36   *Explaining Democratic Survival in Indonesia*

their agendas, observers of Indonesian politics have been reminded of the importance of deep-rooted ideological divisions in this diverse country. Second, the rise of a new brand of more populist and polarized politics has at times drawn on historical ideological divisions and ingrained ethnic stereotypes to mobilize consensus and denigrate the opposite camp, as seen most notably in Prabowo Subianto's 2014 presidential campaign. Thus, the appeal of the division over political Islam as a framework to explain Indonesian politics was strong in the immediate aftermath of authoritarian breakdown, declined during the 2000s (reaching its nadir with the electoral reform of 2009) and began to regain ground in the mid-2010s, with the onset of democratic backsliding.

This historical introduction shows that the conflict between pluralism and Islamism in Indonesia can be considered a typical case of political cleavage as conceptualized by Lipset and Rokkan.[4] As in Western European cases, this cleavage emerged from deep structural transformations triggered by nationalist formation and capitalist expansion; is linked with specific consequential ideational orientations and a sense of collective identity; has been mobilized through political institutions such as mass organizations and parties; and has shown remarkable resilience despite challenging historical circumstances. To be sure, as Ufen (2008a) observes, the division over political Islam does not overlap neatly with economic divisions stemming from demographic (e.g. capital–labor or urban–rural) differences, but the same can be said of many religion-based cleavages elsewhere. It should also be emphasized that characterizing the division over political Islam as a "religious" or a "religion-based" cleavage does not imply a conflict between Islam and religious minorities. Certainly, in a Muslim-majority yet diverse society such as Indonesia, religious denomination is significantly associated with preferences regarding state-Islam relations. However, the division over political Islam is an ideological conflict that unfolds primarily *within* Islam; thus, it would be misleading to regard it as a conflict between Islamic and minority groups. In this respect, again, Indonesia's division over political Islam is not dissimilar from conflicts between secularism and religion observed in societies with greater religious homogeneity.[5]

---

[4] See also Bartolini and Mair (2007).

[5] As religious organizations remain powerful actors in Indonesia's nominally secular state (Menchik 2014), however, the term "pluralist," as opposed to "secularist," is more accurate in the Indonesian context. I therefore use the term "pluralist" in discussing ideological orientations in modern Indonesia.

2.3 *Representation and Participation in Indonesian Politics* 37

Research on twenty years of democracy in Indonesia acknowledges political Islam as a crucial feature of Indonesian politics. The literature on the subject is rich, spanning academic disciplines to provide compelling accounts of the various social, cultural and strategic aspects of the relationship between Islam and politics (Fealy and White 2008; Robinson 2008; Bush 2009; Tanuwidjaja 2010; Hefner 2011; Hicks 2012; Menchik 2016). However, the extent to which the division over political Islam influences voting behavior and political participation is a matter of debate, and research in this area has some important limitations, as follows.

First, while scholars of Indonesian politics generally agree that political parties differ in their positions on political Islam, most measures of party positions are based on evaluations by individual researchers. As we lack systematic measures based on surveys of politicians or experts, it is difficult to provide an accurate overview of the ideological choices available to Indonesian voters. Second, the association between political Islam and other important ideological and attitudinal orientations, such as policy preferences and national identity, remains unclear. For example, the recent wave of Islamic populism suggests that Islamist views may be associated with economic grievances or a preference for more assertive redistributive policies, but this potential link is not thoroughly explored. Third, and most importantly for the purposes of this book, we lack systematic studies of political Islam as a dimension for substantive representation. As we have yet to measure political Islam with indicators that enable easy and meaningful comparison of citizens' and politicians' attitudes, the degree to which the views of political elites on this crucial issue mirror those of their constituents is unclear. As such, the implications of patterns of substantive representation for political legitimacy, participation and satisfaction with democracy are unknown.

2.3.2 Formal and Informal Participation

In the early years of the nationalist movement, nationalist leaders with various ideological orientations established associations to mobilize for the anti-colonial struggle. In this context, civic engagement was treated with suspicion by the Dutch authorities. Although most of these associations were modest in size and their activities were closely monitored by the colonial regime, the most successful of them, Sarekat Islam (Islamic Union), grew to over a million members and was crucial in demonstrating the political viability of the nationalist movement. However, many

Indonesians experienced their first political involvement during the Second World War, when the occupying Japanese encouraged mass mobilization to muster support for their war efforts, especially among young people (Anderson 1972, 29–30), and provided military training for thousands of Indonesians from all political backgrounds. After the Japanese left, many Indonesians continued to join political and military activities in the tumultuous years of the National Revolution, during which high levels of mass mobilization consolidated the political–ideological divisions between Islamists and secularist–pluralist factions that had emerged during the colonial period and the Japanese occupation (Vickers 2013, 116). At this point, the Indonesian public became an integral part of Indonesian politics, and the success of future political projects came to depend in part on political leaders' ability to mobilize ordinary citizens.

After the end of the revolutionary war, Indonesian political parties competed freely in a democratic political system, and they made great efforts to mobilize social groups through various affiliated organizations. As previously mentioned, one of the two main Islamic parties, NU, was a mass organization itself, providing cultural, religious and social services to its members; and the second main party, Masyumi, drew its support from Muhammadiyah, another well-established mass organization. Regarding secularist–pluralist parties, both the PNI and the PKI formed various organizations to mobilize support among specific social groups, including youth, women, professionals, veterans, farmers and workers. Such top-down organizations were key avenues for the political participation of ordinary citizens, and they played a crucial role as channels of communication between the elites and the masses (Pauker 1958). The years of liberal democracy were thus a period of intense political engagement featuring high levels of partisan polarization. This is not to say that ideological factors alone explain polarization and participation at this time, as political organization in this period was also a vehicle for patronage, corruption and nepotism. Yet the experience of liberal democracy in the first half of the 1950s depicts close relationships between top-down mass mobilization, intense ideological debate and electoral politics.

This political model would be replaced by authoritarianism, first in the Guided Democracy and later in the New Order; the patterns of participation in the New Order in particular presented a stark contrast with liberal democracy. Although the first few years of the new regime featured remarkable levels of participation by various social groups (Liddle

2.3 Representation and Participation in Indonesian Politics 39

1978), the New Order soon propagated a paternalistic view of popular participation in which the masses were positioned as subordinate within the power hierarchy, disenfranchised, disconnected from political and ideological debate, and active only during elections. In the 1990s, however, a reinvigorated labor movement and newly established civil society organizations that gave voice to an expanding middle class saw a resurgence of participatory politics (Aspinall 1996; Hadiz 2002). An Islamic revival that had unfolded over two decades gave rise to more assertive demands by Islamic groups for participation and inclusion, and student activism re-emerged and ultimately played an important role in Suharto's downfall. When the authoritarian regime collapsed in 1998, Indonesia had a vibrant associational life and various social groups had been mobilized to take advantage of the new opportunities brought about by the regime change.

Today, high levels of civic engagement are still considered a crucial feature of Indonesian politics. The country's two largest Islamic organizations, NU and Muhammadiyah, continue to thrive as the backbone of Indonesian associational life, alongside a constellation of national and local Islam-based associations with various ideological leanings (Van Bruinessen 2013). The connections between Islam and civic and political engagement, which are also documented in survey research (Mujani 2003), are thus still visible in Indonesia, and religious associations provide an important arena for the development of political skills and political selection. Some scholars emphasize the importance of this social makeup, arguing that Indonesia's vibrant associationalism provides a crucial channel for ordinary citizens to constrain the potentially undemocratic preferences of political elites (Lussier and Fish 2012; Lussier 2016). In recent years, beyond associational life in general, there has been growing interest in more explicitly political informal participation by actors at both ends of the spectrum of ideology on political Islam. Some pursue a progressive agenda on issues on which Indonesian public opinion remains conservative, such as women's and LGBT rights and economic issues such as labor rights and inequality (Dibley and Ford 2019). Others are illiberal Islamist forces emboldened by the success of the mass demonstrations "in defense of Islam" in 2016–2017, in which thousands of protesters gathered in Jakarta to demand the criminal prosecution of the incumbent Christian governor. The increasing mobilizational ability of radical Islamist forces is an especially novel development in the context of post-Suharto Indonesia, and it indicates a link between mass participation and political illiberalism.

A strong associational life coupled with a tradition of participatory politics is thus a defining feature of Indonesian politics. Just like ideological contestation, popular participation has characterized foundational events in Indonesian political history. Although repressed under authoritarian rule, it resurfaced when restrictions to political rights were eased or lifted. However, existing research focuses predominantly on informal participation; ordinary citizens' participation through formal institutions is often overlooked. Most importantly, studies of electoral participation are rare, as scholars of Indonesian politics devote scant attention to electoral turnout and its determinants.[6] While studies of democracy in Indonesia generally recognize the importance of electoral participation for democratic consolidation, electoral turnout is rarely, if ever, the primary focus of analysis. The few studies in which more than one or two sentences are dedicated to the subject focus on the decline in electoral turnout from 1999 to 2009, which is attributed to decreasing public trust in institutions (see Tan 2012) or described as an unavoidable side-effect of socioeconomic development (Mujani, Liddle, and Ambardi 2018, 151–152).

Because of this lack of attention to the drivers of electoral turnout, we are unable to fully account for the patterns of political participation in modern Indonesia. Consider the data displayed in Figure 2.1, which plots electoral turnout in various historical periods. Overall, the chart shows that electoral participation in post-Suharto legislative elections has been quite robust; indeed, turnout in Indonesia can be described as high from a comparative perspective (Schraufnagel, Buehler, and Lowry-Fritz 2014). Even more interestingly, Figure 2.1 shows that electoral participation has fluctuated substantially in democratic Indonesia. After an exceptionally large turnout (92.6%) in the first elections in 1999, electoral participation fell to 84.1% in 2004 and 70.7% in 2009; however, it then increased to 75.2% in 2014 and 81.9% in the most recent elections of 2019. Similar to the patterns of satisfaction with democracy reported in Figure 1.1, these figures defy established accounts of political participation. Using clientelistic mobilization as a framework to explain participation, we should observe a spike in turnout in 2009, when the new electoral system provided strong incentives for clientelistic appeals. Yet we see exactly the opposite, as turnout plummeted to its lowest ever point in that year. Meanwhile, if we view declining turnout rates as a function of rising levels

---

[6] See Fossati and Martinez i Coma (2020a) for an exception.

2.3 Representation and Participation in Indonesian Politics

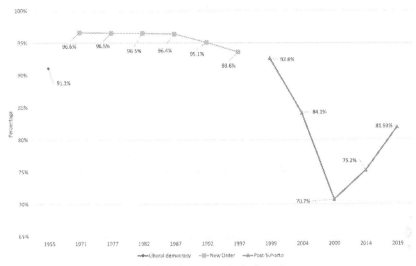

FIGURE 2.1. Electoral turnout in Indonesia, 1955–2019

of education and the "normalization" of electoral participation after the collective euphoria of 1999, the recent trend of increasing electoral participation remains unaccounted for.

Figure 2.1 presents a puzzle similar to the one outlined at the beginning of this book. Political participation, like satisfaction with democracy, has increased since the onset of democratic erosion in the mid-2010s. Again, existing explanations fail to account for this pattern. Most notably, some have reported anecdotal evidence that the incumbent administration mobilized government bureaucracy during the electoral campaign to secure a higher turnout, fearing that low participation would favor opposition candidates.[7] Yet evidence of a campaign of electoral intimidation systematic, sweeping and successful enough to explain the substantial increase in electoral participation (+6.7% compared with the previous election in 2014) is lacking. Furthermore, as I show in Chapter 3, increases in electoral turnout in 2019 were more substantial in districts where Islamist parties were stronger and pro-government parties were weaker. Based on the theoretical framework outlined in this chapter, I argue instead that substantive representation along the division over political Islam is key to explaining this puzzle. While recent years have been marked by increasing illiberalism, partisan polarization and corrosive populist

---

[7] See, for instance, Power (2020, 288–289).

rhetoric, these forces have also helped to improve political representation in the eyes of Indonesians, as they have strengthened perceptions that Indonesian politics offer meaningful choices to voters. Such perceptions have consolidated democratic legitimacy in Indonesia, as indicated by rising public satisfaction with democracy and electoral participation.

2.4 CONCLUSION

This chapter reviews the theoretical and empirical work on the importance of representation for political legitimacy and satisfaction with democracy. Functioning patterns of substantive representation are crucial to foster satisfaction with democracy and trust in democratic institutions, as well as to induce citizens to participate in civic and political life. In turn, an engaged citizenry committed to democracy is a formidable resource for the consolidation and maintenance of democratic regimes. In the context of Indonesian politics, to study representation is to study the ideological division over the role of Islam in public affairs that has shaped political debate since the birth of the independent Indonesian state. In Chapter 3, I begin my empirical exploration of political Islam in Indonesia with an analysis of aggregate electoral data.

3

The Ideological Roots of Electoral Politics

3.1 A CLIENTELISTIC DEMOCRACY?

In Chapter 2, I sketch the history of the division over political Islam in Indonesia. To recapitulate, ideological debate over the role of Islam in public affairs has characterized Indonesian politics since the colonial era. The heyday of ideology-based politics was in the polarized climate of the 1950s, in which political parties could be broadly classified into three families based on their stance on state–Islam relations. Pluralist–secularist forces (mainly the PNI and PKI) advocated for a clear demarcation between the state and Islam; the traditionalist Islamic NU called for a larger role for Islam within the boundaries of a pluralistic republic; and modernist Islamic parties, led by Masyumi, represented a more radical form of political Islam and at times advocated for the establishment of an Islamic state. Although the salience of the division over political Islam has varied over time, it has been resilient enough to survive the vicissitudes of various historical circumstances and political regimes. In recent years, the resurgence of radical Islamism has provided new evidence that state-Islam relations are still an important political issue in Indonesia.

Although the historical significance of the division over political Islam is clear, whether it can still be considered the main feature of political competition in Indonesia is a matter of debate. In his anatomy of Indonesian political parties, Mietzner (2013) argues that accounts of the "end of ideology" in Indonesian politics are premature, as parties still maintain distinct positions on the issue of state-Islam relations and, when appraised in comparison with other young democracies, they present reasonably high levels of institutionalization. However, the consensus among scholars is that ideological issues have had marginal effects on the structure of political competition and voting behavior in post-Suharto Indonesia. Clientelism is a particularly influential framework for the study of citizen–politician linkages in Indonesia, especially among qualitative scholars who study electoral dynamics at the grassroots level (Aspinall and Sukmajati 2016; Aspinall and Berenschot 2019). Most quantitative studies of public opinion and voting behavior highlight the preeminence of economic factors and candidate traits, and they suggest that the effectiveness of parties' religious appeals is contingent on economic considerations (Pepinsky, Liddle, and Mujani 2012; Mujani, Liddle, and Ambardi 2018). Even in the wake of increasing polarization and the recent resurgence of radical Islamism, many scholars emphasize the proclivity of Indonesian political elites to engage in cooperative (or perhaps collusive) power-sharing arrangements rather than competing on ideological–programmatic grounds (Ambardi 2008; Slater 2018).

These studies thus suggest that ideology may not greatly shape how ordinary Indonesians evaluate political candidates and decide which political party to support when they cast their ballots. However, despite the rich and insightful body of literature on the subject, no empirical analysis to date examines the full temporal and spatial spectrum of available electoral data. Although a dealignment from historical partisan affiliations has occurred, we lack conclusive evidence of its extent, its trajectory over the last four electoral cycles, its subnational variations, its variations across parties and its causal mechanisms. Similarly, we know little about how deep-seated partisan affiliations are associated with patterns of clientelism and electoral participation, or exactly how the emergence of new parties has contributed to this partisan dealignment.

This chapter proposes answers to these questions based on an analysis of aggregate district-level electoral data for the five national electoral cycles that took place in Indonesia from 1999 to 2019. This first step of my empirical analysis enables me to begin to substantiate the argument that I present in this book, namely that ideological considerations structure voting behavior in modern Indonesia and have repercussions for democratic legitimacy. A clear implication of this broad proposition is that if the division over political Islam still plays an important role in voting behavior today, we should be able to observe continuities between modern electoral patterns and those of the mid-1950s, when Indonesia was a democracy and ideological competition was a salient feature of its politics. Similar to King (2003), I analyze macro-level electoral returns in search of a connection between historical partisan

3.2 District-Level Analysis

affiliations, rooted in ideological competition in postcolonial Indonesia, and modern voting patterns.

In Section 3.2, I present the research design of my analysis of aggregate electoral returns and offer an overview of the data, focusing on subnational patterns of historical and contemporary partisanship as well as electoral participation. I then present the regression analysis and discuss the findings in Section 3.3.

3.2 DISTRICT-LEVEL ANALYSIS

Indonesia is a large and highly diverse country, whose regions differ substantially in terms of economic development, economic structure, sociodemographic composition, local governance and political culture, among various other factors. As districts and cities vary in their historical legacies of ideological competition, partisan affiliation, religious makeup, socioeconomic modernization, incidence of clientelistic practices and so forth, we can examine how each factor has affected electoral politics since democratization. Furthermore, by considering the five national legislative elections since 1999, we can analyze longitudinal trends in the relationship between historical partisan affiliation and modern electoral outcomes and study how these changes are related to national-level developments such as institutional reforms, as the district-level aggregate data provide sufficient diversity to study variation over time and space.

To determine whether to what degree and why historical ideology-based partisan affiliations have weakened over time, I use the association between past and present electoral geography as a proxy for the strength of deep-seated partisan identity. To gauge the district-level strength of historical partisan affiliations (pluralist, traditionalist Islamic and modernist Islamic), I use data from the national elections in 1955, the last democratic election before the transition to authoritarianism (1957–1966) and the New Order (1966–1998). I then match these data with electoral outcomes in post-Suharto Indonesia's five legislative elections for political parties that can be identified as appealing to one of the three focal ideological traditions. The general approach that I follow is thus to compare historical and recent electoral results and to consider a high degree of empirical association between the two as evidence that historical ideology-based affiliations still drive voting behavior in Indonesia today.

This approach makes some important assumptions. The first is that political ideology – and the division over political Islam specifically – has played an important role in shaping historical partisan affiliations in the

46 *The Ideological Roots of Electoral Politics*

Indonesian context. Of course, this premise should not be interpreted as suggesting that ideology was the exclusive driver of partisan affiliations and voting behavior in the 1950s. For example, clientelism was a key feature of the Indonesian political system in that era, as it is today. Yet the 1950s were undoubtedly a time in which political competition was much more polarized along ideological lines compared with contemporary Indonesian politics (Mietzner 2008). This suggests that aggregate voting patterns from that period carry valuable information about a region's ideological profile. For example, it is plausible to conclude that a district in which the PNI and PKI receive the majority of votes has a more pluralist political culture than one in which Islamic forces prevail.

The second and more general premise is that voting can be treated to a considerable degree as an expression of partisan identity. Again, I make no claim that partisanship should be viewed as the primary driver of voting behavior in Indonesia, especially as mass partisan identities have eroded substantially since democratization in the late 1990s. Yet the aforementioned premise is defensible even in the context of weak partisan identities and in Indonesia specifically. For example, Mujani et al. document that party identity has long been a driver of voting behavior in democratic Indonesia, even though its relevance in accounting for party choice has declined steadily from election to election (Mujani, Liddle, and Ambardi 2018, 199). While these data indicate that historical partisan identities may be less salient now than in the immediate aftermath of authoritarian breakdown, they also show that partisan identity has affected voting behavior in post-Suharto Indonesia.

Third, I assume that deep-rooted partisan identities may be transmitted over generations and persist for long periods of sustained political and socioeconomic change. Considering the extraordinary upheavals that have marked Indonesia's history since the mid-1950s, this premise may sound less plausible than the previous two. Could the partisan affiliations that developed in the aftermath of the National Revolution have survived the authoritarian turn of the late 1950s, the Tragedy of 1965–66, thirty years of authoritarianism and socioeconomic development during the New Order, and then twenty years of democracy marked by patronage politics and ideologically promiscuous coalitions? As discussed in Chapter 2, research on political divisions demonstrates that historical legacies of partisanship are powerful and resilient, as they can show decades of continuity. The case of Eastern Europe, where politics quickly reverted to pre-communist divisions after decades of Soviet rule, is a particularly trenchant illustration (Evans 2006; Ekiert and Ziblatt 2013). It should be acknowledged that the

3.2 *District-Level Analysis* 47

exact mechanisms responsible for such surprising resilience are difficult to verify empirically and that the meanings of such partisan identities today may be quite different from those more than six decades ago. Yet such patterns of continuity suggest that pre-authoritarian partisan legacies linked to specific positions on the issue of state–Islam relations may still have consequential effects on modern Indonesian politics.

3.2.1 Data and Measures

This chapter is centered on the analysis of a panel dataset with district-level electoral returns from 242 districts for all five national legislative elections in post-authoritarian Indonesia (1999, 2004, 2009, 2014, 2019) and from the foundational democratic elections of 1955.[1] By "districts," I refer to the important political and administrative units of the Indonesian government that can be further divided into administrative districts (*kabupaten*) and cities. Note that this unit of analysis does not correspond to *electoral* districts, which are typically larger than administrative districts and cities. However, electoral districts cannot be used as the unit of analysis because electoral district boundaries may be redrawn between elections. Furthermore, the control variables that I use in quantitative analysis are measured at the district level, and building aggregate measures would require calculating averages that may obfuscate variation patterns. Using administrative districts and cities thus enables a more precise analysis of empirical associations across time and space. For convenience, I will use the term "districts" to refer to administrative districts (*kabupaten*) and cities.

Indonesia is currently divided into 34 provinces and 508 districts. Many of these districts were established in the ongoing process of administrative proliferation that began in the early 2000s.[2] To restrict the

---

[1] All electoral data are from official sources. Data for the 1955 election were collected from historical archives at Cornell University. Because data for the province of West Java are missing for 1955, I use returns from the local elections of 1957 for this province. The 1999–2019 electoral data were retrieved from the Electoral Commission (KPU). I am grateful to Kevin Evans for supplying most of these data and to Ray Hervandi, Pearlyn Pang and Emilia Yustiningrum for their research assistance.

[2] As district proliferation, or *pemekaran daerah*, is often driven by the goal of establishing more homogeneous jurisdictions to diffuse ethnic tensions, district splitting is more prevalent in more diverse outer regions. Of the 108 districts located in Java in 1999, only 6 were split into two or more regions between 2001 and 2012, when almost all such proliferation took place. During the same period, district splitting occurred in 92 of the 240 districts outside Java (about 38%).

48   The Ideological Roots of Electoral Politics

analysis to readily comparable units, I drop from the sample districts that underwent territorial changes between 1999 and 2019 and districts that were newly established after democratization. As historical electoral data are not available for the capital region of Jakarta and districts in the Island of Papua, I also exclude these districts from the panel analysis. This leaves us with a balanced panel of 242 districts observed over five electoral cycles. As for the geographic distribution of the districts, 102 districts, 42%, are in Java, and the remaining 140 are in other islands of the Indonesian archipelago.

To operationalize the main independent and dependent variables, I build indicators of past and contemporary electoral support for the three political–ideological groups in Indonesian politics, namely pluralism, traditional Islam and modernist Islam. During the Old Order (1950–1957), the values of pluralist nationalism were most closely associated with the PNI, which consistently advocated an inclusive political model that embraced Indonesia's exceptional social and religious diversity. NU presided over the traditionalist Islam camp, and Masyumi represented modernist Islam and its more uncompromising ideological views. In Indonesian politics today, the PDI-P continues the PNI's ideological tradition of prioritizing inclusive nationalism over Islam. At the opposite end of the ideological spectrum, a number of parties compete for the Islamic legacy, with the National Awakening Party (PKB) maintaining close ties to NU's traditionalism, parties such as the Prosperous Justice Party (PKS), National Mandate Party (PAN) and Crescent Star Party (PBB) typically being described as modernist, and the United Development Party (PPP) attempting to appeal to both constituencies, as it did during the New Order. Table 3.1 offers an overview of these three party families and their 1950s counterparts.[3]

In a regression analysis, I estimate fractional logistic models (Papke and Wooldridge 1996) in which electoral returns from 1999 to 2014 are regressed on 1955 data. This model choice is suitable for response variables that, resulting from the aggregation of multiple observations measured on a binary scale, present values ranging from 0 to 1, such as

---

[3] By focusing exclusively on these ideology-based (i.e., either pluralist or Islamic) political parties, other prominent parties in Indonesian politics are excluded, most notably Golkar, a party established during the authoritarian New Order. As previously discussed, this choice is consistent with the historical development of social cleavages and partisan affiliations in Indonesia. Furthermore, it is dictated by the lack of availability of district-level data on Golkar support during the New Order. I briefly discuss the ideological profiles of Golkar and other new parties in Section 3.3.1.

3.2 District-Level Analysis

TABLE 3.1. *Ideological groups and political parties, past and present*

	Pluralist	Traditionalist Islamic	Modernist Islamic
1950s	Indonesian Nationalist Party (PNI)	Nahdlatul Ulama (NU)	Masyumi
Today	PDI-P (Indonesian Democratic Party of Struggle)	PKB (National Awakening Party) PPP (United Development Party)	PAN (National Mandate Party) PKS (Prosperous Justice Party) PBB (Crescent Star Party) PPP (United Development Party)

aggregate vote shares calculated from individual votes. All of the pooled models are estimated with cluster-robust standard errors for districts and include fixed effects for year and region (a binary variable that distinguishes between Java and Bali and other regions) and a number of covariates as controls, namely district type (city versus administrative district), total population, population density, socioeconomic development, poverty, inequality, religious fractionalization and ethnolinguistic fractionalization.[4]

I first estimate three panel models, one for each political–ideological stream (pluralist, traditionalist Islamic and modernist Islamic), in which binary indicators for years are interacted with 1955 election data. This enables a full analysis of changes in the relationship between historical partisan legacies and contemporary electoral results from the transitional election of 1999 to the most recent one in 2019. Second, I analyze patterns of regional variation, especially differences between what is often considered the historical "core" of Indonesian politics, namely Java and Bali, where partisan affiliations have been traditionally strong, and more peripheral regions where the three ideological traditions may have been less consolidated. I pay special attention to the role of ethnolinguistic fractionalization, as ethnic divisions may hinder the development of programmatic politics and facilitate the establishment of clientelistic linkages. Finally, I explore the relationship between political–ideological

---

[4] Data are from the World Bank's INDO-DAPOER (Indonesian Database for Economic and Policy Research) except for the indexes of religious and ethnolinguistic fractionalization, which is built from the 2010 Population Census data. For missing data in the time series, I use the nearest available year.

50   *The Ideological Roots of Electoral Politics*

traditions and contemporary patterns of electoral participation. I investigate whether, as suggested by my argument, the recent increase in participation is associated with the resurgence of more radical forms of political Islam, which are represented by the modernist tradition. Section 3.2.2 provides an overview of past and present Indonesian electoral geography based on the collected data.

3.2.2 Electoral Geography

The general elections of September 1955 were Indonesia's first experience of free and fair democratic elections. An exceptionally large number of national and local parties (172), with more than 1,000 candidates, competed for seats in the 260-member unicameral parliament. The election saw a very high degree of popular participation, with an estimated turnout of about 91% (about forty million voters, about three-quarters of whom were located in Java alone), and eventually witnessed the emergence of four roughly equally sized electoral blocs, namely the nationalist PNI (22.3% of the vote), modernist Islamic Masyumi (20.9%), traditional Islamic NU (18.4%) and communist PKI (16.4%). The role of ideological considerations in determining this outcome is a matter of debate. For example, some scholars argue that for many voters in rural areas, voting was oriented by traditional power relations (i.e., loyalty to prominent local figures) rather than programmatic issues, and that different appeals were formulated to target different groups of voters (Van der Kroef 1957, 243). Yet the four main political parties maintained distinct ideological positions that featured prominently in campaign communication (Bone 1955). Voters were therefore presented with clear programmatic alternatives in this election, especially with regard to the division over political Islam. In this respect, the aggregate results of the 1955 elections provide insights into the ideological profile of voters in various regions.

With regard to the geographic distribution of preferences for these three ideological streams, a mapping of district-level electoral returns enables us to identify regions of particular strength (or weakness) in terms of pluralism, traditional Islam and modernist Islam. Figures 3.4, 3.5 and 3.6 map electoral support in 1955 for the PNI, NU and Masyumi, respectively, with darker colors indicating higher shares of district-level votes.[5] Overall, these three maps show a substantial degree of subnational heterogeneity in local-level voting behavior, as support for these three parties varied

---

[5] Boundaries between classes are determined using Jenks natural breaks.

3.2 District-Level Analysis

dramatically across districts. In the map shown in Figure 3.1, the PNI appears to be a fairly nationalized party, with a median vote share of 17% in the 242 selected districts and a standard deviation of 0.15. About 60% of these districts recorded vote shares of 10% or higher for the PNI, indicating that this party had a non-negligible presence in most Indonesian regions. However, the map in Figure 3.1 also shows that PNI electoral support was concentrated in Java, the island where most voters resided, which gave this party a crucial advantage in electoral competition. As suggested by the party's pluralist ideology, support for the PNI beyond Java was strong in areas with substantial populations of religious and ethnic minorities, such as North Sumatra, the Bangka-Belitung archipelago, Bali, Eastern Nusa Tenggara and North Sulawesi.

For traditional Islamic ideology (Figure 3.2), represented by NU, the median vote share across selected districts of 11% and the standard

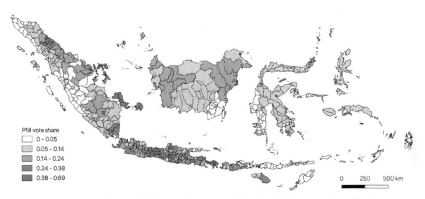

FIGURE 3.1. Map of electoral support for the PNI (1955) by district

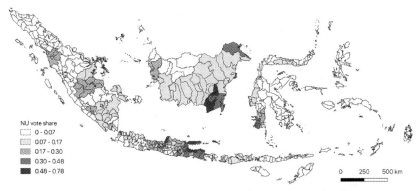

FIGURE 3.2. Map of electoral support for NU (1955) by district

deviation of 0.18 suggest that support for this party varied subnationally to a higher degree than did support for PNI. The strongholds of traditional Islam appear more concentrated geographically than those for pluralism, as they are confined to East Java, some coastal regions of Central Java and Southern Kalimantan. Because a very high share of NU votes came from a limited number of populous Javanese districts, this party could be considered as being more regionalized than the PNI or Masyumi. In addition, NU had very limited support, not only in most regions of Eastern Indonesia and Sumatra but also in many districts in Java. From this perspective, traditional Islam, as measured by past electoral support for NU, may not be easily characterized as being "Java-centric." Support for NU was weak in several Javanese regions, and NU performed well in some Sumatran regions, Kalimantan and southern Sulawesi.

Finally, Figure 3.3 shows electoral support for Masyumi, representing modernist Islam, which has a higher median score than the other two parties, at 25% and displays a much higher regional variation, with a standard deviation of 0.21. As shown in Figure 3.3, support for Masyumi varied more substantially across regions than support for the other two parties, but this does not necessarily mean that this party was more regionalized than the other two. Although there was extreme variation in support for Masyumi, which exceeded 80% in some districts in Aceh but was close to zero in many PNI strongholds, Masyumi had a strong presence in Sumatra and most regions outside Java. However, because its support in vote-rich Java was largely limited to Banten and some districts in West Java, Masyumi was at a disadvantage in securing a prominent position in national politics. This imbalance in the geographic distribution

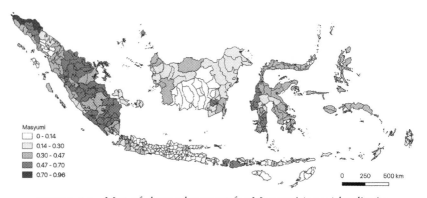

FIGURE 3.3. Map of electoral support for Masyumi (1955) by district

3.2 District-Level Analysis

of electoral support for modernist Islam and its weakness in Java contributed to the relative marginalization of radical Islamic forces in Indonesian politics that persists today.

Thus, in the mid-1950s, Indonesia appears to have been a country with a fairly regionalized party system. The case of PKI features even more uneven patterns of local support, as votes for this party were almost exclusively concentrated in some populous regions in Central and East Java and modern-day North Sumatra. Certainly, all of the major parties had national aspirations and strived to be competitive wherever they could. In this sense, none of them could be characterized as "regionalist" political parties, unlike the many other smaller local parties that contested the 1955 elections. Yet the patterns of regional variations in support for these three electoral blocs are striking, and they indicate that a regression analysis of district-level data can leverage sufficient variation in these variables.

To what extent, then, are these historical results associated with electoral politics in post-Suharto Indonesia? The maps in Figures 3.1, 3.2 and 3.3 suggest some continuity between past and present electoral geography. For example, Bali appears today to be as much a PDI-P stronghold as it was once a core constituency for the PNI, and the same is true of most districts in Central Java and Yogyakarta. Similarly, traditionalist Islam today is strongest in East Java and other Javanese regions where NU used to be the largest party, and the Sumatran regions of Aceh, West Sumatra, Riau and Jambi are today's bastions of modernist Islam. This provides initial evidence that historical legacies of partisan identity may still loom large in contemporary Indonesian politics despite the increasingly competitive electoral landscape and the diffuseness of clientelism.

Beyond visual inspection, an initial approach to addressing this question is to analyze how the correlation coefficients between historical and contemporary electoral returns have changed over time. Table 3.2 displays the full range of variation in correlations between past and present,

TABLE 3.2. *Correlation coefficients for three ideological streams*

	Pluralist	Traditional Islamic	Modernist Islamic
1999	0.69	0.69	0.55
2004	0.71	0.74	0.57
2009	0.58	0.65	0.23
2014	0.45	0.55	0.47
2019	0.55	0.56	0.54

both over time and across ideological groups, and it shows two interesting patterns. First, the figures indicate that the empirical association between historical and contemporary returns has generally diminished since the 1999 elections. The correlation coefficients for pluralism and traditional Islam are weaker today than they were twenty years ago, while modernist Islam shows about the same degree of correlation in 2019 as in 1999. Second, dealignment has not shown a linear downward trend but has oscillated throughout the years. This decline is noticeable for all ideological groups in the first decade of democracy, but evidence for the partisan dealignment hypothesis is much weaker after 2009. The 2019 elections in particular show higher correlation coefficients than those in 2014, especially for pluralism and modernist Islam.

In Section 3.3, I further subject these data to regression analysis, which enables me to control for various sociodemographic factors and analyze interactions with factors such as ethnic diversity. Yet these simple correlation coefficients already provide some intriguing insights into the debate on partisan dealignment in post-Suharto Indonesia. The figures reported in Table 3.2 suggest that a process of dealignment has indeed occurred since the foundational elections of 1999. However, the data also indicate that this process may not have occurred to the same extent for all ideological groups and, even more importantly, that dealignment may be reversible, as suggested by the 2014 and 2019 data. Regarding the discussion on increasing polarization and the resurgence of political Islam in recent years, it is important to note that, as expected, the correlation coefficients for modernist Islam, the group most closely associated with radical Islamism, increased substantially in 2014 and 2019 after reaching a nadir in 2009. More generally, Table 3.2 suggests that political ideology and, specifically, the division over political Islam played a more important role in the 2019 elections than in the previous electoral cycle.

3.3 EXAMINING MACRO-LEVEL ELECTORAL PATTERNS

In this section, I apply regression analysis techniques to answer the main research questions that I address in this chapter. The first asks whether deep-seated partisan affiliations are still a strong driver of voting behavior in Indonesia and how their effect has evolved over the twenty years of democracy beginning in 1999. I then consider the role of ethnolinguistic fractionalization, which I use as a proxy for the incidence of clientelistic linkages between voters and politicians, in the relationship between historical and contemporary electoral patterns. I conclude by considering

3.3 Examining Macro-Level Electoral Patterns 55

some data that indicate a relationship between historical partisan affiliations and electoral participation.

3.3.1 Dealignment or a Resurgence of Ideology?

As mentioned in Section 3.1, research suggests that the importance of ideological-partisan legacies has declined since the transitional elections of 1999, when many Indonesian voters seemed to follow deep-rooted patterns of mass partisanship in their voting behavior. Therefore, in the regression estimation, the interaction terms between historical partisan affiliations and years should be negative, denoting an erosion of mass partisan identities from 1999 to 2019. However, the recent debate on ideological and partisan polarization and the resurgence of radical political Islam indicate that the conventional wisdom about the marginality of political ideology may need to be reassessed.

The estimation results reported in Table 3.3 suggest that the relationship between historical and contemporary electoral politics is more complex than often assumed. The first row of the table reports the estimated coefficients for historical electoral results. They are large in magnitude, positive and significant at the .01 level for all three ideological groups, indicating that overall, in the twenty years of Indonesian democracy, historical partisan-cultural legacies have been a powerful driver of electoral behavior, as electoral geography in post-Suharto Indonesia is indeed strongly correlated with the patterns observed in the mid-1950s. However, as suggested by the dealignment hypothesis, most of the interaction terms between the historical electoral returns and the binary indicators for years are negative, indicating that deep-seated partisan affiliations have eroded. In particular, the interaction term for 2019 is negative and significant for all groups, suggesting a weaker empirical association between historical and contemporary electoral patterns in 2019 than in the baseline year of 1999.

The extent of partisan dealignment that occurred between 1999 and 2019 can be well illustrated with plots of estimated vote shares, such as those reported in Figure 3.4. Each of these three charts shows two curves of estimated support for contemporary pluralist (PDI-P), traditional Islamic (PKB, PPP) and modernist Islamic (PKS, PAN, PPP, PBB) parties, one for 1999 and one for 2019, as a function of past electoral support for PNI, NU and Masyumi, respectively. All of the curves show a positive and substantial relationship between past and present electoral geography, and the differences between 1999 and 2019 are noticeable, especially

56 The Ideological Roots of Electoral Politics

TABLE 3.3. *Historical and contemporary district-level electoral outcomes for three ideological groups*

Variables	(1) PNI/PDI-P	(2) Traditional Islam	(3) Modernist Islam
Historical electoral returns	2.497***	2.636***	2.012***
	(0.284)	(0.240)	(0.305)
Historical electoral returns#2004	0.128	0.425***	−0.446**
	(0.233)	(0.136)	(0.187)
Historical electoral returns#2009	−0.514*	−0.666***	−1.586***
	(0.289)	(0.243)	(0.243)
Historical electoral returns#2014	−1.495***	−1.224***	−0.985***
	(0.238)	(0.293)	(0.277)
Historical electoral returns#2019	−0.794***	−1.054***	−0.628***
	(0.264)	(0.331)	(0.234)
Year = 2004	−0.855***	−0.362***	0.286***
	(0.0612)	(0.0430)	(0.0465)
Year = 2009	−1.134***	−0.633***	0.270***
	(0.0857)	(0.0631)	(0.0724)
Year = 2014	−0.520***	−0.0390	0.292***
	(0.0793)	(0.0781)	(0.0808)
Year = 2019	−0.596***	−0.182**	0.0216
	(0.0813)	(0.0730)	(0.0739)
City	−0.221**	0.252***	0.292***
	(0.105)	(0.0878)	(0.0844)
Population (thousands)	−8.79e-05	0.000148***	0.000106**
	(5.85e-05)	(5.22e-05)	(4.56e-05)
Population density (thousands per km²)	−0.0124	−0.0419***	0.0275***
	(0.0153)	(0.0132)	(0.0103)
GDP per capita (IDR millions)	−0.00463	0.00151	0.000891
	(0.00402)	(0.00207)	(0.00363)
Poverty rate	−0.0147***	0.0172***	−0.00128
	(0.00570)	(0.00472)	(0.00560)
Inequality (Gini coefficient)	0.0109*	−0.0114*	0.00806
	(0.00633)	(0.00602)	(0.00689)
Religious fractionalization index	2.361***	−1.025***	−1.139***
	(0.288)	(0.263)	(0.215)
Ethnic fractionalization index	0.313*	−0.0345	−0.138
	(0.168)	(0.136)	(0.122)
Java or Bali	0.985***	0.344***	−0.101
	(0.121)	(0.0965)	(0.111)
Constant	−2.127***	−2.009***	−2.038***
	(0.224)	(0.202)	(0.246)
Observations	1,161	1,161	1,161
Log-likelihood	−366.0	−331.8	−410.4

Robust standard errors in parentheses. *** $p < 0.01$, ** $p < 0.05$, * $p < 0.10$

3.3 Examining Macro-Level Electoral Patterns

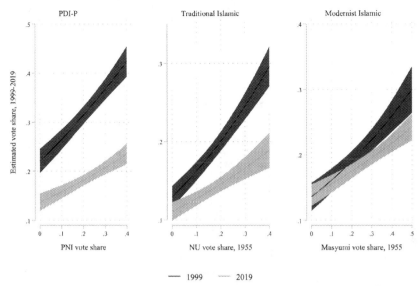

FIGURE 3.4. Historical and contemporary electoral returns in 1999 and 2019 for the pluralist and traditional Islamic parties. In both cases, the 1999 curves are steeper than their 2019 counterparts, indicating a significantly closer empirical association. For example, consider the hypothetical case of a district with a history of robust support for NU in the 1950s and a vote share of 20% for NU in the 1955 election. The model estimates support for traditional Islamic parties in this district at 20% in the 1999 elections, but only at 14.6% twenty years later. These numbers reflect the negative effect of increasingly competitive electoral politics on support for political parties that appeal to deep-seated partisan identities. Figure 3.4 also shows important variation across party families. While the gaps between 1999 and 2019 are substantial for pluralist and traditional Islamic parties, the curves are much closer for modernist Islam, suggesting that partisan dealignment has been significantly less severe for parties in this group.

There is thus robust evidence of the erosion of traditional partisan identities from 1999 to 2019. However, it must be emphasized that this process has not been even in its impact across party families or linear. Figure 3.5, which shows plots of the coefficients of historical electoral returns disaggregated both by party group and by year, provides an exhaustive overview of how the effects of historical partisan legacies have varied over time and across party families. In these charts, higher estimated coefficients indicate a stronger association between historical and

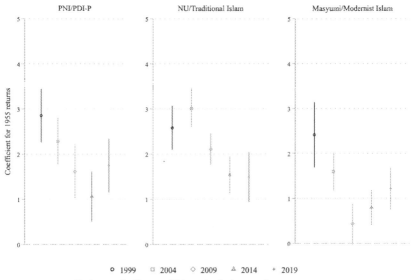

FIGURE 3.5. Estimated effects of historical electoral returns on contemporary elections, 1999–2019

contemporary electoral support, and an effect on contemporary electoral outcomes is statistically significant when the point estimate and the 95% confidence interval are above zero. The first observation based on this figure is that the coefficient plots confirm the two findings that historical partisan affiliations have been significantly associated with contemporary electoral outcomes and that a general process of dealignment has occurred over the last twenty years.

This general trend toward dealignment shows important variations across party families and over time. The legacy of the pluralist ideological stream, shown in the left panel, has weakened substantially between 1999 and 2014, and it witnessed a resurgence in the elections of 2019, for which the estimated coefficient is the highest since 2004. Similarly, the legacy of traditional Islam weakened significantly from 2004 to 2014, but this erosion appears to have stopped in 2019. Finally, the trajectory of partisan dealignment for modernist Islam is somewhat different from those of the other two party families, as it was much more dramatic between the high of 1999 and the low of 2009, and a process of realignment appears to have started in 2014 and continued in 2019.

These patterns suggest three conclusions regarding the role of the deep-seated division between pluralism and Islamism in contemporary Indonesian politics. First, the process of dealignment has not been a

3.3 Examining Macro-Level Electoral Patterns

linear. The elections of 2009 indicate an important discontinuity, as the effect of historical partisan affiliations weakened substantially in that year for all parties, especially for traditional and modernist Islam. Plausibly, this discontinuity results from the introduction of a system of open-list proportional representation that gave candidates unprecedented incentives to cultivate the personal vote as opposed to emphasizing party identity and ideology. This suggests that partisan dealignment has not been driven exclusively by increasing levels of socioeconomic development and mass education, which have been identified as determinants of partisan dealignment in other settings, but also by institutional change. Other institutional developments that have been implemented since democratization, such as direct elections for president, governor and district heads, may also have contributed to this trend by increasing the personalization of political competition.

Second, although historical partisan legacies are weaker now than they were in 1999, a process of realignment appears to have taken place in the last elections of 2019. As noted by numerous observers of Indonesian politics, this electoral cycle featured levels of partisan polarization unprecedented in post-Suharto Indonesia, and this qualitative observation resonates with the aforementioned analysis of district-level electoral returns. As Indonesian politics have become more polarized in recent years, support for pluralist PDI-P and modernist Islamist parties has become more closely aligned with pre-authoritarian patterns of partisan support. Given our qualitative knowledge of recent trends in Indonesian politics, we can infer that this realignment could be due to these ideology-based parties appealing more explicitly to historical partisan identities and the ideological positions. This may particularly be the case for constituencies where, because of their electoral history, such appeals may be especially effective. Concerning the near future of Indonesian politics, the 2019 data suggest that the process of partisan dealignment could be reversible.

Third, the trajectory and the extent of partisan dealignment vary across the three party groups, and the case of modernist Islam is particularly distinctive. Dealignment for this party family began with a substantial drop in the estimated coefficient for the Masyumi historical vote in 2004 and continued in 2009 with an even larger drop. This suggests that the 2009 electoral reform was particularly transformative for parties in this group and for PKS especially, as this party embraced a more moderate ideological profile that may have substantially changed its electoral base in that electoral cycle (Tanuwidjaja 2012). However, realignment had already begun in 2014, and it consolidated further in 2019, consistent with the broader trend of the increasing political clout of radical Islamist forces in Indonesian politics observed in recent years. As radical Islamists have become more vocal since the mid-2010s, modernist Islamist parties, who have traditionally represented a more uncompromising form of political Islamism, may have sought to capitalize on this development by increasing religious-ideological appeals, especially in regions with electoral histories favorable to modernist Islam.

Most of the sociodemographic factors included in the models reported in Table 3.3 have a minor or inconsistent effect on contemporary support for the three party families. The major exception is the index of religious fractionalization, which is quite large in magnitude and significant at the .01 level in all three models. Religious diversity is positively associated with support for PDI-P and negatively associated with support for Islamic parties of any ideological orientation. Figure 3.6 shows the estimations of the expected vote shares for each party group at various levels of religious fractionalization based on the data presented in Table 3.3, and it shows that religious diversity is strongly correlated with electoral outcomes. For example, in a homogenous district with a low religious fractionalization

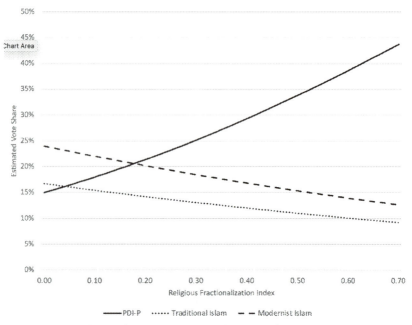

FIGURE 3.6. Religious fractionalization and support for pluralist, traditional Islamic and modernist Islamic parties

3.3 Examining Macro-Level Electoral Patterns 61

index value of 10%, estimated support for modernist Islam is slightly higher than that for PDI-P (22% and 18%, respectively). However, in a more diverse district with a religious fractionalization value of 35%, expected electoral support for PDI-P increases to 27%, while support for modernist Islamic parties declines to 18%. This chart thus contrasts sharply with analyses of voting behavior that depict religion as a marginal factor in shaping voters' choices. On the contrary, when we analyze the full range of variation in available electoral data and focus on the exceptional subnational diversity in the religious composition of Indonesian regions, we find that *religion matters in Indonesian politics*, as it is a powerful driver of voting behavior.[6]

A final point on the relationship between past and present electoral geography regards parties that cannot easily be classified as belonging to one of the three party families studied in this chapter. These include Golkar, the former electoral vehicle of the New Order regime, and other parties that were established by previous Golkar cadres or military figures, such as former president Susilo Bambang Yudhoyono's Partai Demokrat, media tycoon Surya Paloh's NasDem and Prabowo Subianto's Gerindra. For Golkar and most of the parties in this group, drawing a connection between the history of electoral politics in the 1950s and the present day is problematic, as these parties are generally seen as occupying a centrist ideological position, and they may be reminiscent of "catch-all" parties in other contexts that attempt to appeal to voters of various backgrounds and ideological orientations. An exception to this rule is Gerindra, which, to support its leader's presidential ambitions, cultivated from 2014 to 2019 a well-defined oppositional stance to various national cabinets, siding fairly consistently with modernist Islamic parties in various national and subnational electoral competitions. We could therefore hypothesize that patterns of electoral support for this party may mirror those of modernist Islamic parties in showing a connection with pre-authoritarian partisan legacies. The data shown in Table 3.4 suggest that this is indeed the case. Support for Prabowo Subianto's Gerindra in the 2019 elections was significantly higher in districts with a legacy of Islamist mobilization and significantly lower in districts where PNI support was stronger. Furthermore, support for Gerindra was

---

[6] Again, given the substantial ideological heterogeneity among Indonesians Muslims, this finding should not suggest that the political Islam cleavage represents an ideological conflict between Muslim and non-Muslim Indonesians.

TABLE 3.4. *Determinants of electoral support for Gerindra, 2019*

Variables	(1) Gerindra	(2) Gerindra	(3) Gerindra
PNI vote share	−0.791***		
	(0.271)		
NU vote share, 1955		0.0912	
		(0.263)	
Masyumi vote share, 1955			0.818***
			(0.252)
City	0.367***	0.368***	0.303**
	(0.120)	(0.120)	(0.120)
Population (thousands)	0.000254***	0.000275***	0.000235***
	(4.76e-05)	(4.83e-05)	(5.04e-05)
Population density (thousands per km^2)	−0.000679	0.00637	0.00292
	(0.0148)	(0.0147)	(0.0133)
GDP per capita (IDR millions)	−0.00483	−0.00438	−0.00562*
	(0.00338)	(0.00342)	(0.00338)
Poverty rate	−0.0121	−0.0123	−0.0135*
	(0.00795)	(0.00812)	(0.00818)
Inequality (Gini coefficient)	0.00967	0.0125	0.0175
	(0.0110)	(0.0110)	(0.0110)
Religious fractionalization index	−1.547***	−1.688***	−1.242***
	(0.257)	(0.267)	(0.250)
Ethnic fractionalization index	−0.148	−0.186	−0.178
	(0.197)	(0.203)	(0.195)
Java or Bali	−0.376***	−0.569***	−0.257**
	(0.131)	(0.123)	(0.123)
Constant	−1.835***	−1.976***	−2.470***
	(0.303)	(0.314)	(0.350)
Observations	239	239	239
Log-likelihood	−62.99	−63.07	−62.92

Robust standard errors in parentheses. *** $p < 0.01$, ** $p < 0.05$, * $p < 0.10$

systematically lower in religiously diverse districts, as it was for traditional and modernist Islamic parties.

Prabowo accepted a position in President Jokowi's cabinet shortly after losing the 2019 presidential elections, and the extent to which Gerindra will continue to maintain its profile is therefore unclear. Nevertheless, these data suggest that Gerindra has succeeded in differentiating itself from other new parties by developing a somewhat more distinct ideological profile. More broadly, Gerindra's case illustrates how a strategy of ideological differentiation can be successfully pursued

3.3 Examining Macro-Level Electoral Patterns 63

in contemporary Indonesian politics, and it underscores that non-Islamic parties can fruitfully engage in ideological appeals to mobilize Islamist constituencies.

3.3.2 Regional Variation and Clientelism

The electoral maps shown in Section 3.2.2 indicate a high degree of subnational variation in support for pluralism, traditional Islam and modernist Islam in the mid-1950s. As I have discussed, some important differences in electoral patterns can be identified between the political core of the Indonesian archipelago, comprising Java and Bali, and the outer regions.[7] Nationalist support was substantially higher in Java and Bali than elsewhere, with the exception of some religiously heterogeneous provinces; traditional Islam drew most of its support from rural districts in East and Central Java; and modernist Islam was stronger overall in the outer regions and particularly in Sumatra. To a certain degree, this geographical patterns correspond with a political division between the center and the periphery similar to those observed in other countries (Ufen 2008a): Java-based PNI, NU and PKI represented the interests of the vote-rich center of Indonesian politics, while Masyumi channeled the demands of the less-influential and resource-rich regions off Java. Yet the fact that pluralist parties were substantially weaker outside Java also suggests that ideological debate between pluralism and Islamism may have been a less-salient feature of politics in many peripheral regions, where local factors and ethnic divisions may have been more prominent drivers of electoral competition.

Indeed, the idea that a religious division was the key feature of Indonesian politics in the 1950s stems from anthropologist Clifford Geertz's analysis of Javanese religion, which differentiated between the *abangan*, nominal Muslims who practice a syncretic version of Islam with strong Hindu-Buddhist influences, and the *santri*, who adhere to a more orthodox, ideological form of Islam (Geertz 1960). The *abangan* tended to support nonreligious parties such as PNI and PKI, while NU and Masyumi were more popular among the *santri*. As this conceptual framework was developed primarily with reference to Javanese society, it may have applied only loosely, if at all, to other regions. With reference to the analysis conducted in this chapter, this suggests that the relationship

---

[7] See Hindley (1970) for a more comprehensive analysis of subnational variations in support for ideology-based parties in the 1950s.

64   *The Ideological Roots of Electoral Politics*

between historical and contemporary patterns of electoral support for these three political–ideological streams may vary substantially across districts.

An especially important factor that may account for such subnational diversity is ethnolinguistic diversity, in which Indonesian districts vary dramatically. Ethnic fragmentation is generally very low in Java, as most districts in Central and East Java are almost entirely Javanese in their ethnic composition.[8] In the 102 districts included in our analysis located in Java, the index of ethnolinguistic fractionalization (ELF), which assumes values of 0 for completely homogenous districts and 1 for extremely diverse districts, has a fairly low median value of 0.06. Although the outer regions may be more homogenous in terms of religion, they are in general more ethnically diverse. The ELF index median value is 0.13 in Bali, a relatively homogenous society, and much higher in Kalimantan (0.74), Sumatra (.65), Sulawesi (0.38) and other eastern islands (.60). Subnational variation in district-level ethnic diversity thus correlates strongly with the center–periphery dichotomy between Java and the rest of the archipelago, as non-Javanese districts show on average a much higher level of ethnolinguistic heterogeneity.

Ethnolinguistic fractionalization can have important implications for political competition. Ethnic tensions and economic competition between ethnic groups are more likely to be observed in ethnically diverse societies, and many studies suggest that high levels of ethnolinguistic fractionalization are tied to governance pitfalls such as underprovided public goods, corruption and clientelism (Alesina, Baqir, and Easterly 1999; Keefer 2007). For political elites, ethnic groups provide convenient and clear boundaries to delimit the coalitions that would benefit from their patronage, so they encourage ethnic-based appeals and facilitate the establishment of clientelistic linkages between politicians and citizens (Fearon 1999). In turn, when politics are driven by ethnic appeals and competition between ethnic groups for government resources, voters are less likely to be interested in programmatic and ideological debates, as they prioritize patronage considerations and vote for coethnic candidates. This relationship between ethnic diversity and clientelistic politics is well established in various ethnically diverse societies, including Indonesia, where

---

[8] The Madurese, concentrated in a few districts on the island of Madura and northeastern East Java, are an exception. In terms of political behavior, however, these people are closely aligned with traditional Islam, just like Javanese majorities in many other Javanese-dominated localities in this province.

3.3 Examining Macro-Level Electoral Patterns 65

ethnolinguistic fractionalization is strongly associated with preference voting, a key channel for establishing clientelistic linkages (Allen 2015). In short, ethnic fragmentation and the clientelistic practices that it encourages may have played an important role in the erosion of deep-seated, ideology-based partisan identities documented in Section 3.3.1 above. We can therefore hypothesize that the relationship between historical and contemporary electoral returns is systematically stronger in more homogeneous districts, where more voters may be more engaged in programmatic-ideological debates than in ethnically divided societies.

In the regression analysis, this hypothesis can be tested by estimating multiplicative models such as those reported in Table 3.5, in which past electoral returns are interacted with the ELF index. If the effect of historical partisan identities on contemporary electoral outcomes is indeed weaker in more ethnically diverse districts, the estimated interaction term should be statistically significant and negatively signed. The results of the model estimation indeed show this pattern, as the interaction term (the third row in the table) is signed negatively for all of the models. This indicates that historical partisan legacies may have a negligible effect on contemporary voting behavior in districts where ethnic divisions may foster clientelistic linkages between politicians and voters. However, the coefficients for the interaction terms are only statistically significant at the 0.05 level for pluralism and traditional Islam; the coefficient for modernist Islam, although negatively signed, is not significant at conventional levels. The role of ethnolinguistic fractionalization in moderating the relationship between past and present electoral behavior thus varies across party families. Perhaps this could be explained by the regional distribution of past support for modernist Islam, which was especially high outside Java. As these outer regions present higher levels of ethnic diversity, modernist Islam may have had to address early on the challenge of articulating an ideological platform rooted in the division over political Islam while simultaneously appeasing multiple ethnic groups demanding representation and patronage. It should also be noted that ethnic diversity in many regions outside Java correlates weakly with religious diversity, as most non-Javanese ethnic groups are predominantly, if not exclusively, Muslims.[9] This may also have helped modernist Islamist leaders to

---

[9] Exceptions include eastern Indonesian regions such as North Sulawesi, East Nusa Tenggara, Papua and West Papua, where many ethnic groups are predominantly Protestant or Catholic.

66 *The Ideological Roots of Electoral Politics*

TABLE 3.5. *Historical partisan legacies and ethnolinguistic fractionalization for three ideological groups*

Variables	(1) Pluralism	(2) Traditional Islam	(3) Modernist Islam
Historical electoral returns	2.491***	2.704***	1.454***
	(0.296)	(0.243)	(0.283)
Ethnic fractionalization index	0.642***	0.344**	0.112
	(0.193)	(0.169)	(0.241)
Historical electoral returns*EFL	−2.611***	−2.392***	−0.633
	(0.830)	(0.639)	(0.545)
City	−0.194*	0.200**	0.289***
	(0.102)	(0.0826)	(0.0840)
Population (thousands)	−5.85e-05	0.000138***	9.75e-05**
	(5.66e-05)	(5.29e-05)	(4.61e-05)
Population density (thousands per km²)	−0.0120	−0.0399***	0.0262**
	(0.0146)	(0.0129)	(0.0103)
GDP per capita (IDR millions)	−0.00286	0.00209	0.000448
	(0.00318)	(0.00203)	(0.00350)
Poverty rate	−0.0150***	0.0141***	−0.00138
	(0.00558)	(0.00454)	(0.00559)
Inequality (Gini coefficient)	0.00786	−0.00515	0.00838
	(0.00634)	(0.00579)	(0.00693)
Religious fractionalization index	2.520***	−1.287***	−1.186***
	(0.293)	(0.255)	(0.216)
Java or Bali	0.935***	0.322***	−0.0653
	(0.119)	(0.100)	(0.116)
Year = 2004	−0.821***	−0.275***	0.168***
	(0.0318)	(0.0243)	(0.0315)
Year = 2009	−1.246***	−0.814***	−0.203***
	(0.0504)	(0.0460)	(0.0541)
Year = 2014	−0.848***	−0.338***	0.00392
	(0.0537)	(0.0558)	(0.0590)
Year = 2019	−0.770***	−0.448***	−0.153***
	(0.0472)	(0.0568)	(0.0514)
Constant	−2.052***	−2.063***	−1.895***
	(0.221)	(0.206)	(0.254)
Observations	1,161	1,161	1,161
Log-likelihood	−366.2	−332.2	−411.4

Robust standard errors in parentheses. *** $p < 0.01$, ** $p < 0.05$, * $p < 0.10$

subsume ethnic identities into a common religious identity and to link religious identity with an Islamist political agenda.

Figure 3.7 illustrates the results reported in Table 3.5 with plots of the estimated marginal effects of historical support for PNI, NU and Masjumi

3.3 Examining Macro-Level Electoral Patterns

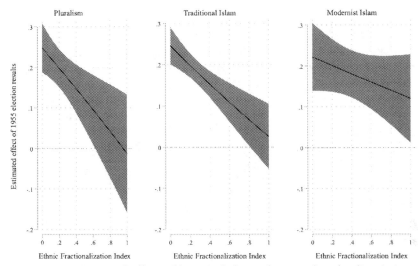

FIGURE 3.7. Marginal effects of historical electoral returns by ethnolinguistic fractionalization

on 2019 support for PDI-P, traditional Islamic and modernist Islamic parties, respectively, for different levels of ethnolinguistic fractionalization. The relationship is negative in all of the panels, but it is especially strong for pluralism and traditional Islam, indicating that the effect of historical partisan returns is significantly weaker in more ethnically fractionalized constituencies. For example, although the estimated marginal effect for previous PNI support is higher than 0.2 in highly homogenous districts (those with an ELF index value of about 0, including several districts in Central and East Java), the effect becomes nonsignificant for ELF index values higher than 0.65, where the lower confidence interval bound of the estimates becomes negative. In summary, these results suggest that local-level factors may be consequential in moderating the effect of historical partisan identities in contemporary politics. In ethnically homogenous districts, ideological appeals based on deep-rooted partisan identities are more likely to resonate with voters; in more diverse districts, ethnic divisions may facilitate the emergence of a more clientelistic, patronage-based type of politics in which ideological factors are less prominent drivers of voting behavior.

3.3.3 Resurgent Islamism and Electoral Participation

As I discussed in Chapter 2, high levels of civic engagement and electoral participation have been a key feature of Indonesian politics since the breakdown of the New Order regime in the late 1990s. Most research on political participation in Indonesia focuses on informal participation though civic associations, nongovernment organizations and advocacy groups, and few studies consider formal participation in elections. The dataset that I have assembled for this chapter allows a unique opportunity to study the relationship between electoral participation and the division over political Islam, especially in light of the increase in electoral turnout over the last two electoral cycles. Electoral turnout reached a historical low in 2009, when only 70.7% of registered voters cast a ballot, and has increased steadily since, reaching 75.2% in 2014 and 81.9% in 2019.

This variation over time suggests a connection between patterns of electoral participation and the role of deep-seated partisan affiliations. As shown in Figure 3.5, the 2009 elections were not only a nadir for electoral participation but also an important point of discontinuity for historical partisan identities, whose effect on voting behavior was substantially eroded by the introduction of a new electoral law that encouraged clientelistic appeals. Afterward, as mass partisanship (especially for the modernist Islamic camp, but later for pluralism as well) began a process of realignment with historical affiliation, electoral participation increased. This observation is of course based only on a correlation and a limited number of data points, but it is consistent with the idea that historical partisan identities based on the division over political Islam play a crucial role in giving substance to Indonesian democracy in the hearts and minds of ordinary citizens. More specifically, these figures suggest a connection between the increasing influence of radical Islam in Indonesian politics, a realignment with historical partisan affiliations for modernist Islamist parties, and an increase in electoral participation. We can therefore hypothesize, as I suggested in Chapter 1, that the rise of radical Islamism in Indonesian politics in recent years, while deleterious from a liberal conception of democracy, may have had positive effects on representation and participation. As ideological appeals to a stronger role for Islam in political life have become more prominent in recent years, Islamist voters, whose ideas have long been at the margins of Indonesian politics, may have felt a stronger sense of representation and belonging in the political debate. Such feelings may have fostered higher levels of satisfaction with democracy and political engagement among members of this ideological group.

The available data on electoral turnout do not allow a comprehensive analysis over five electoral cycles like the one I conducted for partisan affiliations. Nevertheless, district-level data for 2014 and 2019 are

3.3 Examining Macro-Level Electoral Patterns

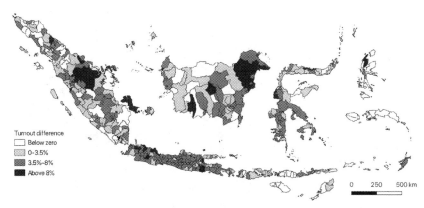

FIGURE 3.8. Differences in electoral turnout, 2014–2019

available, and they can shed light on the determinants of the surge in electoral participation in the last election. Again, as suggested by the map in Figure 3.8, subnational variation of this variable is substantial, as districts differ significantly in their 2019 turnout compared with previous elections. Of the 448 districts for which data are available for both 2014 and 2019, the median increase in turnout was 4%, but 75 districts witnessed a decrease rather than an increase in electoral participation. In contrast, 58 districts reported turnout increases of 8% of higher, a surge that could substantially alter electoral dynamics. The increase in participation was also much more visible in Java and Bali, where the median turnout increase was 5.8%, than in other regions (+2.9%). These data indicate that local-level factors may have played an important role in determining the increase in participation observed in the aggregate national-level data, and again, this subnational variation can be exploited for inferential purposes. If a connection exists between the resurgence of Islamism, representation and electoral participation, we should observe higher increases in turnout in districts with a stronger modernist Islamic tradition.

Visual inspection of the electoral turnout map substantiates this hypothesis, as many areas where participation decreased or increased below the median have sizable religious minorities, such as Maluku (median difference of -4.6%), East Nusa Tenggara (-1.2%), North Sumatra (+1.9%) and West Kalimantan (+2.3%). In contrast, provinces with strong Islamist traditions have large increases, such as Riau (+7.3%), West Java (+7.2%), Banten (+6.4%) and Southeast Sulawesi (+6.1%). Interestingly, the top two districts with the highest increases in electoral

70 *The Ideological Roots of Electoral Politics*

participation are cities in predominantly Islamist Sumatra, namely Padang (+21.5% in turnout) and Pekanbaru (+20%), both of which recorded exceptionally high levels of support for modernist Islamic parties in 2014: 36.8% and 35.1%, respectively.

In addition to visual inspection, a simple linear regression model in which turnout differences are a function of previous electoral participation and support for the three ideology-based party families could further clarify the relationship between resurgent Islamism and increased electoral participation. The results of the regression estimation for this model, which also includes a dummy variable to investigate differences across regions (Java or Bali versus other islands), are reported in Table 3.6. The key finding is that of the three estimated coefficients for previous partisan support, only the coefficient for modernist Islam is statistically significant. Electoral participation in 2019 increased more substantially in districts with higher previous support for modernist Islamic parties, while pluralist and traditional Islamic legacies do not appear to have had significant effects. For example, the estimated increase in electoral turnout in a district in Java with low levels of previous electoral support for modernist Islamic parties (say 5%) is estimated to be 4.4%, but it would increase to

TABLE 3.6. *Support for ideology-based parties and electoral turnout*

Variables	(1) Turnout difference, 2014–2019
Electoral turnout (share) in 2014	−0.434***
	(0.0513)
PDI-P vote share, 2014	0.0105
	(0.0220)
Traditional Islam vote share, 2014	−0.0197
	(0.0291)
Modernist Islam vote share, 2014	0.0647***
	(0.0211)
Java or Bali	0.0256***
	(0.00494)
Constant	0.347***
	(0.0357)
Observations	442
R-squared	0.470
Log-likelihood	882.6

Cluster (province)-robust standard errors in parentheses. *** $p < 0.01$, ** $p < 0.05$, * $p < 0.10$

3.3 Examining Macro-Level Electoral Patterns 71

5.7% in a district with a 2014 share of votes for modernist Islamic parties of 25%. To be sure, most districts reported higher levels of participation in 2019 compared with previous elections, and the surge in national-level aggregate turnout is probably due to higher participation in populous Javanese districts, in many of which support for modernist Islam is low. Yet these data show that more ideologically conservative districts have witnessed relatively higher increases in electoral participation. The renewed prominence of radical Islamist discourse may thus have inspired politicians in these Islamist-friendly regions to give greater emphasis to ideological factors in their campaigns, and such appeals may have resonated with voters in these regions. The structural advantage of the pluralist camp in populous Javanese districts ultimately tilted the results of the presidential elections in favor of the incumbent president, but the opposition-Islamist camp was nevertheless highly successful in mobilizing its traditional constituencies.

The coefficients for the three party groups have different signs: Previous support for PDI-P and modernist Islamic parties is positively associated with increases in electoral participation, but this relationship is negative for traditional Islam. Recall that the results plotted in Figure 3.5 show that the estimated coefficients for the effect of historical partisan legacies in 2019 increased (i.e., realignment) for PDI-P and modernist Islam and decreased (further dealignment), albeit only slightly, for traditional Islam. However, these figures do not imply that dealignment necessarily leads to electoral losses for ideology-based parties. For example, in 2019, PKB clearly outperformed its 2014 results, attracting more than two million additional votes despite further partisan dealignment, and PKS gained several seats in the disruptive 2009 elections. Citizen–politician linkages are complex, and ideological appeals are only one of the strategies that political parties have at their disposal to win votes. Politicians of ideology-based parties may sideline ideological appeals to broaden their vote base, especially when to entice swing voters from other parties. Yet these results suggest that there is a close connection between ideology-based appeals and a party's ability to mobilize voters *in their core constituencies*. Emphasizing the party's platform on the division over political Islam may not be a universally successful electoral strategy, but it resonates with voters in regions with strong, deep-rooted ideological-partisan traditions, and ideology-based politics may have important ramifications for political participation in these constituencies.

3.4 CONCLUSION

The division over the role of Islam in politics was foundational to the emergence of the Indonesian nation and the establishment of the Indonesian republic as an independent state. In this chapter, I document that this cleavage continues to cast a shadow over modern Indonesian politics. It is difficult to overemphasize the tremendous social, cultural and institutional differences that set today's Indonesia apart from the Indonesia of the mid-1950s, when ideological issues featured prominently in political debate. Yet the data analyzed in this chapter show that history still matters. Although voting may remain a transactional matter, devoid of programmatic and ideological considerations, for some Indonesian citizens, this chapter reminds us that for a much more substantial proportion of the population, electoral participation is about connecting with historical identities that have been consolidated over generations, pondering deeply felt and consequential issues that go back to the era of the country's founding fathers, and expressing a position on the future path of Indonesia's democracy.

4

Political Elites and Ideological Competition

4.1 IDEOLOGICAL COMPETITION IN YOUNG DEMOCRACIES

In established Western democracies, political competition is often structured along a left–right axis. In most of these countries, a relatively clear and stable distinction between left and right emerged in the early or mid-twentieth century, with political parties differentiating themselves largely in terms of how much fiscal redistribution and state intervention in the economy they favored. However, the dynamics of left–right ideological competition in consolidated democracies have changed substantially over the last few decades. For example, leftist parties have largely abandoned their most radical economy policy platforms and many have pivoted toward more centrist positions; at the same time, the far right, long at the fringes of politics, has witnessed a robust revival, and cultural issues such as immigration have become increasingly important in structuring voters' left–right identification (De Vries, Hakhverdian and Lancee 2013). Accordingly, a simple left–right schema cannot fully account for the complex and possibly multidimensional structure of the preferences of political elites and citizens (Kriesi et al. 2008; Albright 2010). However, despite the limitations of the left–right heuristic and the changing nature of its ideological content, most voters in advanced Western democracies are able to position major parties on the left–right spectrum and to describe their own ideological orientations in left–right terms (Mair 2007, 209). The stability of this pattern of left–right organization in advanced democracies has thus underpinned representation by ensuring a sufficient variety of political alternatives and assisting voters in evaluating parties' ideological positions and making electoral choices accordingly.

Patterns of ideological competition in new democracies may be more difficult to identify, as a clear divide between the left and right may not be consolidated in the minds of political elites and ordinary citizens. In many non-Western settings, late capitalist development, often under authoritarian rule, has entailed different patterns of working-class formation and organization. As labor unions and leftist parties in such settings have historically been weaker than their Western counterparts, issues of economic redistribution have often failed to emerge, and economic–fiscal issues may be marginal in the structuring of ideological competition. In such settings, political parties often propose very similar economic policy platforms (Bleck and Van de Walle 2013), and voting is often based on clientelistic relationships rather than programmatic preferences (Mainwaring and Torcal 2006). However, this does not imply that politics in these settings are devoid of ideological competition, as the left–right ideological axis may carry different substantive meanings (Zechmeister and Corral 2013). For example, while Western publics understand the left–right continuum mainly in economic terms, associations with cultural issues related to nationalism, religion and tradition are more prevalent in Asian societies (Dalton 2006). This suggests that context-specific political ideologies may be an important driver of political behavior in political systems in which clientelism is prevalent.

The Indonesian case presents an ideal empirical context in which to investigate ideological competition on noneconomic issues as a dimension of political representation in young democracies. On the one hand, party differentiation on economic and fiscal issues is notably absent from Indonesia's political landscape. Since the brutal eradication of the PKI in the mid-1960s and with three decades of repression under the New Order's authoritarian rule, an assertive political left has not yet emerged. Although the labor movement has at times been successful in advancing its agenda in post-Suharto Indonesia (Caraway and Ford 2020) and various social policy programs have alleviated some aspects of inequality (Hidayat et al. 2004), the economic platforms offered by Indonesian political parties are barely distinguishable and are generally supportive of the status quo. For example, no Indonesian political party appears to have articulated a robust and consistent agenda of economic redistribution or, at the other end of the ideological spectrum, to have convincingly supported market reform to curb Indonesia's historically high levels of state intervention in the economy. However, as mentioned earlier, the historical division over political Islam is a distinctive feature of Indonesian politics. Throughout the twenty years of democracy in Indonesia, and

4.2 Surveying Elites

especially over the last few years, recurring debates on state–Islam relations have anchored the Indonesian party system to this deep-seated historical division and provided opportunities for political parties to differentiate their ideological profiles.

In this chapter, I analyze data from an original survey of Indonesian politicians to determine the extent to which the ideological division over political Islam is rooted in the minds of Indonesia's political elites and to shed new light on the substantive meaning and political organization of this division. After describing the survey method and some key measures, I describe the distribution of policy preferences regarding political Islam and economic issues in our sample, and I analyze the empirical associations between political Islam and other ideational variables of interest. I then focus on the role of political parties by leveraging the survey data to analyze whether and to what extent their positions on various ideological and policy issues differ. This analysis enables me to empirically test some of the premises upon which my argument is based. For political Islam to function as a dimension of ideological representation, sufficient heterogeneity in views on state-Islam relations must exist in the political class, and political parties must propose a sufficiently diverse range of policy platforms on this issue. An analysis of the views collected from this sample of politicians helps to determine whether this is indeed the case.

4.2 SURVEYING ELITES

The dataset upon which this chapter is based is from a survey of Indonesian politicians designed by Edward Aspinall, Burhan Muhtadi, Eve Warburton and me, and implemented by Lembaga Survei Indonesia.[1] This survey was administered in late 2017 and early 2018 to 508 Indonesian politicians sitting on elected provincial legislative councils (DPRDs). Surveying local rather than national politicians has two main advantages. First, this population is highly representative of the Indonesian political class. Members of provincial DPRDs are from the same small set of parties represented in the National Assembly (DPR). These parties generally have high levels of vertical integration, and local politics are a key arena for recruitment for national politics. Furthermore, this strategy offers an accurate and comprehensive view of political elites in a large, decentralized and diverse country such as Indonesia, which

---

[1] The dataset is also used in three journal articles, namely Fossati et al. (2020), on which Chapter 6 builds; Aspinall et al. (2020); and Warburton et al. (2021).

displays dramatic subnational variation in history, economic development, social formation and local politics. Second, this population is more easily accessible than are members of the national legislature, who are likely to be subject to more severe time pressure. The choice of DPRD respondents therefore ensured the feasibility and timely completion of this important data collection project.

The sampling procedure was based on a population of 2,073 politicians, including all of the members of provincial DPRDs, with the exception of a few representatives of small local parties in Aceh, the only Indonesian province where local parties are allowed. This population was first stratified into three main regions to ensure that the sample would match the relative population quota: Sumatra accounted for 29.5% of the total legislator population, Java accounted for 26.8% and the other provinces accounted for 43.7%. Provinces constituted the primary sampling unit in this sampling design, and they were selected in each region according to each province's proportion of the population. The sample selected according to this procedure included thirty-one of the thirty-four provinces in Indonesia, namely all of the provinces in Sumatra, all of the provinces in Java and fifteen provinces randomly selected from other regions.[2] Finally, we randomly selected an average of fifteen DPRD members in each selected province (with the number of legislators selected in each DPRD varying because of different DPRD sizes across provinces), and we conducted face-to-face interviews with the resulting 508 politicians between December 2017 and March 2018.

I therefore rely on high-quality data for the analysis presented in this chapter. Face-to face interviews tend to be longer and provide more information than do surveys conducted via Web-based methods, and random sampling ensures a higher degree of sample representativeness than do surveys with non-probability samples. This was easily one of the largest surveys of legislators ever conducted in a single country, enabling me to make fine-grained comparisons of attitudes across all ten of Indonesia's major parties. Furthermore, this is one of very few studies of non-Western political systems in which estimates of party policy positions are based on elite interviews. While such studies are typically limited by very small samples and low response rates (Laver 2014, 214), our methodology ensures a substantially larger and more representative sample. With a wide range of questions measuring views on political

---

[2] The only provinces excluded because of random selection were North Kalimantam, West Sulawesi and West Papua.

4.2 Surveying Elites

Islam, policy preferences on various economic issues and many more attitudinal orientations, this dataset is ideal for studying the views of Indonesia's political elite.

4.2.1 Indonesia's Political Elites at a Glance

The data collected via the elite survey enable us to construct an accurate sociodemographic profile of the Indonesian political class. In general terms, and not surprisingly, the Indonesian politicians surveyed were older, comprised a larger proportion of men than women and had a higher socioeconomic status than the broader Indonesian population. The median age in the sample was forty-nine years, well above the figure for the general population, for which the median is below thirty years old. Women are dramatically underrepresented among local politicians; female respondents constituted only 16.3% of the sample. More than 90% of the respondents held a college or a postgraduate degree. Regarding professional background, the overwhelming majority of the sample came from private business or white-collar occupations. Many of the respondents – 42.7% – reported having been businesspeople in various industries before becoming legislators; a smaller group worked in civil service or legal occupations (22.8%); 7.7% were involved in politics in various capacities (e.g. community organizer, executive role in local government); and only 2.6% reported having a working-class background. Finally, in terms of ethnoreligious heritage, our respondents were more likely to be drawn from the dominant ethnic (Javanese) and religious (Muslim) groups, as more ethnically diverse regions outside of the main island of Java are overrepresented. About 77% of the respondents were Muslim and only 17% identified as Javanese. The picture that emerges from these data is one of low levels of descriptive representation, as groups such as women and less-affluent classes were severely underrepresented. This imbalance is important for the argument proposed in this book because it has implications for substantive representation. As I show in Chapters 5 and 6, attitudes on political Islam are associated with sociodemographic factors such as education and income. The exclusion of individuals of lower socioeconomic status from Indonesia's political elites thus implies that some ideological groups are better represented than others within this group, as I discuss in Chapter 6.

As shown in Figure 4.1, our sample comprised politicians of all major political parties in Indonesia, with the PDI-P and Golkar as the two major groups. Party-switching by local politicians appears to be common but

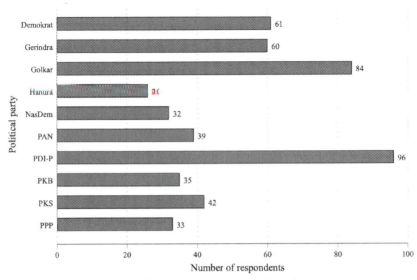

FIGURE 4.1. Elite survey respondents by political party

not extremely widespread in Indonesia; 28.2% of the respondents reported being a member of a different party in the past and only 4.7% reported being members of more than two parties. Beyond party membership, it is interesting to note the legislators' involvement in associational life and informal political engagement. For example, several respondents reported being or having been members of the two major Islamic organizations Nahdlatul Ulama (21.7%) and Muhammadiyah (15.8%), as well as of other Islamic and non-Islamic religious associations (11.6% and 5.5%, respectively). Activism in student organizations was also a common trait, as about 64% of the legislators reported being active members of student associations of various ideological and religious orientations. Civic engagement during college may thus be an important way to develop important political skills and relationships to sustain future careers in formal institutions. Finally, to explore connections with the authoritarian past in local governance, we asked the respondents if they had any family member who held an important political position in local government, the bureaucracy or the military during the New Order. About one-third of the respondents (32.9%) answered this question in the affirmative, indicating a certain degree of intergenerational continuity among local political elites in Indonesia and suggesting that democratization has created opportunities for new groups to acquire direct political influence.

4.3 POLICY ATTITUDES OF INDONESIAN POLITICIANS

In this section, I analyze the elite survey data by focusing on two key areas of political attitudes, namely views of political Islam – the key cleavage in ideological competition in Indonesia – and attitudes toward economic policy. Given our prior knowledge of the Indonesian case, we should expect substantial heterogeneity in the former area, given that state-Islam relations have been a salient and controversial issue throughout Indonesian political history. In contrast, legislators should be less divided on economic policy issues, as conservative fiscal attitudes and high levels of support for state intervention in the economy should be observed across the political spectrum.

4.3.1 Measuring Political Islam

As mentioned in this book, I understand political Islam as an ideological dimension regarding the role of Islam in politics. At one end of the spectrum, pluralist Indonesians favor a clear demarcation between Islam and the state. Although these individuals may not necessarily be opposed to religious values playing a role in public life, they do not see Islam, or any other religion, as deserving of a special status in state–religion relations. At the opposite end of the spectrum, Islamist Indonesians believe that Islam should have a privileged position in public life over all other religions, a principle that can have broad and consequential ramifications in various policy domains. Between these two extremes, individual-level positions vary as to whether Islam should play a more or less prominent role in Indonesian public affairs.

Measuring individual positions on this ideological continuum is challenging because political Islam, like many other ideational constructs, is complex and unobservable.[3] Asking our elite respondents where they stand in general terms on this issue may have been feasible given the high degree of educational attainment and political knowledge of these professional politicians. However, to study substantive representation, we need to compare the orientations of the elite with those of the public, and many citizens may be unable to directly estimate their own position on political Islam given their lower levels of political information or cognitive skills. A seven-item scale was therefore developed to measure political Islam by

---

[3] The same applies to the concept of Islamic piety as discussed in, for instance, Pepinsky, Liddle and Mujani (2018).

80 Political Elites and Ideological Competition

probing agreement or disagreement with a series of specific policies and issues pertaining to state-Islam relations. This approach has the advantage of asking easy-to-understand questions on salient issues that are familiar even to less sophisticated respondents, and it is therefore appropriate for both politicians and voters. The data obtained enable us to meaningfully compare the attitudes of the elites and masses, as I do in Chapter 5. Furthermore, rather than relying on a single question to measure a complex construct, we can combine responses to these items into a single composite indicator that offers a more accurate measure of where each individual stands on the cleavage over political Islam.

Table 4.1 reports the full scale used to measure political Islam, where support for each item was measured with a simple 5-point Likert scale (1 = strongly disagree, 2 = disagree; 3 = neither disagree nor agree, 4 = agree, 5 = strongly agree). The summary statistics displayed in Table 4.1 show the share of respondents who reported (strong) agreement or (strong) disagreement with each statement. These figures show substantial variation across the items. For the most radical items, such as those stating that sharia law should be implemented in the whole country (Item 4) or that Islam should become Indonesia's only official religion (Item 7), support seemed to be confined to a very narrow group. For other items, however, such as the idea that voting for candidates belonging to religious minorities should be avoided (Item 6) or that blasphemy against Islam should incur harsher punishment (Item 5), support was much more widespread. The figures reported in Table 4.1 thus indicate that Indonesian politicians are divided on the key issue of the role of Islam

TABLE 4.1. *Views on political Islam among Indonesia's political elite*

	Item	Disagree	Agree
1	The government should prioritize Islam over other religions	50%	38%
2	Islamic religious leaders should play a very important role in politics	37%	47%
3	Indonesian regions should be allowed to implement sharia law at the local level	55%	32%
4	Sharia law should be implemented throughout Indonesia	77%	10%
5	Blasphemy against Islam should be punished more severely	19%	67%
6	When voting in elections, it is very important to choose a Muslim leader	26%	60%
7	Islam should become Indonesia's only official religion	85%	7%

4.3 Policy Attitudes of Indonesian Politicians

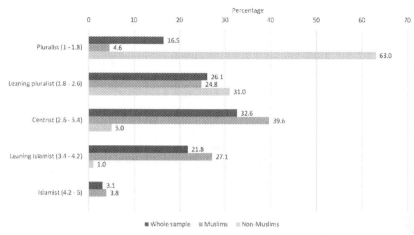

FIGURE 4.2. Ideological groups among Indonesia's political elite

in political life. However, none of the statements analyzed in isolation enable me to draw more general conclusions about the distribution of Indonesian legislators' preferences regarding political Islam.

By calculating the arithmetic mean of the seven items reported in Table 4.1, we can build a composite index, called the Political Islam Index (PII), that offers an exhaustive measure of policy positions on the role of Islam in politics. The PII ranges from 1 to 5, where lower values indicate that individuals are more supportive of secularism and higher values indicate that individuals support a larger role for Islam in political life. When respondents are divided into five groups according to their PII score, as shown in Figure 4.2, we can more easily gauge the distribution of support for secularism and Islamism among Indonesia's political elite.[4] The chart shows the overall prevalence of pluralist views among the legislators that we interviewed. About 42.6% of the sample were pluralist or pluralist-leaning, 24.9% reported Islamist or Islamist-leaning views and the remaining 32.6% could be characterized as ideologically centrist. However, an inspection of the data that disaggregates the PII distribution by the respondent's religion presents a different picture. When we exclusively consider Muslim respondents, the prevalence of pluralist understandings of state-Islam relations disappears, as the distribution is virtually normal. Although there was a degree of ideological heterogeneity

---

[4] To group the respondents into various ideological categories and generate Figure 4.2, I simply divide the range of the scale into five segments of equal size.

among both Muslims and non-Muslims, the difference between the two groups was substantial, as the median PII value is 3 for Muslim respondents and only 1.76 for respondents with other religious affiliations. The gap in the first group (pluralist) is especially noteworthy, as it suggests that clearly pluralist views are highly concentrated in religious minorities. Although the majority of non-Muslim respondents (63%) appeared to be pluralist, few Muslims (4.6%) shared the same views.

Given the importance of Islamic associations and organizations in Indonesian social and political life and the fact that many of the legislators in our sample had been members of such organizations, it is worth exploring the association between organizational membership and views on political Islam. Figure 4.3 shows the share of pluralist/pluralist-leaning (as opposed to Islamist or Islamist-leaning) respondents among for Muslim respondents in general (45% of whom had never joined an Islamic organization or association) and three groups defined by their experience of Islamic associational life, namely current and former members of Nahdlatul Ulama (NU), Muhammadiyah and other Islamic associations. The data suggest that members of NU are just as likely to be Islamist-leaning or Islamist than are Muslim respondents on average (about 31%) but more likely to be pluralist-leaning or pluralist (33.6%

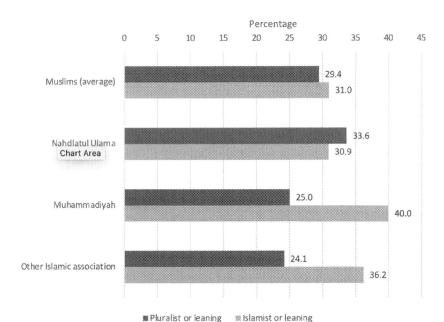

FIGURE 4.3. Ideological profile of Islamic organizations

4.3 Policy Attitudes of Indonesian Politicians

versus 29.4% for Muslims of any associational background). These findings resonate with studies suggesting that grassroots NU members are about as likely to show intolerant views as are Indonesian Muslims in general (Mietzner and Muhtadi 2020), and they are also consistent with a common view that identifies NU with more pluralist understandings of political Islam. In contrast, membership of Muhammadiyah and other Islamic associations appears to be a strong predictor of more radically Islamist views among Indonesian politicians. This is again in line with an established view in research on Indonesian political Islam that modernist Islam, represented by Muhammadiyah and a constellation of smaller, more radical groups, is associated with stronger support for Islamist views. More generally, these findings suggest that engagement in social organizations is an important factor in the development of Indonesian politicians' attitudes toward state–Islam relations.

4.3.2 The Economic Dimension

To measure attitudes toward economic policy, I again asked the respondents to what extent they agreed or disagreed with certain policy propositions. As in the case of political Islam, economic policy preferences may be considered sufficiently complex to warrant measurement with a scale and a composite index rather than with individual questions. Furthermore, economic policy preferences may be multidimensional in that views of various aspects of economic policy may vary independently from one another. However, given constraints on survey time and our expectation that this dimension is marginal in ideological competition in Indonesia, I adopted a simplified approach whereby I focused exclusively on two crucial dimensions of economic policy, and I measured each with one survey item. The first dimension was fiscal redistribution, which was examined using a commonly used question in survey research, which asked the respondents to what extent they agreed or disagreed with the following statement: "The government should spend more on helping the poor, even if it means increasing taxes." The second dimension can be defined as "statism," or support for a high level of state intervention in the market economy. To measure preferences over this dimension, I asked the respondents whether they agreed or disagreed that the government should intervene in the economy to set the price of gas and other basic goods. This is, of course, only one of the many ways in which governments can intervene in the economy, but it is particularly relevant to the Indonesian context, in which debates about state subsidies for fuel, rice

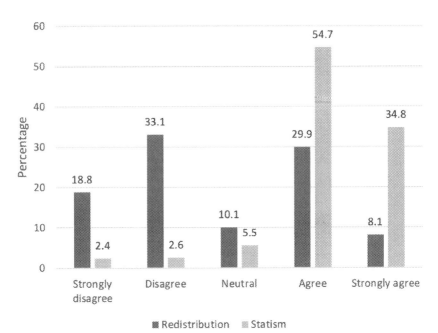

FIGURE 4.4. Economic policy preferences of Indonesia's political elite

and other basic commodities have long been salient.[5] Both questions therefore referred to issues with which our respondents were familiar, and they were straightforward enough that they could be addressed to both knowledgeable politicians and less-sophisticated ordinary citizens to obtain measures for meaningful comparison.

The distribution of the economic policy preferences of Indonesia's political elites, as measured by these two questions, is presented in Figure 4.4. Somewhat surprisingly, the data for fiscal redistribution show that views on this important issue were quite varied. Although conservative fiscal attitudes prevailed (for example, the number of respondents who strongly disagreed that more redistribution is needed was more than double the number of those who strongly agreed), a significant minority of the sample – 38% – supported a higher level of redistribution even if this would entail an increase in fiscal pressure. This suggests that although no political party consistently and assertively espouses a redistributive agenda,

---

[5] Another question included in the survey instrument concerned support for government intervention in labor markets by setting minimum salaries. Responses to this question were highly correlated with the question used in this section to measure statism.

4.3 Policy Attitudes of Indonesian Politicians

within each party, there may be substantial heterogeneity in views of this aspect of economic policy. In contrast, support for statism was overwhelming among the respondents, as only a small minority, about 10%, did not agree that the government should impose price limits on basic goods. This strong skepticism regarding free markets' ability to regulate consumption prices resonates with Indonesia's long history of policymaking, in which price controls, subsidies and other market distortionary measures have been used as tools to alleviate poverty and economic inequalities.

Finally, an important question pertaining to Indonesian politicians' policy preferences among is whether and to what extent the cleavage over political Islam intersects with economic policy preferences. The opinions expressed by the legislators we interviewed suggest that this is not the case for either economic redistribution or statism. For example, agreement with fiscal redistribution was at 43.4% for pluralist and pluralist-leaning respondents and only slightly lower, at 41.6%, for Islamists and Islamist-leaning respondents, while support for statism was above 90% for both groups. This indicates that these two dimensions of ideological competition are independent of one another, as the key ideological cleavage in Indonesian politics, political Islam, is not connected with economic policy positions.

However, there are some important differences in the policy priorities of pluralist and Islamist legislators, as shown in Figure 4.5. The question

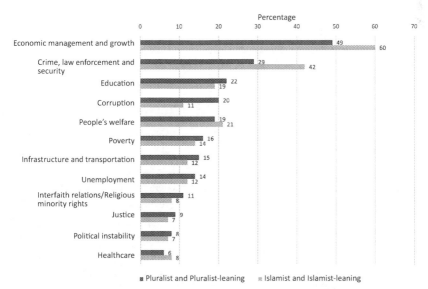

FIGURE 4.5. The policy priorities of Indonesia's political elite

86   *Political Elites and Ideological Competition*

on which the figure is based asked the respondents to indicate up to three issues that they consider the most important for Indonesia, and the bar chart in Figure 4.5 shows the share of respondents in each ideological group who mentioned a specific policy issue as a top-three priority. On most of these issues, the preferences of the two camps appear to have been aligned, but Islamists were significantly more likely to indicate economic management and growth as a priority (60%, as opposed to only 49% of pluralists). Pluralists, in contrast, were about twice as likely as Islamists to mention corruption as a policy priority. Although there are no significant differences between these two ideological blocs in economic policy positions, there could thus be a difference in issue salience, as Indonesians who support a larger role for Islam in politics may be more inclined to see economic public goods such as macroeconomic growth and good economic management as a top priority.

4.4 ISLAM AND OTHER ATTITUDES

In this section, I delve further into the substantive content of the cleavage over political Islam by analyzing its relationship with ethnic prejudice, specifically with stereotypes toward Chinese Indonesians, and with views of democracy. This exercise allows me to obtain a comprehensive view of how this crucial ideological cleavage intersects with attitudes about national identity and democratic governance. In studying the relationship between political Islam and these attitudinal constructs, I thus document the importance of the division over political Islam, as I show that it is closely connected to two crucial domains of political attitudes, namely conceptions of nationhood and democracy.

4.4.1 Anti-Chinese Prejudice

In Indonesia, citizens of Chinese descent constitute about 2% of the population. During the colonial era, the Dutch relied on Chinese settlers to incorporate their colonies into the global economy, and they encouraged immigration from China as a source of labor. Throughout the colonial period, the Chinese in Indonesia lived in social segregation from the native populations, being classified by colonial authorities as a distinct racial group subject to different legal and fiscal systems (Sidel 2008, 130). With independence in 1949, the colonial distinction between indigenous people, or *pribumi*, and Asians of foreign descent was maintained, and the sentiment that Chinese Indonesians, while citizens, did not "belong"

4.4 Islam and Other Attitudes

to the newborn "Indonesian nation" (*bangsa Indonesia*) was widespread. Indonesians of Chinese descent suffered substantial discrimination in social and political life and were often accused, even by prominent revolutionary leaders such as Sukarno and Mohamad Hatta, of being disloyal to the national cause and responsible for the economic deprivation faced by native Indonesians (Suryadinata 2005, 19–39). After a decade of rising anti-Sinicism in the 1950s, discrimination against the Chinese minority peaked during the authoritarian New Order, when Chinese Indonesians were forced to change their names to indigenous names and all manifestations of Chinese culture, such as schools, religious festivals, newspapers and magazines, were either severely limited or banned (Chua 2004).

Although hostility toward the ethnic Chinese in Indonesia is sometimes overstated, anti-Sinicism is deep-rooted in this country, where members of the Chinese minority have been the target of cyclical eruptions of ethnic violence from the colonial period (Shiraishi 1997) to the democratic transition and beyond (Purdey 2005; Sidel 2006). Studies on the subject often emphasize that economic competition with native populations is the most important driver of hostility toward the ethnic Chinese in Indonesia (Wertheim 1964; Wang 1992, 269–270). Since the colonial era, the prominent position of the Chinese in the Indonesian economy and their visible wealth have fueled economic resentment and racial animosity from indigenous Indonesians, as Chinese Indonesians have been easy scapegoats in times of economic turmoil. Other scholars, while not dismissing the importance of economic factors, emphasize cultural distance as a key factor in explaining anti-Chinese animosity. The religious status of the Chinese as non-Muslims has received particular attention, as ethnic violence against the Chinese has often overlapped with Islamic radicalism (Mackie 1976, 80–82). Perhaps the most compelling recent illustration of this connection between Islamism and anti-Chinese sentiments is the case of the Christian-Chinese former Jakarta governor Basuki Tjahaja Purnama, known as Ahok, where dubious allegations of blasphemy against Islam enabled radical Islamic groups to mobilize large crowds in Jakarta in late 2016, which eventually led to the governor's prosecution, electoral defeat and imprisonment.

Our survey of local legislators provides an unprecedented opportunity to measure anti-Chinese sentiments among Indonesian political elites. Drawing from qualitative knowledge of the Indonesian case and survey research on ethnic stereotypes in other contexts (Zick, Küpper and Hövermann 2011), we designed the series of questions reported in Table 4.2 to measure elite attitudes toward two main dimensions of

88 *Political Elites and Ideological Competition*

anti-Chinese prejudice in Indonesia. The first entails perceptions of economic privilege and is closely related to the specific position held by the ethnic Chinese in the Indonesian economy regarding the indigenous *pribumi* majority. The second recurring dimension of anti-Sinicism in Indonesia depicts the Chinese as cultural aliens, a non-Muslim ethnic group that poses a serious threat to cultural homogeneity and established norms in Indonesian society. This dimension includes various stereotypes describing Chinese Indonesians as socially and culturally exclusive and as bearers of a foreign culture that is incompatible with Indonesian "traditional values." The statistics reported in Table 4.2 suggest that these two tropes about Chinese Indonesians resonate among Indonesia's political elite, as for most of them, respondents who agreed with the statements outnumbered those who disagreed. Item 3, which tapped into the idea of economic domination, was by far the most widely accepted, with 77% support, followed by stereotypes about Chinese exclusivity (Item 1) and, perhaps more surprisingly, the idea that Chinese Indonesians may still hold some allegiance to their supposed ancestral motherland (Item 4). Other more radically worded stereotypes about cultural distance (Items 2 and 6) received substantially lower levels of support.

An analysis of the survey responses further reveals a strong association between support for the six statements in Table 4.2 and political Islam. Endorsement for stereotypes about Chinese Indonesians was limited among the pluralist respondents, who on average agreed or strongly agreed with only two of the six statements in Table 4.2. However, the average value for the endorsed stereotypes increases steadily as we move away from the pluralist end of the ideological spectrum, reaching 2.4 for those leaning pluralist and 2.9 for centrists, and then jumping to 3.7 and 4

TABLE 4.2. *Support for stereotypes about Chinese Indonesians among politicians*

		Disagree	Agree
1	Chinese Indonesians only care about their own kind	36%	50%
2	Chinese Indonesians have their own culture, which is incompatible with Indonesian culture	47%	33%
3	Chinese Indonesians have too much influence on the Indonesian economy	16%	77%
4	Chinese Indonesians still harbor loyalty to China	32%	46%
5	Chinese Indonesians have too much influence on Indonesian politics	41%	43%
6	It is difficult to be close friends with Chinese Indonesians	53%	31%

4.4 *Islam and Other Attitudes*

for Islamist-leaning and Islamist respondents, respectively. An additional question in the survey instrument asked the legislators whether they were comfortable with a Chinese Indonesian holding an important public role such as district head, province governor or minister in a national government. Again, the answers to this question were strongly associated with political Islam, as the share of respondents who were comfortable with a Chinese Indonesian leader was dramatically lower among Islamist and Islamist-leaning legislators (only 16% were somewhat or very comfortable) than in the pluralist camp (70%). These figures resonate with research showing that in the Indonesian context, higher levels of religious piety are associated with ethnocentrism and a preference for coethnics in voting behavior (Allen and Barter 2017).

These findings are consequential for our understanding of political Islam in Indonesia, as they show a close relationship between this ideological cleavage and conceptions of Indonesian national identity. A higher level of agreement with stereotypes about Chinese Indonesians, a minority group that has long been a target of exclusion, resentment and violence, suggests that Islamist Indonesians are significantly more likely than pluralists to understand the boundaries of the national community in ethnic rather than civic terms. More specifically, this ideological group has yet to fully accept citizens with Chinese ancestry as legitimate members of the Indonesian nation. I return to this point in Chapter 5, where I use public opinion data to analyze more directly the relationship between political Islam and the structure of Indonesian national identity.

4.4.2 Democracy

A long-standing question in public debates on and theoretical studies of representation regards how representatives are supposed to behave in fulfilling their roles in office (Pitkin 1967). According to one view, representatives should be primarily understood as delegates. As their role is defined by a well-specified mandate, they should serve their constituents by expressing views and adopting behaviors that mirror and implement constituent preferences. A different view argues that representatives should enjoy a higher degree of autonomy over their constituents. Representatives should ultimately behave according to their own personal beliefs, which at times may contradict their constituents' preferences. This dichotomy has its limits (Rehfeld 2009), but it is a good starting point to study alternative conceptions of representation, as it portrays a moral tension that is well understood and experienced by representatives themselves. In our survey, we asked the legislators directly what they believed about their role: Should representatives act as delegates and do what voters want, or should they do what they think is right, as a trustee would? The survey responses show that the differences in views of representation between ideological groups are not large, as delegate view of representation prevailed across the groups (59.3% of the respondents said that a representative should do what voters want). However, trustee understandings of representation were somewhat more common among Islamists (45.5%) than among pluralists (41%). Interestingly, the group that most strongly rejected trustee-based representation comprised centrist respondents, whose support for delegate conceptions of representation was at 64%. Perhaps these legislators, not having strong positions on what is supposed to be "right" as defined by the cleavage over political Islam, were more inclined to see popular preferences rather than political ideology as the guiding factor.

Our survey instrument measured support for democracy by asking about agreement or disagreement with three statements: "Democracy, although not perfect, is the best form of government for Indonesia," "Democracy can overcome the various issues that Indonesia is facing today," and "If Indonesia has to choose between economic development and democracy, democracy is more important." Support for each of these three items was very high and cut across ideological groups, although the third statement was somewhat more controversial than the others, as it was supported by 62% of the respondents, as opposed to 95% for the first and 81% for the second statement.

Although there was no significant difference in support for democracy as a form of government between Islamists and pluralists, differences emerged in how democracy was evaluated. We did not directly ask about satisfaction with democracy, but one of the survey questions asked the respondents to evaluate the state of democracy in Indonesia on a 10-point scale, where lower values corresponded to lower levels of democracy. The median score for the whole sample is 8, which indicates that the assessments were quite positive on average. However, the share of respondents who gave evaluations below this median value and could therefore be described as less satisfied with how democracy is now working in Indonesia varied across ideological groups. The share was 40.8% among those who were pluralist-leaning or pluralists, 54.4% among centrists and 59.8% among Islamist or Islamist-leaning respondents. Islamist politicians thus appear to be substantially more dissatisfied with the practice of democracy in Indonesia than pluralist legislators are.

4.4 Islam and Other Attitudes

This dissatisfaction may have multiple sources, and it is plausibly associated with the legacy of marginalization of the more Islamist voices in Indonesian politics that I previously described. The survey data also suggest that one of these sources is economic, as dissatisfaction appears to be related to perceptions of economic inequality. First, Islamist-leaning and Islamist respondents were much more likely to believe income distribution to be unfair than respondents who were pluralist-leaning or pluralist: Only 24% of the Islamists described the income distribution in Indonesia as "very fair" or "fair," whereas 38.7% of the pluralists did so. Second, the respondents who believed income distribution to be unfair were substantially more likely to evaluate Indonesian democracy critically. Less-satisfied democrats (i.e., those who gave the state of democracy a score of 7 or below) constituted only 33.6% of the respondents who saw income distribution as fair, compared with 57% of those who evaluated the income distribution in Indonesia as unfair or very unfair. This evidence suggests strong and important connections between political Islam, economic grievances and dissatisfaction with democracy, which I further analyze when I discuss Islamic populism in Chapter 5.

Finally, the survey instrument included a series of statements designed to measure support for liberal values on a 4-point scale. These statements, reported in Table 4.3, solicited opinions on various key principles of liberalism, such as pluralism, horizontal accountability, separation of powers and the rule of law, and they were worded so that agreement with them denotes illiberal attitudes. As Table 4.3 shows, the legislators

TABLE 4.3. *Support for liberal principles among Indonesian politicians*

		Disagree	Agree
1	Harmony in society will be disrupted if people are allowed to establish many organizations	65.31%	34.69%
2	When a judge has to decide an important case, the judge must accept the views of the head of government	84.72%	15.28%
3	If the government is overseen too tightly by the House of Representatives, it cannot achieve important goals	91.38%	8.62%
4	If citizens have too many different views, then society will be chaotic	56.8%	43.2%
5	When a country faces a difficult situation, the government may ignore the law in an effort to resolve the issue	78.46%	21.54%

generally reported low levels of agreement with these statements, which indicates the prevalence of liberal views among them. By building an additive index from these four questions, we can obtain a better understanding of variation among legislators in support for liberal values. A plurality (38.2%), who can be described as liberal, did not support any of the statements in Table 4.3; 26.4% leaned toward liberal views, as they supported only one of the statements; 20.9% can be seen as illiberal-leaning, as they agreed with two of the statements in Table 4.3; and 14.6% had pronounced illiberal attitudes, as they agreed with three or more of the statements. Is this index of support for liberal values related to political Islam? Figure 4.6 shows a cross-tabulation of the PII data for the three main ideological groups, and it indicates some important differences in support for liberalism across ideological blocs. Although centrist and Islamist respondents were rather similar in their distributions of support for liberal values, with illiberal individuals constituting only a small minority in each group, illiberal respondents were the second largest group of pluralists, representing 24%. This suggests that according to this measure, pluralist legislators have a more illiberal ideational profile than the other two ideological groups do.

Considering the association between the rise of Islamism and the illiberal turn in Indonesian politics, which is often discussed in academic

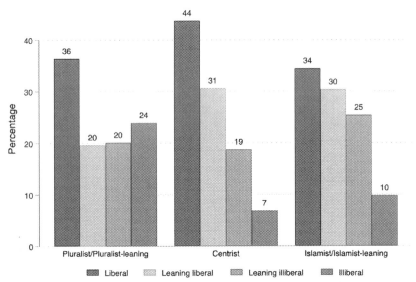

FIGURE 4.6. Political Islam and support for liberalism among Indonesia's political elite

research and public debates, this finding is somewhat surprising. Perhaps this could be at least partially explained by the fact that Islamist political parties and factions have often been marginalized or excluded from political power, especially during periods when the liberal values measured in Table 4.3 were not upheld, such the Guided Democracy and the New Order. This historical legacy may account for the suspicion regarding a strong state and unrestrained executive power, to which some of the items in the index allude. Furthermore, there are no strong reasons to expect genuine, consistent liberal political thought in the pluralist camp. Its ideological tradition has been strongly influenced in the Indonesian context by organicist political thought, which emphasizes communitarianism and traditional values and could be regarded as an alternative to liberalism (Bourchier 2014). In any case, these results should be interpreted cautiously, as they only concern support for the general principles of liberal politics. The aforementioned discussion of anti-Chinese prejudice suggests that when such general principles are applied to more concrete cases, especially to the controversial status of ethnoreligious minorities in Indonesia, Islamists do indeed harbor more sectarian and exclusionary political views.

4.5 POLITICAL PARTIES

As discussed in Section 4.4.2, political Islam is an important ideological dimension in Indonesian politics that is associated with distinct conceptions of national identity, policy priorities and evaluations of democratic performance. The next question is whether political parties play a significant role as avenues of substantive representation on this ideological cleavage. One indicator is whether parties display a sufficient level of ideological differentiation. To assess the degree of ideological differentiation between Indonesian political parties, I start by analyzing some of the general questions that we asked in the legislator survey about party ideological and programmatic profiles, party strategy and citizen–party linkages. I then focus in greater detail on parties' ideological positions on political Islam and economic policy.

4.5.1 How Much Do Political Parties Differ from Each Other?

In two questions, our survey asked the respondents whether they believed that Indonesian political parties could be considered the same in terms of ideology or policy platform. The results suggests that politicians are divided in their views. For ideology, 54.6% of the respondents agreed or strongly agreed that political parties all follow the same ideology, while the remaining 45.5% disagreed or strongly disagreed. The general opinion was that parties are more differentiated in their policy platforms than in their ideology, as only 47.1% agreed that they are the same, while 52.9% disagreed. Thus, for both issues, Indonesian provincial legislators were split into two groups of roughly equal sizes, one of which perceived significant differences across parties that the other does not recognize.

However, a closer look at the data reveals that opinions about parties' lack of ideological differentiation varied significantly across parties, which may indicate that significant ideological differences do exist. The belief that political parties all share the same ideology was most common among members of Golkar (79%), a party that is often described as ideologically centrist and as seeking to find a middle ground between the pluralist and Islamist camps, followed by members of Golkar splinter parties such as Hanura (71%), Demokrat (66%) and NasDem (65%). In contrast, members of parties that are considered as having a clearer ideological profile were substantially less likely to agree that parties are ideologically the same. This group includes the pluralist PDI-P (37% agreement) and Islam-based parties such as PPP (27%), PKS (41%) and PKB (42%). This breakdown shows that Indonesian political parties are far from being the same ideologically, as partisanship is closely associated with perceptions of parties' ideological differentiation, or lack thereof. Regardless of the perceived ideological differences, however, an overwhelming majority of the sampled legislators agreed that such differences can be put aside to work with other parties, as 94.7% of them stated that their party could form coalitions with any other party on issues such as passing certain legislation or choosing a candidate for direct elections for district head or governor.

Another way to investigate ideological differences between political parties is to study their electoral strategies. In appealing to citizens for votes, parties and candidates can articulate a variety of appeals, such as emphasizing candidate traits, informing about party policy programs and stressing the ability to deliver material benefits. Parties and candidates usually implement a mix of these strategies, and differences in party structure, ideology and programmatic platforms can be linked with campaign strategy. Studying what parties do during electoral campaigns could therefore provide valuable insights into party differentiation.

We asked our respondents a battery of questions on what factors they considered effective in mobilizing voters, including organizational factors

4.5 Political Parties

(recruiting consultants, mobilizing local elites, relying on party machines, etc.) and appeal-making strategies. The most popular type of appeal made to voters was personal, as 50.9% of the respondents stated that emphasizing their own traits as candidates was very important to their victory. This is not surprising given the candidate-centric nature of Indonesia's legislative electoral system. Other popular electoral appeals include talking about the party's policy programs (46.1%) and the party's competence in running the economy (31.1%) and emphasizing the party leader's positive qualities (40.7%). Regarding appeals based on social identities, only a small group of respondents – 11.1% – described religious appeals as a very important election strategy, whereas larger shares of the interviewees considered appeals based on national and ethnic identity to be very important (35.2% and 22.4%, respectively). Again, however, these aggregate figures mask important variations between parties. While the shares of respondents who valued nation-based appeals varied little between parties, opinions on religion-based appeals varied substantially between pluralist parties such as NasDem and PDI-P, for which the shares of respondents considering religious appeals as important or very important were 34.4% and 45.7%, respectively, and Islam-based parties, where members were much more likely to express this view (81.2% for the PPP, 78.6% for the PKS, 82.9% for the PKB and 74.4% for PAN). Variation in this measure across parties is consistent with the idea of ideological differentiation on religious issues.[6]

Finally, we asked the politicians about their beliefs about why voters choose to vote for their party, instructing them to name up to three factors that they consider the most important to explain party vote. The results are consistent with those discussed previously for party strategy in showing the importance of appeals based on candidates, party leaders and party platforms. For example, nearly half of the respondents (49.8%) believed that voters choose their party because it fields better candidates, 51% because the party supports political change and reform, 30.3% because voters agree with the party policies and 26.8% because the party represents the voters' economic interests. Religion ranked fairly low as a driver of party choice in the legislators' minds, as only 7.5% included it among their top three factors. However, the share of respondents who mentioned religion varied dramatically between parties, ranging from 0% for NasDem to 36% for the PPP. It is interesting to observe the

---

[6] See also Kuipers (2019).

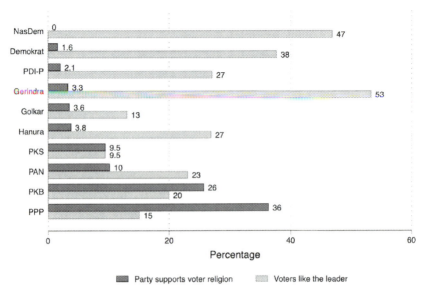

FIGURE 4.7. Voter party choice as seen by Indonesian politicians

correlations between religion and party leadership as determinants of party choice, which are reported in Figure 4.7. For pluralist parties, liking the party leader was considered a much more important driver of voting behavior than voting according to one's religious beliefs or endorsements from religious organizations. However, for most Islam-based parties, religion-based voting was considered as important as, if not more important than, party leadership. This again indicates a connection between a party's ideological profile and the nature of the citizen–politician linkages that it may pursue as an electoral strategy.

4.5.2 Party Positions

In contrast with democracies in Europe, for which scholars can draw on a range of data sources, Indonesia does not benefit from a systematic approach to measuring parties' ideological positions and programmatic platforms. Party manifestoes, for example, have yet to be analyzed as a source of information on party positions, and mass surveys have yet to be conducted to ask voters to assess parties' ideological profiles. Here, to measure and analyze ideological divisions in modern Indonesian politics, most importantly on the issue of political Islam, I rely on politicians' own assessments of party positions. This approach is a radical departure from

4.5 Political Parties

prior studies of party positions in Indonesia in which scholars rely on their individual expert judgment to evaluate Indonesian parties' ideological positions on political Islam (Baswedan 2004; Mietzner 2013, 167–191).

I focus here on four broad ideological dimensions measured on a 10-point scale. The first dimension is a general left–right ideological continuum that captures politicians' own assessment of their party's positions on a 10-point party scale. Although "left" and "right" are analytical categories that may not be applicable to modern Indonesian politics, this question allows for the possibility that political attitudes are more structured around this spectrum than prior studies assume. Furthermore, including this question enabled empirical investigation of the associations between left–right positions and preferences regarding social and economic policy issues. For the second dimension, the ideological cleavage about political Islam, we designed two survey items. The first directly asked whether a party supports a smaller or larger role for Islam in politics. The second asked whether the party's ideology is based more on Islam or on the *Pancasila*, Indonesia's official ideology, encapsulating principles of religious tolerance and pluralism.[7] The third dimension measured preferences regarding sociocultural issues, first by presenting a general contraposition between social progress/renewal and traditionalism and then with a more specific reference to gender. The final dimension was economic, and it was measured with three items related to issues of economic redistribution and the role of the government in the economy.

To determine the structure of ideological competition in Indonesian politics, I analyze how the responses to these questions were associated with one another. A suitable technique for this aim is factor analysis, which can be used to identify the drivers of common variance regarding how our respondents evaluate their party positions on the four ideological dimensions described in the previous paragraph. Factor analysis is a data-reduction technique that identifies patterns of common variation among a series of variables, in this case party positions on various issues. In brief, this method examines the correlations between the various items to identify categories of "similar" statements – that is, statements that can be attributed to a common underlying factor (in this case, a dimension of ideological competition between political parties). For each extracted factor, the factor analysis calculates a coefficient called the eigenvalue,

---

[7] See Latif (2018); Pepinsky et al. (2018, 73–75).

98 Political Elites and Ideological Competition

TABLE 4.4. *Factor analysis of self-assessed party positions*

Variable	Factor 1 Cultural	Factor 2 Economic
Left/right	0.3166	−0.2043
Religious		
Role of Islam in politics	0.4524	−0.1603
Pancasila or Islam?	0.6427	0.0572
Social		
Traditionalism	0.4026	0.1552
Women's rights	0.4098	0.1721
Economic		
Supporting the poor versus business interests	−0.0376	0.2504
Economic policy priority	0.1434	0.3699
Statism	0.0539	0.4342
Eigenvalue	1.164	0.453
Correlation between the two factors: 0.156		

Note: Factor extraction is carried out using principal factors and the list-wise deletion of missing observations (N = 460). The factor loadings are based on oblique rotation. Loadings higher than 0.30 are in bold.

which represents the amount of information condensed in the factor, and we can determine the number of underlying dimensions of Indonesian national identity by comparing the eigenvalues between factors.[8] Once the number of relevant factors is identified, we can interpret their substantive meaning by analyzing the various loadings, i.e., the empirical associations between the factors and the variables. For example, a strong association between one of the extracted factors and the question on statism would indicate that the factor captures an economic dimension of ideological competition.

The results reported in Table 4.4 identify two factors but suggest that only one is a strong driver of common variation. The first extracted factor has an eigenvalue of 1.16, and the factor loadings reported in the table indicate that this ideological dimension encompasses religious and cultural issues. The loadings on the religion items are particularly strong (0.45 and 0.64), and the association with traditionalism and gender is also robust (loadings of 0.40 and 0.41, respectively). The loading for the left–right dimension suggests that the first factor is also positively

---

[8] The Kaiser criterion, a rule of thumb commonly used in empirical research to decide how many factors to retain for further analysis, suggests dropping all factors with an eigenvalue lower than 1.

4.5 Political Parties

associated with a general left–right ideological spectrum. However, the loadings for the left–right item for both factors are fairly weak, suggesting that this dichotomy resonates little in the context of Indonesian politics.

Political parties that are evaluated by their representatives as advocating a larger role for Islam in politics are therefore more likely to be described as right-wing, conservative, traditional and supportive of women's maintaining their traditional social role. In contrast, pluralist parties are perceived as being more left-wing, progressive, reformist and supportive of women's emancipation. The data analysis thus suggests that political Islam functions in Indonesia in a manner reminiscent of left–right division on cultural issues in other political systems even if our respondents do not associate this substantive cleavage with the labels of "left" and "right." Regarding the second factor, the low eigenvalue (.45) indicates its marginality as a driver of the ideological differentiation between Indonesian political parties. An inspection of the factor loadings reported earlier reveals that this second factor is associated with economic issues, especially with the questions on economic policy priorities and the role of government in the economy. Interestingly, this economic dimension is negatively (although weakly) correlated with left–right positions, which suggests that leftist–pluralist parties are more likely to be perceived as endorsing pro-market economic policies. The factor analysis thus identifies economic policy as a dimension of ideological competition, but it appears to be marginal compared with the religious–cultural dimension. Furthermore, these two dimensions do not significantly overlap, as suggested by the low value of the correlation coefficient between the two factors (0.16). In other words, the Islamist–pluralist division is indeed the sole axis of ideological competition in Indonesian politics.

The second step is to analyze the patterns of variation within and across parties. To this end, Table 4.5 reports a series of descriptive statistics for the responses aggregated by political party and an index of ideological polarization for each item.[9] The polarization indexes suggest that the ideological space is significantly polarized on religious issues, while political parties offer a more modest range of policy positions on social issues and an even narrower one on economic issues.[10] Of

---

[9] The index is derived from Dalton (2008). It has a value of 0 when all parties occupy the same position on the ideological scale and takes higher values for higher levels of polarization.

[10] To put the indexes into context, the average left–right polarization indexes for the Asian countries included in Dalton's sample range from to 0.90 for the Philippines to 1.16 for Taiwan, 2.13 for South Korea and 3.30 for Japan.

TABLE 4.5. *Party positions: Measurements and descriptive statistics*

Dimension	Coding	Mean	SD	Min	Max	Polarization
1. Left/right						
Left–right self-placement	1 = Left, liberal, progressive	5.97	0.7	5.18	7.21	1.15
	10 = Right, conservative					
2. Religious						
Role of Islam in politics	1 = Smaller role for Islam	6.39	1.38	4.51	8.3	2.75
	10 = Larger role for Islam					
Pancasila or Islam?	1 = Ideology is based on *Pancasila*	3.69	1.78	1.82	7.22	3.39
	10 = Ideology is based on Islam					
3. Social						
Traditionalism	1 = Encourages social renewal	2.85	0.78	2.18	4.55	1.35
	10 = Supports tradition					
Women's rights	1 = Encourages emancipation	3.48	0.81	2.66	5.12	1.40
	10 = Supports a traditional role					
4. Economic						
Supporting the poor versus business interests	1 = Supports interests of the poor	2.7	0.48	2.09	3.34	0.94
	10 = Supports interests of employers					
Economic policy priority	1 = Prioritizes equality	5	0.53	4.26	5.58	1.00
	10 = Prioritizes growth					
Statism	1 = Bigger role for the state	3.83	0.59	3.05	4.88	0.89
	10 = Bigger role for private sector					

4.5 Political Parties

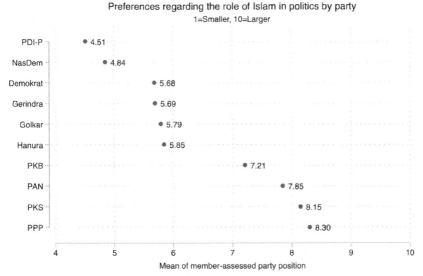

FIGURE 4.8. Party ideology: A smaller or larger role for Islam in politics?

particular interest is the item that measures party preferences regarding the role of Islam in politics, which offers the most direct measure of ideological polarization regarding political Islam. As shown in Figure 4.8, although no party supports an unequivocally pluralist position, the spectrum ranges from Indonesia's largest party, the PDI-P (4.51), whose members tend to advocate a clearer demarcation between Islam and the state, to the PPP (8.30), the most Islamist party in the group. In contrast, Indonesian parties are much more tightly clustered on economic issues. Their elected representatives view them as trying to strike a balance between economic growth and equality and as championing the interests of the lower and middle classes. Elites also invariably see their parties as supporting vigorous state intervention in the economy. Furthermore, an analysis of within- and between-group variance shows that the differences between political parties account for a larger share of variation for some issues than for others. For example, differences between parties account for 38.8% of the total variance for *Pancasila* and 24.7% for Islam, but only 3.2% for statism and 0.8% for the economy. This again corroborates the finding of high party differentiation on religious issues coupled with low or no differentiation on economic issues.

A final important question concerns within-party cohesion in political ideology, especially with regard to political Islam. To what extent are legislators sorted into political parties according to their own personal ideological orientations, as measured by the PII? To answer this question, we can analyze simple measures of variance such as standard deviations, which provide a ready indicator of internal ideological heterogeneity for the ten parties. Our data show that there is substantial variation in ideological cohesion across parties. The most ideologically heterogeneous party is Demokrat, whose legislators' PII has a standard deviation of 0.85, and the most homogeneous is PPP, whose legislators' PII has a standard deviation of 0.52. Whereas about 61% of PPP legislators can be described as Islamist or Islamist-leaning according to the classification adopted earlier, Demokrat's members show remarkable ideological diversity, with 49% being pluralist or pluralist-leaning, 29% being centrist and 22% being Islamist or Islamist-leaning. This suggests a relationship between party ideology and within-party ideology cohesion, which is depicted in Figure 4.9. As the figure shows, internal ideological heterogeneity appears to be higher for centrist parties such as Demokrat and Hanura and lower for parties with a clearer ideological profile at either end of the spectrum. This is especially the case for more unequivocally Islamist parties, because, as mentioned earlier, no party shows an average position that could be described as clearly pluralist. Ideological ambiguity is therefore associated with a more ideologically diverse party base among local legislators.

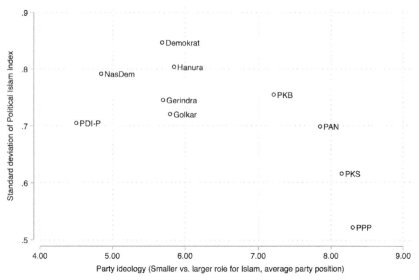

FIGURE 4.9. Party ideology and internal ideological cohesion

4.6 CONCLUSION

This chapter analyzes data from an original survey of Indonesian politicians to test the argument that political Islam is the key dimension of ideological competition in Indonesian politics and that political parties differ clearly on this issue. This argument is amply supported by analysis of the personal ideological orientations of a sample of provincial legislators, their experience of electoral campaigns and their assessment of party policy positions. In Chapter 5, I turn to public opinion surveys to analyze how ordinary citizens in Indonesia conceptualize the division over political Islam.

5

Public Opinion on Political Islam

5.1 STUDYING POLITICAL ISLAM IN MASS ATTITUDES

Political Islam is a salient political issue in many Muslim-majority societies where, as in Indonesia, Islam has been closely intertwined with politics since colonial domination. Political scientists acknowledge the centrality of ideological cleavages about political Islam as a driver of political competition in these settings, and survey research has been used to gauge the extent of public support for Islamism and to explore the implications of political Islam for various attitudinal orientations.[1]

In the Indonesian context, early studies of political Islam in public opinion champion the idea that Indonesian Muslims are ideologically moderate and that religious considerations play only a marginal role in voting behavior. In a series of articles based on quantitative data and survey research, Saiful Mujani and William Liddle portrayed Indonesia as a secular democracy – a feature they attribute to the historical legacies of pluralism and ideological moderation (Mujani and Liddle 2009, 2010). Factors such as assessments of macroeconomic performance and leader personalities appear to be more important for voting choice than ideology and religion, which explains the overall poor performance of Islamic political parties and the marginality of radical Islamism. In a similar vein, Pepinsky, Liddle and Mujani (2018) show, using an experimental research design, that Islam-based parties may enjoy an advantage under

---

[1] See, for example, Blaydes and Linzer (2008); Jamal and Tessler (2008); Tessler, Jamal and Robbins (2012); and Fair, Littman and Nugent (2018).

5.1 Studying Political Islam in Mass Attitudes

some circumstances, but economic factors generally trump religious ones in influencing party choice. This body of research thus portrays Indonesian voters as being more concerned with economic development than religious and social issues, and this view has been an influential explanation of Indonesia's success in keeping extremist political forces at bay for most of its democratic history.

However, the Islamist mass demonstrations of 2016–2017 have obfuscated this image of Islam as being essentially moderate and tolerant in Indonesia, and they have generated new interest in the study of public opinion regarding political Islam. Some studies analyze Indonesian public opinion from a comparative perspective and conclude that ideologically the Indonesian public is better described as a typical case in the Islamic world rather than a moderate outlier (Sumaktoyo 2019). Other studies measure the extent of support for an Islamist political agenda using cross-sectional and longitudinal data. Recent surveys suggest that about a quarter of the Indonesian population supports an Islamist political agenda, and public opinion trends point to increases in Islamist views of politics following the mass demonstrations (Mietzner and Muhtadi 2018; Mietzner, Muhtadi and Halida 2018). Furthermore, recent research indicates that evaluations of the economy, long thought to have an independent effect on voting behavior, are to a significant extent endogenous to partisanship in Indonesia's newly polarized political climate (Muhtadi and Warburton 2020). These studies suggest the increased salience of the cleavage over political Islam in public opinion and invite further investigation of the substantive meaning of this ideological divide. To what extent is political Islam associated with political participation and behavior among ordinary Indonesians? Does this religious-ideological cleavage intersect with national identity? Does it have implications for how Indonesians evaluate democracy and conceptualize public policy in specific areas?

I use two main data sources in this chapter to answer these questions. The first is the Indonesia National Survey Project (INSP), on which Section 5.2 and most of Section 5.4 are based. As I mentioned in Chapter 1, this survey was conducted on a nationally representative, randomly selected sample of Indonesian citizens, who were interviewed face-to-face. The high representativeness of this sample makes the INSP an ideal data source for drawing descriptive statistics about the population as a whole. This survey was the first to use the PII to measure ordinary citizens' attitudes toward state-Islam relations. The analysis of survey data can provide an accurate picture of how public attitudes on this important issue vary, and the dataset also provides a reliable basis for the study of ideological congruence that I conduct in Chapter 6.

In addition to this dataset, I have implemented an online survey to study in greater depth the relationship between political Islam and two other powerful narratives in Indonesian politics, namely nationalism (Section 5.3) and populism (Section 5.4.2). This survey, conducted between August and September 2018, was designed specifically for this purpose, and it measures national identity and support for populism as a political ideology using indicators derived from comparative survey research on these subjects.[2] The respondents were recruited with the help of a local contractor, who incentivized participation with various material inducements. A total of 1,422 responses were collected from a respondent pool with remarkably diverse socioeconomic, demographic and ideological backgrounds. To ensure that various sociodemographic groups would be included in the sample, quotas were set for age, gender, region (urban or rural), religion and education. While the final sample, as is the case for most surveys based on an online pool of respondents, was skewed toward male, younger and better-educated respondents, the sufficiently large sample size ensures that hundreds of responses were collected even for underrepresented population segments. Furthermore, studies of political ideology suggest that the relationships between political ideology and other ideational constructs are virtually identical across the samples collected online and via face-to-face interviews (Clifford, Jewell and Waggoner 2015). This offers reassurance that the findings reported here are highly likely to apply to the Indonesian population as a whole.

As in Chapter 4, my aim here is to test some of the important foundations of the argument put forward in this book. For the cleavage over political Islam to serve as an axis for ideological representation, this issue should be well understood and salient in the minds of ordinary citizens. Voters should display substantial heterogeneity in how they conceptualize state–Islam relations, as this ideological dimension should have implications for their political behavior. I substantiate these hypotheses in Section 5.2, after which I further explore the associations between political Islam and other pivotal ideological constructs, such as national identity, populism and various policy preferences.

---

[2] I designed this survey in collaboration with Duncan McDonnell at Griffith University, and the dataset was also used for a journal article that analyzes populist attitudes in the Indonesian context in greater detail than I do in this chapter (Fossati and Mietzner 2019).

5.2 A DEEP-ROOTED CLEAVAGE

In this section, I draw from the analytical approach outlined in Chapter 4 to measure ordinary Indonesians' orientations toward political Islam. As this sample is much more diverse than the elite sample studied in Chapter 4, I am also able to investigate how political Islam is associated with sociodemographic factors, political knowledge and political participation.

5.2.1 A Profile of Political Islam in Indonesia

In line with the discussion in Chapter 4, we can build a simple arithmetic mean of the responses to the seven items on the political Islam scale to generate the PII, an accurate indicator of where each respondent stands on the issue of state–Islam relations. Again, the PII ranges from 1 to 5, where lower values indicate respondents more supportive of secularism and higher values indicate individuals who support a larger role for Islam in Indonesian political life. When respondents are divided into five groups according to their scores, as I did in Chapter 4, we can gauge the distribution of support for secularism and Islamism in the Indonesian electorate, as shown in Figure 5.1. At both ends of the PII spectrum, we find groups of fairly equivalent size that represent the two ideological "extremes" of pluralist and Islamist Indonesians. In between, 27.5% of respondents can be described as centrist, 17.9% as pluralist-leaning and 34% as Islamist-leaning. This distribution suggests that, although there is

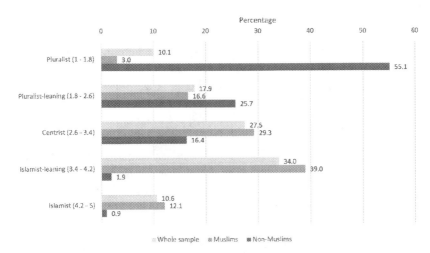

FIGURE 5.1. Ideology groups in the Indonesian electorate

substantial heterogeneity in views about state–Islam relations, the respondents favoring a larger role for Islam in politics outnumber those with more pluralist leanings. This skew is much more pronounced if we only consider Muslim respondents, of whom only 3% can be categorized as pluralist and 12.1% as Islamist. This means that only forty-one Muslim respondents in the sample qualify as pluralist, while more than four times as many show an Islamist ideological profile.

The overall picture emerging from these data is one of a fairly conservative electorate in which uncompromisingly pluralist attitudes are held only by Indonesians belonging to religious minorities and a very small share of progressive Indonesian Muslims. The median value of the PII for a Muslim respondent in the sample is 3.43 on a five-point scale, which suggests that most Muslim respondents are comfortable with the idea that Islam should be primus inter pares among the religions practiced in Indonesia. These numbers suggest that for many Indonesian Muslims, support for pluralism may be conditional on some form of acknowledgment of Islam as having a privileged status in Indonesian law and public policy. This finding is consistent with the view that although Indonesia's state–religion relations are characterized by tolerance toward religious minorities, they differ from a Western secularist ideal based on individual rights and a clear separation between religion and the state (Menchik 2016).

Although the political elite studied in Chapter 4 were highly homogeneous in their socioeconomic backgrounds, the INSP sample is highly representative of the Indonesian population because of its sampling strategy. The respondents are thus highly diverse in terms of age, location of residence, gender, education and income, and they provide a valuable opportunity to study how political Islam is associated with these sociodemographic factors. Table 5.1 focuses on Muslim respondents and displays how the distribution of the ideological groups identified in Figure 5.1 varies across different social sectors. Age does not appear to have a clear relationship with political ideology, as older respondents are about as likely as younger ones to embrace pluralist or Islamist views.[3] However, there is a clear difference between male and female respondents: Although only 48% of men can be categorized as Islamist or Islamist-leaning, 55% of women can be so classified. High levels of support for social conservatism and Islamic fundamentalism among women in the Islamic world are well known and are plausibly related to

---

[3] However, support for Islamism is substantially weaker among middle-aged respondents.

5.2 A Deep-Rooted Cleavage 109

TABLE 5.1. *Political Islam and sociodemographic factors among Indonesian Muslims*

	Pluralist and pluralist-leaning (%)	Islamist and Islamist-leaning(%)
Age		
Less than 30	19.37	55.86
30–39	17.61	52.24
40–49	21.07	43.54
50–59	19.5	53.11
60 and above	20.95	54.76
Location		
Urban	19.31	50.07
Rural	20	52.18
Gender		
Male	21.66	47.53
Female	17.6	54.73
Education		
Less than elementary	12.8%	61.61
Elementary	18.4	54.72
Secondary	16.42	53.36
High school or diploma	25.91	42.75
College or above	24.42	38.37
Income quintile		
Fifth	15.94	56.52
Fourth	15.93	56.19
Third	17.63	50.26
Second	18.68	53.11
First	26.51	44.96

women's higher financial vulnerability in these settings (Blaydes and Linzer 2008). In terms of geography, Islamist and pluralist Indonesians do not seem to be concentrated in rural or urban areas, which suggests that a high degree of ideological diversity can be found both in Indonesian cities and in rural regions. However, further investigation of subnational variation in political Islam reveals substantial differences across provinces. Although the INSP sample is not representative at the provincial level, the Muslim respondents interviewed in regions with a deep-rooted history of radical Islamism overwhelmingly fall into the Islamist and Islamist-leaning groups, as in Aceh (76%), West Sumatra (76%) and Banten (66%). In contrast, such views represent only a plurality in provinces where traditionalist Islam has been preponderant, such as Central Java (48%) and East Java (41%).

The data reported in Table 5.1 also suggest a close link between political Islam and social class as defined by education and income. The empirical association with educational attainment is very robust, as support for Islamist understandings of politics is lower among better-educated respondents. The level of endorsement for an Islamist political agenda is highest among Muslims lacking even elementary education, 62% of whom can be described as Islamist or Islamist-leaning, whereas it tends to be lower among more educated respondents: 55% of those with elementary education, 53% with secondary education, 43% with a high school certificate or a diploma and 38% of college-educated respondents. Conversely, the share of pluralist respondents is higher given higher levels of educational attainment. A similar pattern is observed for income levels, as pluralist views are more common in higher-income groups. In the two lowest income quintiles, only 16% of Muslim respondents fall into the pluralist-leaning or pluralist ideological groups, but this share is 18% in the third quintile, 19% in the fourth and 27% in the highest income quintile.[4] These data thus indicate a strong association between social class and ideological orientations, as Indonesian citizens with Islamist worldviews appear to be concentrated in social segments of lower socioeconomic status. This finding is consistent with the association between political Islam and economic grievances revealed in Chapter 4 and in qualitative research (Hadiz 2018).

5.2.2 Political Participation

The association identified previously between socioeconomic status and the cleavage over political Islam may have implications for political behavior. A well-established framework for conceptualizing political participation and explaining how it varies between individuals views participation as a function of the resources available to citizens (Brady, Verba and Schlozman 1995). Some individuals are more likely to engage in political and civic life because they can rely on assets such as disposable time and money and because they have developed the necessary civic skills through education and other channels. Although socioeconomic status

---

[4] Data on income quintiles were compiled by enumerators, who coded a respondent in the lowest quintile when their monthly household income per capita was below 200,000 IDR, in the fourth quintile for 200,000–333,000 IDR, in the third quintile for 333,000–567,000 IDR, in the second quintile for 567,000–875,000 IDR and in the first quintile for incomes above 875,000 IDR.

5.2 A Deep-Rooted Cleavage

alone may not fully explain the variation between individuals and social groups, social and economic inequalities have obvious repercussions for a citizen's ability to meaningfully participate in politics, as these can constrain a citizen's ability to acquire and process the information and time available for civic engagement. Thus, given the patterns discussed earlier, we should expect pluralist Indonesians to be more engaged in politics than Islamists.

A starting point for exploring this hypothesis is a survey question that asks how interested respondents are in politics. Overall, political interest is not particularly high in the Indonesian electorate, as only 28% of respondents describe themselves as being somewhat or very interested in politics. However, this question appears to be closely associated with the cleavage over political Islam. Interest in politics appears to be slightly below average, at about 25%, for the majority of the sample, which could be described as centrist or Islamist-leaning, and above average in the two more ideologically "extreme" groups, namely pluralists (43%) and Islamists (37%). Indonesians with well-defined, unambiguous views of where they stand on state–Islam relations are therefore much more likely to be interested in politics than those whose ideological positions are closer to the median, which I describe as being moderately conservative. This suggests that the cleavage over political Islam is linked with interest in politics and political engagement, and it resonates with this book's broader argument that this ideological cleavage has sustained the legitimacy of democratic institutions in post-Suharto Indonesia.

Interest in politics should be closely related to knowledge about politics, as individuals interested in politics are more likely to spend time acquiring the information necessary to increase their knowledge and understanding of Indonesia's political systems. To measure one's knowledge about politics, the INSP survey asked four factual questions about Indonesian political figures, parties and institutions:

1. Name the vice president of Indonesia. (Open-ended)
2. Which political party has the largest number of seats in the DPR? (Multiple choice)
3. Who is Sri Mulyani Indrawati? (Multiple choice)
4. How long is the term of office for a local leader such as a governor, bupati or mayor? (Multiple choice)

The three main ideological groups defined by the PII differ substantially from their political sophistication. The average number of correct answers is 2.77 for pluralist and pluralist-leaning respondents, 2.53 for centrists and 2.27 for Islamist and Islamist-leaning respondents. The survey answers further show that for each of the questions, the level of political knowledge is highest for respondents with pluralist views and lowest for respondents at the Islamic end of the ideological spectrum. For example, while only 15% of pluralist respondents were unable to name Jusuf Kalla as the vice president of Indonesia, 27% of Islamists were unable to do so. These data indicate that the differences in educational attainment between ideological groups are consequential for how well individuals understand politics, suggesting that Islamist/Islamist-leaning respondents, being less politically sophisticated than their pluralist counterparts, may be more vulnerable to misinformation and manipulation.

We can observe similar differences in political participation between pluralist and Islamist Indonesians across a wide range of indicators of civic engagement. Regarding formal political participation, no substantial differences exist between the two groups: Electoral turnout is, on average, very high in Indonesia, and survey responses tend to overreport voting. Indicators of informal political engagement are a more useful measure of how Indonesians of different ideological orientations vary in their political engagement. As Figure 5.2 shows, pluralist respondents are more likely than Islamists to report various types of political participation, such as contacting a politician to discuss issues they are concerned about; donating money to, or volunteering to help, a political party or candidate; participating in campaign events; talking about politics on social media; and taking part in public demonstrations or protests. These figures suggest that, overall, respondents with pluralist worldviews are more engaged in political life than those favoring a more conservative view of state-Islam relations. Data on association membership, also reported in Figure 5.2, point to a similar finding of pluralists reporting higher levels of membership than Islamists in any type of civil society organization and religious associations/organizations especially.

It is important to note that differences in participation between the two groups remain even after we account for the important disparities in socioeconomic status as identified in Section 5.2.1. Figure 5.3 displays the estimated probabilities (with 95% confidence intervals) of respondents reporting at least one of the informal means of participation listed previously, and these margins are estimated using a simple logistic model in which participation is a function of the ideological group and of the socioeconomic covariates reported in Table 5.1. As shown in the chart, important differences are observed between the ideological groups when we control for factors such as gender, education and income.

5.2 A Deep-Rooted Cleavage

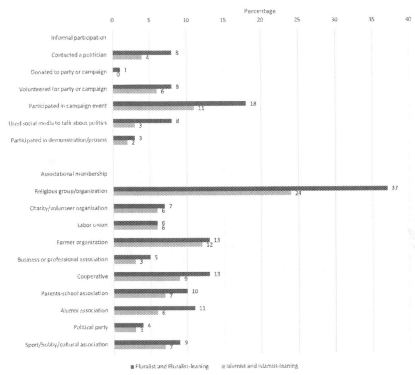

FIGURE 5.2. Political and civic engagement by different ideological groups

The estimated probability of informal participation is highest among pluralists (32%) and lower among leaning pluralists (25%), centrists (21%), leaning Islamists (19%) and Islamists (20%). The cleavage over political Islam is therefore a significant predictor of political participation in the Indonesian context, and data indicate that the pluralist minority is characterized by especially high levels of political mobilization. This inequality between the two ideological camps may thus be rooted not only in present-day socioeconomic disparities but also in the aforementioned historical legacy of political marginalization of Islamist Indonesians.

5.2.3 Party Choice

The INSP includes several questions seeking leverage to an analysis of the relationship between party choice and respondents' views on political Islam. The first question asks, "If elections for the DPR were held today,

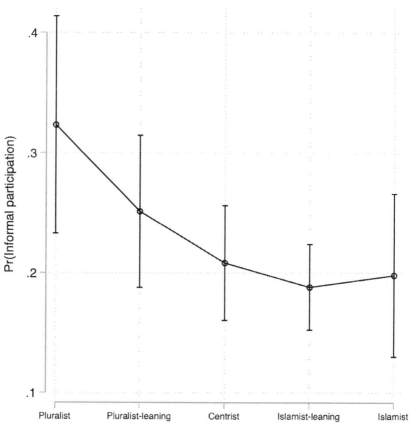

FIGURE 5.3. Estimated probability of informal participation by ideological group

what party would you vote for?" About 68% of respondents indicate they would vote for a specific political party, with the most popular choices being PDI-P (32.8%), Golkar (17%), PKB (10%) and Gerindra (9.8%). To illustrate the degree to which voters make a choice of parties according to their ideological proclivities, Figure 5.4 displays the mean values of PII for Indonesia's ten largest parties on the right axis and the distribution of supporters' ideologies on the left axis (i.e., the shares of supporters falling into the pluralist-leaning/pluralist, centrist and Islamist-leaning/Islamist categories). Data show that there are no political parties having voters who support radically pluralist or Islamist positions, as the mean PII values are clustered in a fairly narrow space, from 2.52 to 3.66 on a five-point scale.

Nevertheless, these values, along with the bar chart showing the ideological profile of each party's voters, suggest that there are some important

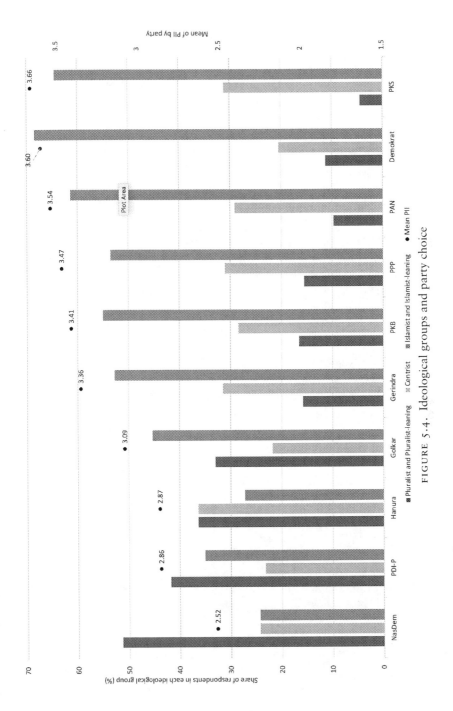

FIGURE 5.4. Ideological groups and party choice

ideological differences among the supporters of different parties. Of all the political parties studied, NasDem is the most pluralist, as its voters have the lowest average PII value and are the only group for which pluralist and pluralist-leaning views constitute a majority (51.4%). At the other end of the ideological spectrum, PKS and Demokrat are the most Islamist parties, with average PII scores higher than 3.6 and with large majorities of Islamist and Islamist-leaning respondents (68.4% for Demokrat and 64.4% for PKS). PDI-P is the only party with a clear majority of pluralist supporters; in all of the other parties, except Hanura and Golkar, Islamist and Islamist-leaning voters account for 50% or more of party supporters. Unsurprisingly, respondents who did not indicate a preference for a specific party or reported an intention not to vote have a less definite ideological profile, as centrist individuals constitute 32.7% of this group, but only 25.1% of those with a party preference.

In sum, these data indicate that voters with well-defined ideological positions are more likely to develop a preference for a political party, which is consistent with the idea that cleavage over political Islam has a positive implication for representation and democratic legitimacy. Some substantial differences emerge when we compare the ideological orientations of different party voters using PII. It is also important to note the clear prevalence of Islamist and Islamist-leaning members in most parties, including nominally pluralist parties such as Golkar, Gerindra and, most notably, Demokrat. In this respect, PDI-P and NasDem, currently the first and fourth largest parties in DPR, respectively, may play an important role in offering a pluralist alternative in a political landscape dominated by conservative party platforms.

Another question, similar to the one we asked in the survey of politicians, asks respondents to account for their party choice, giving them the option to name up to three factors that are important in influencing their vote. The answers are in line with those provided by politicians and analyzed in Chapter 4, as only a few respondents report voting for a specific party because of religious issues. Liking the party leader is the most commonly mentioned factor (23%), followed by the belief that the party has better candidates (16%), support for party policies (14%) and perceptions that the party stands for reform and change (14%). Only 9% of respondents mention religion as a factor, but if we break down this aggregate value by ideological group, a strong correlation emerges. No pluralist respondents mentioned religion, but 6% of pluralist-leaning respondents, 9.6% of centrists, 11.5% of Islamist-leaning respondents and 13.7% of Islamists did. Again, religious considerations alone do not completely explain party

5.3 ISLAM AND NATIONAL IDENTITY

choice, and even the most Islamist parties need to articulate messages that go beyond clarifying their position on the cleavage over political Islam to be electorally successful. Yet this variation across parties corroborates the hypothesis that important differences exist between the parties in terms of their ideology and the appeals that they formulate to mobilize support.

5.3 ISLAM AND NATIONAL IDENTITY

Section 5.2 discussed some associations between political Islam and political behavior. I now explore the relationship between this ideological cleavage and other key ideational orientations in Indonesian politics and society, starting with nationalism. The key question that I address in this section is whether the cleavage over political Islam is associated with conceptions of national identity: Do pluralist and Islamist Indonesian diverge in what they consider crucial to defining the boundaries of national identity? Answering this question will shed light on political Islam's effects on ordinary Indonesians' conceptualizations of nationhood and the role of ethnoreligious minorities in this diverse country, which have repercussions for public preferences regarding policies designed to recognize, protect and advance minority rights.

A key distinction in the literature on nationalism based on the early comparative-historical work of Kohn (1944) is to distinguish between "ethnic" and "civic" conceptions of national identity. From an ethnonationalist perspective, claims of belonging to a specific nation are based on kinship (ethnic or religious), ancestry and "blood," whereas civic nationalism demarcates nationhood based on shared political and civic values. Thus, while civic nationalism is typically characterized as voluntarist and inclusive, ethnic nationalism is portrayed as ascriptive and exclusive.

Many scholars who examine the Indonesian case from a comparative perspective describe Indonesian nationalism as being inclusive, emphasizing its ability to bring together people of different ethnic backgrounds and ideological orientations (Hamayotsu 2002; Sidel 2012, 132). In addition, the dichotomy between ethnic and civic conceptions of national identity is readily applicable to the Indonesian context. Although the variety of nationalism propagated by revolutionary leaders could indeed be characterized as being close to the civic ideal, this conception has coexisted with more exclusionary ethnic understandings of what it means to be Indonesian that view Islamic faith as a key component of nationalist credentials (Laffan 2003; Bourchier 2019). Ideological positions on political Islam may therefore be associated with understandings of national

118 Public Opinion on Political Islam

identity, as Islamist individuals may be more likely to endorse ethnonationalist understandings of nationhood.

To measure attachments to and conceptions of national identity, I rely on indicators that are widely used in comparative research, specifically on those included in the International Social Survey Program (ISSP). A question in the web-based survey asks, "Some people say that the following things are important for being truly Indonesian. Others say they are not important. How important do you think each of the following is?" What follows is a list of nine items that may be associated with ethnic or civic understandings of what it means to be Indonesian: to be born in Indonesia, to be an Indonesian citizen, to have lived in Indonesia most of one's life, to be able to speak Bahasa Indonesia, to be a Muslim, to respect Indonesia's laws and institutions, to feel Indonesian, to have Indonesian ancestry and to be a *Pribumi*.[5] We can thus ascertain whether ethnic and civic conceptions of national identity are present among the Indonesian public as coherent attitudinal constructs. Furthermore, we can construct measures of ethnic and civic conceptions of national identity and use them to analyze their association with political Islam.

5.3.1 Political Islam and the Structure of Indonesian National Identity

Factor analysis, which I used in Chapter 4 to identify the dimensions of ideological competition in the Indonesian party system, is suitable for analyzing the structure of Indonesian national identity, and indeed this method is commonly used in studies of national identity based on survey data (Jones and Smith 2001; Shulman 2002; Reeskens and Hooghe 2010). We can thus identify the number and nature of the dimensions of Indonesian national identity via a factor analysis of the various questions listed earlier regarding what it means to be a true Indonesian. The first factor extracted from the nine items listed in Section 5.3 has a high eigenvalue of 3.94, the second has an eigenvalue of 1.31 and the rest have eigenvalues of 0.75 or lower. Given the eigenvalue threshold of 1, this is evidence that variation in conceptions of national identity can be reduced to two dimensions, as expected.

To define the substantive content of the two factors and to determine whether they fit the conceptual dyad of ethnic and civic nationalism, we

---

[5] The last item is of course not included in international iterations of this battery, and it was added with specific reference to Indonesia's social context.

5.3 Islam and National Identity 119

TABLE 5.2. *Factor analysis of dimensions of national identity in Indonesia*

	Item	Factor 1 Ethnic	Factor 2 Civic
1	To be born in Indonesia	0.7839	0.0573
2	To be an Indonesian citizen	0.1474	**0.667**
3	To have lived in Indonesia most of one's life	**0.6564**	0.199
4	To be able to speak Bahasa Indonesia	0.1973	**0.5589**
5	To be a Muslim	**0.8048**	−0.1124
6	To respect Indonesia's institutions and laws	−0.2233	**0.7758**
7	To feel Indonesian	0.0389	**0.7445**
8	To have Indonesian ancestry	**0.8324**	−0.0077
9	To be a pribumi	**0.8315**	−0.0326

N=1,308. Principal component factors are obtained with oblique rotation (promax).
Loadings higher than 0.5 are in bold.

identify the items most strongly associated with each factor. For example, a strong association (or "loading") between one of the extracted factors and the item "to be a *Pribumi*" would be evidence that the factor captures the dimension of an ethnic conception of national identity. Table 5.2 reports the factor loadings for each item, where higher loading values indicate a closer correlation between the item and the factor. The first factor, which explains most of the overall variation in the survey responses (40.4%), is closely associated with items 1, 5, 8 and 9, and can thus be interpreted as corresponding to ethnic nationalism. Variation in this factor tells us whether a respondent understands Indonesian national identity as being connected to ethnic traits, such as having Indonesian ancestry, being a *pribumi* (as opposed to a *warga keturunan*, or Indonesian of "foreign" ancestry) or being a Muslim. The finding of a well-defined ethnic conception of nationhood is not surprising, as it resonates with the vast body of research that documents the emergence and historical evolution of Islamic nationalism in Indonesia (Laffan 2003; Fogg 2012). However, the strong empirical associations between "to be a Muslim" and other statements such as "to have Indonesian ancestry" and "to be a *pribumi*" also indicate that religious understandings of nationalism are clearly underpinned by ethnocentric sentiments. The second factor is associated with statements that can be more readily understood as representing a civic conception of national identity, such as feeling Indonesian and respecting Indonesian institutions and laws.

The factor analysis thus suggests that both civic and ethnic understandings of national identity resonate with the Indonesian public, as they do in

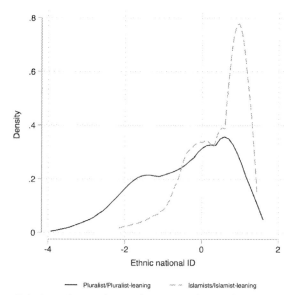

FIGURE 5.5. Ethnic understandings of national identity for two ideological groups

most other societies. To what extent are these two ideas of what is important to be Indonesian associated with the cleavage over political Islam? Because of limited space, the survey questionnaire did not include the full scale used to build the PII, but it did include the first item in the scale, which asked whether respondents agreed or disagreed that the Indonesian government should prioritize Islam over other religions; this question can be used as a proxy for ideological positions on the political Islam spectrum.[6] A first look at the correlations between the responses to this question and the two extracted factors suggest that political Islam is indeed related to conceptions of national identity, but primarily with ethnonationalism, as the correlation coefficient with the first factor is 0.38 and that with the second factor is only 0.10. Figure 5.5 presents the relationship between political Islam and ethnonationalism with two density plots of the first extracted factor (the factor corresponding to ethnic nationalism) for pluralists/pluralist-leaning and Islamists/Islamist-leaning respondents. For pluralists, the median value of the factor is -0.26, and about three-quarters of the observations have values of 0.5 or below. In contrast, the median value for Islamists is much higher, at 0.67, and

---

[6] Survey respondents show substantial diversity in their views, with 38.3% disagreeing or strongly disagreeing (pluralists and those leaning pluralist), 29.4% having a neutral stance (centrists) and 32.3% agreeing or strongly agreeing (those leaning Islamist and Islamists).

5.3 Islam and National Identity

many more observations are clustered around the highest factor values. Islamism is therefore closely related to ethnic-based, ascriptive conceptions of national identity in Indonesia; this resonates with the strong correlation between political Islam and anti-Chinese ethnic prejudice revealed in Chapter 4.

Although conceptions of national identity are associated with political Islam, national identity is a complex construct, and not all of its various dimensions may intersect with this religious–ideological cleavage. For example, an additional question in the survey aims to measure the strength of or attachment to national identity by asking respondents how close they feel to their nation. The answers are recorded on a scale ranging from 1 to 4 (not close at all, not very close, somewhat close, very close), for which higher values denote greater attachment to national identity. The survey responses show that most respondents feel close to their national identity, with about 19% feeling "not close at all" or "not very close" to their nation, 47.2% feeling "somewhat close" and 33.8% "very close." As Figure 5.6 shows, however, this measure of attachment to national identity has a weak relationship with the cleavage over political Islam, as pluralists and those leaning pluralist are about as likely as

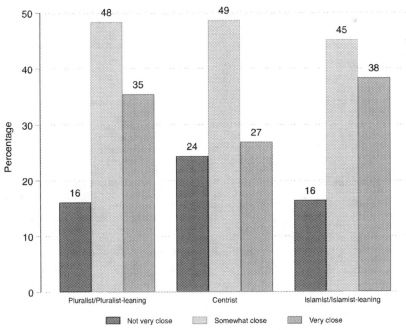

FIGURE 5.6. Political Islam and attachment to national identity

122   *Public Opinion on Political Islam*

Islamists and those leaning Islamist to feel close (or not close) to their nation, although centrists display overall lower levels of national attachment. This chart reminds us that although pluralist nationalism has historically dominated in the Indonesian context, nationalist feelings can be fully compatible with a strong religious identity and with an Islamist understanding of politics.

5.4 POLITICAL ISLAM AND POLITICAL PREFERENCES

The public opinion data reviewed thus far are consistent with the idea that political Islam is a deep-rooted religious–ideological cleavage among ordinary Indonesians and that it has implications for political behavior and understandings of the nature of the Indonesian nation. In this section, I further explore how views on state–Islam relations are associated with mass opinions on various political and social issues, starting with democratic attitudes and then discussing populism and preferences regarding economic policy and decentralization. Analysis of these data is important for the argument developed in this book, as it enables me to assess whether and to what extent the significance of this ideological cleavage goes beyond religious and national identity. The overall picture that emerges from Section 5.4.1 onward indicates that positions on the political Islam ideological spectrum are linked with important political orientations and policy preferences, which underscores that this religious–ideological cleavage may have consequential ramifications for how ordinary citizens conceptualize political issues in Indonesia.

5.4.1 Democracy

Support for democracy can be measured via questions that ask survey respondents to reflect on their opinions regarding democracy as a system of government. Among the most commonly used wordings, the so-called Churchill questions acknowledge the limitations of democracy and ask whether respondents agree that despite such shortcomings, democracy can be considered the best possible system of government. The INSP asked whether respondents disagreed or agreed that democracy, although not perfect, is the best form of government for Indonesia, and the survey respondents overwhelmingly agreed with this statement, with little variation between ideological groups (support was 79.8% on average, 84.2% among pluralists and those leaning pluralist and 79.3% among Islamists). For a question that presented a hypothetical tradeoff between democracy

5.4 Political Islam and Political Preferences

and economic development, support for democracy was lower, as only 49.9% of the sample agreed that democracy is more important than development. Again, however, there was very little variation between pluralist/pluralist-leaning respondents and Islamist/Islamist-leaning respondents, as agreement that democracy should be prioritized was at about 52% for both groups. These results are consistent with previous findings of high levels of support for democracy in Indonesia, and they suggest that support for democracy is not contingent on views on the cleavage over political Islam.

However, generally high levels of support for democracy should not be equated with support for the system of constitutional checks and balances typical of established liberal democracies. Consider, for example, the question often asked in comparative survey research about support for a strong leader who does not need to bother with the parliament and always wins elections. Agreement with this statement varies substantially across ideological groups, as shown in Figure 5.7. Although support for such a strong leader with no accountability is only 33% among pluralist and pluralist-leaning respondents, it rises to 45% among Islamist and Islamist-leaning respondents. Islamist respondents are thus substantially more likely to support authoritarian political leadership than pluralist respondents, who are the only ideological group for which a majority is

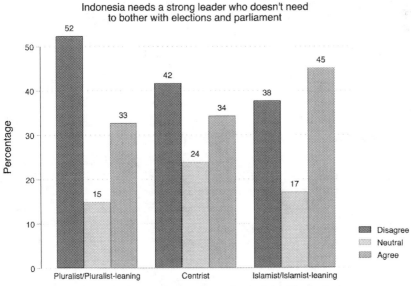

FIGURE 5.7. Preference for a "strong leader" by ideological group

opposed to such a "strongman" figure. This association suggests that the ideological divide over the role of Islam in politics has important implications for the kind of democracy that is perceived as worthy of support. I return to this point in Chapter 7, in which I conduct a more exhaustive analysis of the Indonesian public's various understandings of democracy and their relationship with evaluations of democratic performance.

5.4.2 Populism

Populism has drawn substantial attention in public and scholarly debate in recent years, as populist actors have seen their electoral fortunes rise throughout the world. However, conceptualizing populism is a controversial endeavor, as scholars alternatively understand populism as a political organization strategy or as an ideational construct. For the purposes of this study, I understand populism "as a thin-centered ideology that considers society to be ultimately separated into two homogeneous and antagonistic camps, 'the pure people' versus 'the corrupt elite,' and which argues that politics should be an expression of the volonté générale (general will) of the people" (Mudde 2004, 543). Conceptualizing populism as a thin ideology is especially useful in the context of this book, as this definition allows for the possibility that populist understandings of politics may be coupled with various "thicker" ideologies such as secularism and Islamism.

Populism has deep historical roots in Indonesia. Sukarno, one of the founding fathers of the Indonesian nation, can be considered an archetypical populist, as he was crucial in propagating a narrative that portrayed the Indonesian masses as victimized first by colonialism and then by international capitalism. Sukarno's powerful populist rhetoric played an important role in mobilizing support for the newly established Indonesian republic. In post-Suharto Indonesia, populism has been associated with the political ascent of Prabowo Subianto, whose discursive style mimics Sukarno's populistic panache and includes claims to speak on behalf of "the people" as well as attacks against corrupt elites, democratic institutions and foreign enemies (Aspinall 2015). This new incarnation of populism in Indonesia has striking similarities with cases of right-wing populism elsewhere, as it combines anti-elite sentiment with xenophobia and authoritarianism. One of the most notable features of populism in the Indonesian context is its association with the resurgence of Islamist sentiment and the illiberal turn in Indonesian politics discussed previously. This has prompted some observers to

5.4 Political Islam and Political Preferences 125

TABLE 5.3. *Measurement scale for populist attitudes*

	Item	N	Mean	SD
1	Politicians in Indonesia need to follow the will of the people.	1,391	4.26	0.93
2	The people, not politicians, should make our most important policy decisions.	1,365	3.51	1.13
3	I would rather be represented by a citizen than by a specialized politician.	1,371	3.84	1.01
4	Elected officials talk too much and take too little action.	1,382	3.93	1.23
5	Politicians always end up agreeing when it comes to protecting their privileges.	1,370	3.93	1.17
6	The particular interests of the political class negatively affect the welfare of the people.	1,366	3.94	1.06
7	What people call "compromises" in politics are really just selling out one's principles.	1,355	3.86	1.06

speak of "Islamic populism" (Hadiz 2018; Kusumo and Hurriyah 2018), as Islamist political ideology and populist rhetoric have combined to form a powerful platform for the Islamic masses to express their economic and political grievances. With the debate concerning Indonesian populism primarily concentrated on populist leaders, however, there has been little analysis of populist voters, and it remains unclear whether populist attitudes are indeed more prominent among Islamist than pluralist Indonesians.

To measure support for populist worldviews among the sample of 1,422 respondents recruited for the web survey, comparative analyses of populist attitudes (Van Hauwaert and Van Kessel 2018) were used to build the scale reported in Table 5.3. In combination, these items assess support for various defining features of a populist worldview. The items tap into populist tropes such as the view that decisions should be made directly by voters rather than by a class of professional politicians; various negative stereotypes of politicians as a homogenous group of self-interested individuals; a contraposition of interests between political elites and citizens; and distaste for compromise as a constitutive element of democratic politics. The respondents were asked to evaluate each item on a five-point Likert scale in which higher values correspond to higher degrees of agreement, and the descriptive statistics reported in the table indicate that the level of populist attitudes in Indonesia is comparatively high. Support varies somewhat across the seven items, and the average is 3.90.

To operationalize populism for further analysis, we developed a threshold by which an individual is considered populist or non-populist. A composite index was built by calculating the arithmetic mean of responses to the seven items of the scale reported in Table 5.3. This index, for which higher values indicate greater support for populism, is a convenient measure of the degree to which each individual that we surveyed can be regarded as a populist in their understanding of Indonesian politics. The composite index can also be adapted into a simpler dichotomous measure of populist support. With an index score of 4 taken as the threshold for whether a certain respondent, on average, agrees with the scale items, we classify survey respondents as populist if they score 4 or higher on the composite index (47.7% of the sample) and as non-populist otherwise (52.3%).

To what extent, then, are populist sentiments associated with the ideological cleavage over political Islam? As mentioned earlier, the Web survey measured preferences regarding the role of Islam in politics with a single, easily understandable question: "To what extent do you agree or disagree that the Indonesian government should prioritize Islam over other religions?" The cross-tabulation of the responses to this question and the binary indicator of populist attitudes suggest that support for populism indeed varies substantially across ideological groups. Regarding the other ideational constructs analyzed in this chapter, support for populism was lowest among centrists, at 35.2%, and substantially higher among those with well-defined views on political Islam, increasing to 51.1% for pluralist and pluralist-leaning respondents and 57.3% for Islamist and Islamist-leaning respondents. This indicates that populist rhetoric in Indonesia resonates strongest among individuals who hold well-defined, if not radical, views, in either direction on the issue of the role of Islam in public life. However, the data also show that populists constituted a larger share of the Islamist respondents than the pluralist respondents. Put differently, Islamists accounted for a larger proportion of those who supported populist attitudes (25.9%) than of those who do not (14.5%). This suggests that although Indonesian populism may be associated with both pluralist and Islamic ideological orientations, it is more likely to have an Islamist flavor. These findings warrant further exploration of the interplay between political Islam, populist worldviews and political-economic grievances.

Most studies suggest that populist sentiments thrive on dissatisfaction and grow in parallel with voters' disillusionment with the social, political and economic system. To test whether a correlation between populist attitudes and general discontent with the status quo exists in Indonesia, we examine whether there are higher levels of support for populist

5.4 Political Islam and Political Preferences

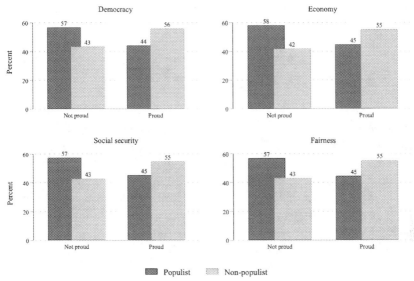

FIGURE 5.8. Populism and pride in Indonesia's achievements

attitudes among respondents who are critical of Indonesia's achievements in the post-Suharto era. For that purpose, the survey instrument asked respondents to state how proud they were of Indonesia's achievements in a wide range of areas using a four-point scale (1 = Not proud at all, 2 = Not very proud, 3 = Somewhat proud, 4 = Very proud). The data suggest that there is an overall significant relationship between dissatisfaction with Indonesia's achievements and support for populism, which is illustrated in Figure 5.8 with some examples. As the figure shows, there is a substantially higher share of populist respondents among those who express dissatisfaction with Indonesia's performance regarding democratic governance, the economy, ach social security and ensuring fairness for all. For example, 56.7% of those who are not proud or not very proud of how democracy is working in Indonesia can be characterized as populists. In contrast, among those who express pride in how democracy is working (somewhat proud or very proud), populists are a minority (44.1%).

These findings show that Indonesian populism, like populism elsewhere, is related to general dissatisfaction with the policy outcomes delivered by the current political system. Does this dissatisfaction overlap with the cleavage over political Islam? Contrary to expectations based on the Islamic populism literature, these data show that in each of the four areas shown previously, Islamists are significantly *prouder* of Indonesia's achievements than pluralists. Although 58.4% of pluralist and pluralist-leaning respondents describe themselves as at least somewhat proud of how democracy works in Indonesia, 71.2% of Islamist and Islamist-leaning respondents do; for economic achievements, these figures are 70.7% versus 73.7, respectively; for social security, 67.2% versus 79.3%; and for fairness, the biggest gap between the two groups is observed, with 73.8% of Islamist and Islamist-leaning respondents expressing pride in their country's achievements and only 58.6% of pluralist and pluralist-leaning respondents expressing the same view. There is therefore little evidence that at the time at which the survey was conducted (late 2018), economic, social or political grievances were concentrated at the Islamist end of the political Islam ideological spectrum. Populist sentiments and the disillusionment that feeds them appear to cut across ideological cleavages. These findings, in contrast with the patterns uncovered in the elite survey, suggest that it is Indonesians with pluralist rather than Islamist ideological preferences that are most disaffected with Indonesian democracy.[7]

5.4.3 Economic Issues

Observers of Indonesian politics have debated whether and to what extent economic factors account for the resurgence of Islamist politics in this country. The data that I have just discussed indicate that grievances regarding many areas of democratic governance, including economic outcomes, are more pronounced among Islamists than among Indonesians with other ideological leanings. However, the question on pride in economic achievements analyzed in Section 5.4.2 is only a starting point for analysis, as it is formulated in rather general terms and based on a nonrandomly selected sample. To more exhaustively and accurately examine the link between political Islam and economic attitudes, this section leverages INSP data to further delve into the association between political Islam and evaluations of economic conditions, policy priorities and preferences regarding economic policy.

The first set of relevant questions in the survey instrument asks respondents to evaluate the economic conditions both of their country as a whole and of their own household using a five-point scale ranging from "very bad" to "very good." When evaluations of Indonesia's macroeconomic performance are broken down by ideological group, Islamist respondents tend to be overall more critical of the national economy. Among pluralist

---

[7] In Chapter 7, I return to this point and conduct a more exhaustive analysis of the interplay between political Islam, conceptions of democracy and satisfaction with democracy.

5.4 Political Islam and Political Preferences   129

and pluralist-leaning respondents, 29.9% describe the economy as good or very good, as opposed to 25.3% as bad or very bad. Among Islamist and Islamist-leaning respondents, 34.4% express a negative assessment and 23.1% express a positive assessment. Nevertheless, it is important to note that this divergence is not rooted in the respondents' perceptions of their actual financial conditions, as Islamists and pluralists differ little in their evaluation of the current economic condition of their households. In fact, Islamist and Islamist-leaning respondents are slightly more optimistic about their own financial situation, with 38.1% of them describing it as good or very good, versus 36.7% of pluralists and pluralist-leaning respondents. We should thus underscore that although differences in evaluations of the national economy between pluralist and Islamist respondents are significant, such divergences do not seem to be related to perceptions of personal economic conditions. This difference in assessments of macroeconomic performance, as is the case for perceptions of economic inequality (Muhtadi and Warburton 2020), may therefore be endogenous to partisan dispositions and various levels of support for the incumbent president.

Regardless of their causes, divergent evaluations of macroeconomic performance between ideological groups suggest that Islamist respondents might be more concerned about the economy and more likely to prioritize issues related to economic policy. To explore this question, we asked the respondents what they believed to be the most important issues facing Indonesia, and they were allowed to mention up to three. The bar charts in Figure 5.9 highlight some differences in policy priorities across ideological groups, but they also show important areas of consensus. Economic management/growth and corruption are clearly the most salient political issues for all ideological groups, followed by infrastructure development and poverty alleviation. This substantial agreement between otherwise very different groups of voters indicates the importance of developmentalist goals in Indonesian political discourse, and it resonates with prior research on voting behavior, which has long identified economic issues as a powerful driver of electoral choices.

Some differences between pluralists/pluralist-leaning and Islamists/Islamist-leaning respondents also emerge. For example, while the former appear to be more concerned than the latter about corruption, crime and security, social services, and protecting the rights of religious minorities, the latter are more likely to mention inflation, unemployment and wages/salaries as the most important issues. Although most voters, regardless of ideological background, are mindful of economic development as a policy priority, Islamist Indonesians appear to be more concerned about vulnerability to

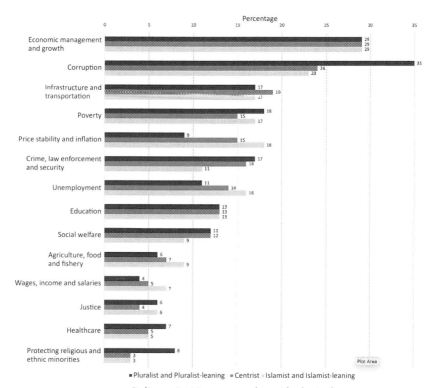

FIGURE 5.9. Policy priorities among three ideological groups

economic fluctuations, such as in the form of exposure to rising consumer prices or higher risk of unemployment. This finding is consistent with the data I analyzed in Section 5.2.1, which show that support for Islamist ideals is more prominent in lower socioeconomic strata of the Indonesian population.

As respondents with Islamist leanings appeared to be more concerned about their economic vulnerability, we can hypothesize that they preferred the state to have a more active role in the economy, especially for policies aimed at improving the economic conditions of the most vulnerable sectors of the population. The INSP included a question asking whether the government should intervene in markets and set the price for basic goods, which I analyze for the elite survey. Similar to the politicians, ordinary Indonesians overwhelmingly approved of these policies (90.1% agree somewhat or strongly with the statement), with no significant differences between ideological groups. However, the INSP data reveal a link between support for economic redistribution and political Islam that was not observed among the legislators. Figure 5.10 shows a cross-tabulation between ideological groups and agreement with the statement, also included in the elite survey, "The

5.4 Political Islam and Political Preferences

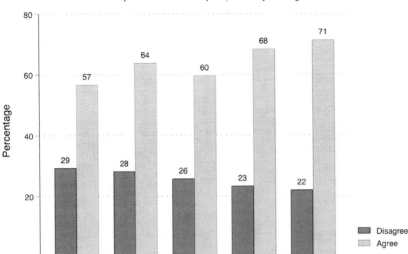

FIGURE 5.10. Political Islam and support for redistribution

government should spend more to help the poor, even if it may require raising taxes." As shown in the bar chart, although most of the respondents in each ideological group supported greater economic redistribution, agreement with this statement increases steadily as we move from more pluralist to more Islamist ideological groups. According to this indicator, the cleavage over political Islam appears to be associated with fiscal policy preferences: The stronger the support for Islam in politics, the greater the support for economic distribution.

The data discussed here offer some insights into the relationship between political Islam and public attitudes toward the economy and economic policy. Preferences regarding political Islam are, to a certain extent, associated with economic policy preferences. This indicates that the ramifications of the cleavage over political Islam could be more complex than often assumed. Islamists Indonesians are more critical of the overall condition of the national economy, more likely to be concerned about inflation and unemployment and more supportive of economic redistribution. As discussed, the real economic inequalities between ideological groups may contribute, at least in part, to explaining these distinctive attitudes. At the same time, however, we must emphasize that such differences in economic attitudes are not as crucial as those on sociocultural issues. As much as Islamist and pluralist Indonesians may diverge in their assessment of economic issues, the salience of economic

Public Opinion on Political Islam

development and support for economic redistribution are so pervasive that they cut across the cleavage over political Islam.

5.4.4 Decentralization

Political Islam and regional autonomy have been closely intertwined in Indonesia, a country in which center-periphery relations have been a crucial issue for state formation. To divide and rule the Indonesian population and its leadership, the Dutch created a federalist state in Indonesia in the mid-1940s. This initiative was strongly opposed by Indonesian nationalists, who viewed support for federalism as collaboration with the country's colonial masters, and advocated instead a unitary vision for the new Indonesian state (Feith 1962, 70–71). This important critical juncture created a strong association between nationalist-pluralist ideology and preferences for centralized governance. At the other end of the ideological spectrum, political Islam has often been identified as supporting, sometimes through violent means, a larger role for regional government. Shortly after decolonization, the first important challenge to the Indonesian state was the secessionist Darul Islam insurgency, in which guerrillas, most of whom were located in the regions of West Java, Aceh and South Sulawesi, proclaimed an independent Islamic state within Indonesian territory. In the late 1950s, the Islamic party Masyumi was disbanded along with other regional parties for their involvement in regional rebellions in Sumatra and Sulawesi (Nordholt 2005, 43–44). This historical legacy suggests that the cleavage over political Islam may be associated with policy preferences regarding decentralization.

To assess whether this is the case, the INSP measures support for regional autonomy by asking whether "[a]llowing different laws in response to different local needs and conditions" is desirable in a political system. To be sure, subnational government autonomy is only one of the many features that distinguish decentralized governance from more centralized political systems, yet allowing local government to implement laws that mirror the preferences of their constituents is a cardinal issue in multilevel systems of government, like Indonesia's following the implementation of decentralization reforms in the early 2000s. In decentralized Indonesia, the tension between allowing local autonomy and preventing excessive subnational inequalities and preserving equal rights for all citizens has been relevant in various policy domains, including discussions of whether local government should be allowed to implement Islamic regulations (Buehler 2016). Responses to this question show an overall high level of support for regional autonomy, as 57.1% of respondents describe this feature as desirable or highly desirable in a political system.

5.4 Political Islam and Political Preferences

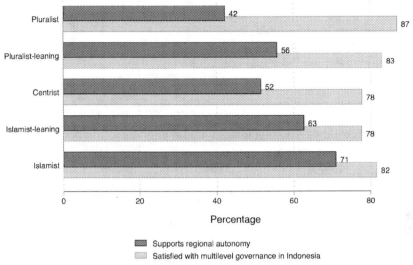

FIGURE 5.11. Support for and satisfaction with regional autonomy by ideological group

The data reported in Figure 5.11 show that there is a close association between political Islam and support for regional autonomy. Islamist respondents are systematically more likely to support regional autonomy than pluralists, as support is lowest among pluralist respondents (42.3%), and it increases as we move closer to the Islamist end of the ideological spectrum, reaching 62.7% for Islamist-leaning respondents and 71% for Islamist respondents. A similar relationship is observed by disaggregating support for regional autonomy over religious groups, as this feature is deemed desirable or very desirable by 58.7% of Indonesian Muslims, but only by 47.1% of Indonesians belonging to a religious minority. Pluralist Indonesians and those belonging to a religious minority display more lukewarm feelings toward regional autonomy, plausibly because of concerns that decentralized governance may empower local governments to implement discriminatory laws and regulations. In contrast, Islamists might be more supportive of the same principle, as decentralization may provide more fruitful opportunities to advance an Islamist political agenda than national politics, where Islamist forces have long been at the margins or members of ideologically diverse coalitions.[8]

---

[8] Drawing from a more recent online survey, I offer a more exhaustive discussion of this issue in Fossati (2022).

Public Opinion on Political Islam

Concerning the practice of the decentralization in contemporary Indonesia, a question included in the questionnaire prompts respondents that in Indonesia, "there are several levels of government, such as national government, province government, and district or city government," and it asks them how well they believe this system of government to be working. Respondents overwhelmingly think that multilevel governance is working well or very well (80.2%), which suggests that decentralization is one of the most appreciated structural features of the post-Suharto Indonesian state. While support for regional autonomy as a principle is associated with the cleavage over political Islam, Figure 5.11 shows that satisfaction with multilevel governance cuts across ideological groups. A vast majority of respondents of all ideological leanings thus acknowledge the benefits of multilevel governance in many regions, especially in terms of electoral accountability and policy responsiveness (Fossati 2016, 2018).

5.5 CONCLUSION

The findings reported in this chapter speak to the relevance of ideology in structuring public attitudes and driving voting behavior. The ideological divide between secularism and Islamism resonates with the Indonesian public: Very few people lack an opinion on the issue of state–Islam relations, and I have documented substantial variation in individual-level attitudes on this issue. This suggests that this ideological dimension is a consolidated and readily available heuristic in the minds of many Indonesians. Furthermore, this chapter has demonstrated an association between the cleavage over political Islam and various attitudinal and behavioral variables, including political participation, party choice, conceptions of national identity, views of democracy and populism, and policy preferences in two crucial policy domains, namely economy policy and decentralization. To be sure, as shown in Chapter 4, these associations are not currently reflected in the Indonesian party system. For example, we have yet to observe Islamic parties coherently and consistently advocate for a higher degree of economic redistribution and more decentralized governance. Yet this analysis of public opinion suggests that the cleavage over political Islam may have implications for public attitudes beyond religious and cultural issues, and it offers a glimpse of how political competition in Indonesia could become more structured and programmatic, as I further discuss in Chapter 8.

6

Ideological Representation

6.1 STUDYING SUBSTANTIVE REPRESENTATION

In Chapter 2, I described substantive representation as a relationship between a representative and those represented, in which the former acts for the latter. In the context of representative democracy, substantive representation therefore concerns what representatives think and do: Do elected officials hold opinions that mirror those of their constituents? Do they behave according to these orientations, such as by supporting legislation consistent with them? As I wrote earlier, substantive representation is a crucial feature of any democracy, as it is closely tied to regime legitimacy, satisfaction with democracy and political participation. In this chapter, I study various aspects related to substantive representation in Indonesia by jointly analyzing the legislator and public opinion surveys on which Chapters 4 and 5 are based. In analyzing these two datasets simultaneously, I am able to ascertain whether and to what extent the preferences of Indonesian politicians and ordinary citizens align, especially regarding the cleavage over political Islam. This empirical analysis thus follows a large body of empirical literature in which substantive representation is understood primarily as ideological–attitudinal congruence between voters and politicians (Powell 2004).

I structure the data analysis into three main sections. First, in Section 6.2, I provide an overview of the similarities and differences between ordinary people and politicians in their views of state-Islam relations and economic issues. Building on the discussion of Chapters 4 and 5, I compare how preferences regarding political Islam and economic policy are distributed in these two populations. This allows me to sketch a

135

general picture of ideological congruence between voters and politicians and to identify inequalities in representation. With this comparison, we can ascertain whether there are groups in the Indonesian population, defined based on their attitudinal profile or socioeconomic characteristics, that are underrepresented in Indonesia's political institutions. Second, Section 6.3 focuses more closely on the role of political parties as avenues of democratic representation. Parties are crucial institutions in a representative democracy, as they can provide a range of meaningful policy alternatives and present sufficient levels of programmatic stability and internal cohesion. Drawing from collaborative work published elsewhere (Fossati et al. 2020), I examine whether Indonesian political parties are fulfilling this basic function and, more specifically, whether they function as institutions that link voters and politicians according to their views of political Islam. Finally, after establishing the importance of political Islam as an axis of representation and of political parties as institutions that structure voter–politician ideological linkages, I analyze in Section 6.4 the interaction between ideological preferences and partisanship. By randomly exposing respondents of a survey experiment to partisan and leader cues, I probe whether and to what degree political elites may affect public preferences on political Islam.[1] This enables me to analyze the stability of voter preferences on this important issue and to gauge the potential for further ideological polarization.

This chapter thus contributes to the general argument proposed in this book by analyzing the core question of whether political Islam is indeed the principal dimension of substantive representation in Indonesian politics. Before we proceed with the empirical analysis, a brief discussion of the methodological approach is in order. In this chapter, the distributions of the voters' and politicians' responses are analyzed in various ways according to the research question and the measures used to compare the elites and masses. One of the most common options is to treat congruence as the ideological distance between the median voter and the median legislator. This is a useful conceptualization if we want to know whether, on average, politicians accurately reflect the ideological positions of their constituents. For example, we can compare the median and mean values of ideological positions on a certain scale (such as the PII) for politicians and voters to obtain a synthetic indicator of how far apart they are on this issue. When studying political parties as institutions

---

[1] This survey experiment was designed in collaboration with Burhanuddin Muhtadi and Eve Warburton. See Fossati, Muhtadi and Warburton (2022) for a full analysis of the data.

of representation, we can create party dyads of voters and politicians in which the analysis of distance between voters and their representatives is carried out at the party level. However, although this is a simple and intuitive method of comparing the ideological dispositions of the populations of interest, it has a substantial disadvantage, as the mean and median values do not convey information about the distribution of ideological positions on a particular issue.

Therefore, in addition to analyzing median and average values, I also consider the full distributions of the preferences regarding political Islam and other issues, as suggested by Golder and Stramski (2010). Focusing on distributions in addition to single parameters such as median and mean values enables us to evaluate the extent to which a legislature reflects the full spectrum of preferences in a given polity, including all of its ideological and demographic groups rather than only the views of a hypothetical median voter. With this approach, we can also ascertain whether any group in the electorate is excluded from democratic representation and whether any group dominates representative politics. This approach therefore can demonstrate the extent to which a country's political class reflects or diverges from the attitudes and preferences of the community it governs.

A general rule for operationalizing congruence when the full ideological spectrum is considered, proposed by Andeweg (2011), is to consider congruence in terms of the "overlap" between citizens and politicians. Given a scale to measure preferences, such as the Likert scales used for the various indicators analyzed in Chapters 4 and 5, we can compare the differences between politicians and voters at each point of the scale and take the lowest percentage for each point. When all of these percentages are added, we obtain a measure of ideological overlap ranging from 0% (no overlap at all) to 100% (complete overlap), which gives an intuitive measure of the ideological distance between political elites and ordinary citizens and which takes into consideration discrepancies between the two populations along the full ideological spectrum.

6.2 IDEOLOGICAL CONGRUENCE IN INDONESIA

In Chapters 1–5, I argued that measuring ideological congruence based on left–right ideological scales alone is problematic for studies of representation because a simple left–right schema is inadequate to account for the multidimensionality of ideological competition. Furthermore, measuring substantive representation on this axis alone risks portraying a

138   *Ideological Representation*

biased picture of ideological congruence, as issues that are important to citizens may be overlooked if they are not closely associated with the overarching left–right dimension. In the case of Indonesia, this issue is exacerbated by the fact that concepts such as "left" and "right" do not resonate with the public. In the INSP survey, for instance, only 66% of respondents were able and willing to report their position on a ten-point left–right ideological scale. This value is substantially lower than those for most other countries, where left–right cognition is often about 90% (Jou and Dalton 2017). In this section, I thus study ideological congruence for two separate issues, namely political Islam and economic policy. Given the analysis carried out on the elite survey, the expectation is that state–Islam relations could be an ideological dimension for which meaningful representation is taking place, as political parties articulate a range of positions on this issue. In contrast, representation on economic issues is expected to be inadequate, as political parties do not differ substantially in their views on statism or economic redistribution.

6.2.1 Political Islam

To analyze whether and to what degree party supporters and elected representatives are aligned, we need a common measure of ideological orientations for voters and politicians. As mentioned previously, the PII provides a suitable composite measure for this purpose. Rather than asking voters where they stand on the broad issue of the role of Islam in politics, a question that some respondents may find difficult to answer, the PII items directly measure policy preferences with seven easy-to-understand statements related to various aspects of political Islam that feature identical wording in the elite and mass surveys. We thus obtain readily comparable measures of elite and mass ideological orientations on the main ideological cleavage in Indonesian politics. In both the elite and mass surveys, the PII presents high levels of internal consistency, with Cronbach alpha coefficients of 0.87 and 0.81, respectively. In the legislator survey, party means of the PII are strongly correlated ($r = 0.95$) with the means of perceived party placement on the political Islam dimension analyzed in Chapter 4. This indicates that the index is a valid measure of ideological positions on the division over political Islam.

On average, voters appear more conservative than politicians on the issue of state–Islam relations. The median and mean values of the PII distributions are 2.86 and 2.75, respectively, for politicians, and 3.29 and 3.15 for voters. This indicates that Islamist views are substantially

6.2 Ideological Congruence in Indonesia

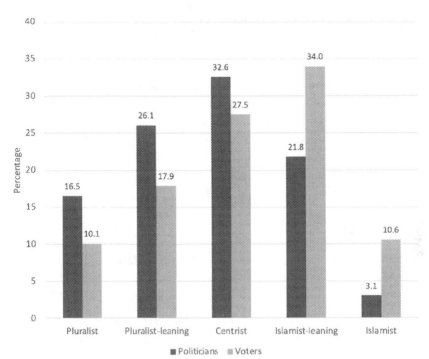

FIGURE 6.1. PII distributions for politicians and voters

more common among the public than among Indonesia's political elite. The distribution displayed in Figure 6.1, which is based on the categorization of respondents into the five ideological groups previously used, confirms this ideological discrepancy between voters and their representatives. Those leaning pluralist and pluralists represent about 28% of ordinary citizens and 42.6% of politicians, whereas Islamist and those leaning Islamist account for 44.6% of the electorate and only 24.9% of legislators. There is thus an imbalance in representation on this ideological cleavage, as Indonesians who favor a larger role for Islam in public life appear to be less well represented than citizens with more pluralist leanings. This gap cannot be attributed primarily to the fact that religious minorities are slightly overrepresented in the legislator sample, as even when we restrict the analysis to Muslim respondents alone, those leaning Islamist and Islamists constitute 51.1% of voters and only 31% of politicians. More plausibly, the socioeconomic differences between the political elite and the population may drive this ideological divergence, as views of political Islam are strongly associated with income and education.

140   *Ideological Representation*

The low levels of descriptive representation identified in Section 4.2.1 can therefore explain why Indonesia's political elite is, in general, more pluralist than the Indonesian electorate. Nevertheless, despite this general discrepancy between the elites and masses, the two distributions displayed in Figure 6.1 show a significant degree of overlap. If we calculate the ideological overlap across these five ideological groups using the method described in Section 6.1, we obtain a score of 80.3%. While this figure is somewhat far from the ideal congruence value of 100%, it nevertheless suggests an overall high level of congruence between elites and masses on political Islam.

6.2.2 Economic Issues

In Chapters 4 and 5, I analyzed statism and fiscal redistribution as two main dimensions of economic policy preferences. Preferences regarding statism, which I have defined as support for state intervention in the economy, were measured with a question on agreement with state policies to set the price of basic goods such as rice and gas. As shown in these two chapters, overwhelming shares of politicians and ordinary people (about 90% in both populations) support such interventionist policies. If we juxtapose the distributions of preferences of the politicians and the masses on this issue, we find a very high level of ideological overlap: 94.8%. This suggests that overall, substantive representation on this issue is well consolidated in Indonesia. Certainly, political parties offer little choice to voters in their policy platforms on state intervention in the economy, as they invariably support statist approaches to economic management. While this lack of differentiation limits the perimeter of substantive representation, it should be noted that skepticism about markets is widespread in Indonesian public opinion. For instance, based on data from the INSP, only about 3% of the public disagree that the government should set the price of basic goods, and only 4% disagree that the government should set a minimum wage for workers. The consensus expressed by legislators on this issue thus mirrors the preferences of the population quite closely, as a strong preference for statism cuts across differences in political ideology, partisanship and socioeconomic background.

A different picture of economic redistribution emerges when we compare the preferences of the Indonesian public with those of their representatives. As mentioned in Chapter 5, support for redistribution is quite high among the Indonesian public, with 64.6% of our public respondents agreeing or strongly agreeing that the government should spend more to help the poor, even if it means raising taxes. Another question included in the INSP asks about support for employment subsidies for workers who

6.2 Ideological Congruence in Indonesia

lose their jobs. Again, support among ordinary citizens is very high at 71.1%. Although this latter statement should be understood more as a measure of support for social insurance than for fiscal redistribution, together, the responses to these two questions suggest a high level of support for expanding social security programs to benefit Indonesians in low- and middle-income groups. However, the same degree of agreement with these statements is not found among politicians, for whom support for redistribution is 38% and support for social insurance is 45.5%.

Figure 6.2 depicts this discrepancy between voters and politicians by plotting the distributions of a simple index obtained by averaging the two questions on spending more to help the poor and providing unemployment subsidies. Like the five-point scales used to record the responses to these questions, this index ranges from 1 to 5, where higher values denote higher levels of support for economic redistribution. The difference between political elites and ordinary citizens is striking: While only 24.3% of politicians score 4 or higher on the index, more than double this percentage (55.6%) of voters do so. If we calculate the ideological overlap between the two populations using the now-familiar method, we obtain an overlap value of 68.3%, which is well below the scores calculated for statism (94.8%) and political Islam (80.3%). This is a clear indication that the ideological link between citizens and politicians in this pivotal policy area is weak. First, as shown in Chapter 4, Indonesian

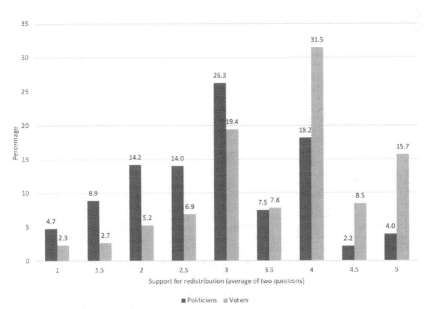

FIGURE 6.2. Distribution of economic policy preferences of politicians and voters

142 *Ideological Representation*

political parties do not provide meaningful alternatives in their fiscal policy platforms, as all parties seem to support a conservative approach of striking a balance between sustaining economic growth and addressing inequality through fiscal redistribution. Second, when we consider the Indonesian political class as a whole and compare its ideological orientation toward economic policy with that of the public, the substantial disconnect shown in Figure 6.2 emerges.

6.2.3 Inequalities of Representation

The two ideological dimensions that I analyzed in this section, namely political Islam and views of economic redistribution, vary in terms of their overall congruence between voters and politicians, as elites are more closely aligned with voters on political Islam than on economic issues. This difference is consistent with the hypothesis that political Islam is a significantly more salient issue than economic redistribution in Indonesian politics, which I investigate further in the remainder of the chapter. However, these two dimensions are similar in one respect, as the ideological discrepancies between voters and politicians suggest that in both cases, some common views held by ordinary Indonesian citizens lack adequate representation among legislators. In the case of political Islam, voters are significantly more conservative than politicians, whereas for economic redistribution, the opposite is true. This indicates that some ideological groups, specifically those supportive of economic redistribution and a larger role for Islam in public affairs, are systematically underrepresented in the Indonesian context.

Figure 6.3 displays the inequalities of representation for these two dimensions with 3D bar charts that show the percentages of voters (Figure 6.3b) and politicians (Figure 6.3a) who fall into various ideological groups based on their positions on political Islam and economic redistribution. For political Islam, the figure follows the familiar pluralist/pluralist-leaning, centrist and Islamist-leaning/Islamist categorization. For fiscal policy, I use the index calculated for Figure 6.2 to classify respondents as fiscally conservative (index value of less than 3), moderate (3) or progressive (higher than 3). The charts show that there are important ideological differences between these two populations. Although voters are divided in their attitudes on state-Islam relations, they overwhelmingly fall into the progressive category on fiscal issues. In contrast, legislators' ideological profiles are more evenly distributed across the various groups of this two-dimensional ideological space. Pluralist positions are more prevalent among the political elite regardless of fiscal policy orientation, as are conservative and moderate positions on fiscal policy. As expected, the most

6.2 Ideological Congruence in Indonesia

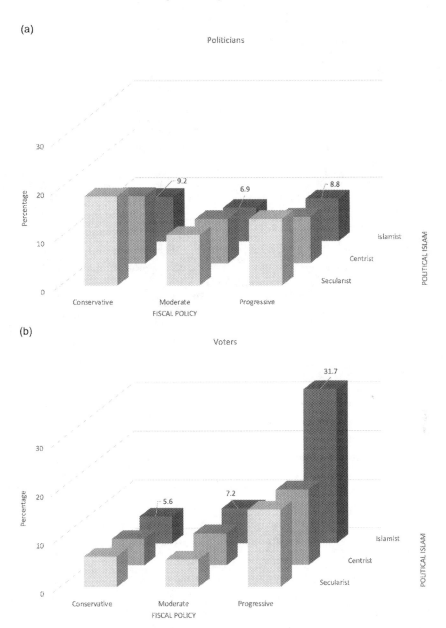

FIGURE 6.3. (a) Politicians' and (b) voters' preferences regarding political Islam and economic redistribution

striking difference between the two joint distributions is for fiscally progressive Islamist-leaning and Islamist Indonesians, who constitute almost one-third of the mass public but only 8.8% of legislators.

It is important to note that the inequalities of representation across ideological groups depicted in Figure 6.3 may have roots in the socioeconomic differences between Indonesia's political elite and the general population, as legislators are on average substantially better educated and wealthier than ordinary Indonesians. I showed in Chapter 5 that attitudes regarding political Islam are related to socioeconomic factors, especially to educational attainment, as poorly educated Indonesians are much more likely to support Islamism than individuals with tertiary education. Furthermore, support for redistribution is also linked to the respondent's socioeconomic background to a considerable extent. For example, fiscally progressive individuals account for 78.4% of respondents with less than elementary education but only 44.1% of college-educated respondents; similar differences are observed across income groups, as the share of support for redistributive policies increases from 54.7% of Indonesians in the highest quintile of income distribution to 74.2% of those in the lowest bracket. This suggests that the quality of representation may vary dramatically across socioeconomic groups, as the preferences of Indonesians of more affluent social classes are systematically better represented by political elites.[2] Figures 6.4a and 6.4b explore this hypothesis by plotting the scores for ideological overlap between political Islam and economic redistribution disaggregated by education and income groups, and the coefficients indeed show that class differences are a powerful driver of inequalities in representation. Looking at the differences across education groups, for example, the ideological overlap on political Islam is between 69% and 75% for low-education Indonesians and much higher, around 90%, for those with higher levels of educational attainment. For ideological congruence on issues of economic redistributions, the inequalities between low-education and high-education Indonesians and between poorer and wealthier social groups are even starker.

In Indonesia, as in many other countries, the policy preferences of the most privileged social segments are better represented in political institutions. Regarding the mechanisms that produce such disparities in substantive representation, we can hypothesize that Indonesian political elites are more responsive to affluent social groups than to citizens with lower

---

[2] See Warburton et al. (2021) for a more exhaustive discussion of this point.

6.2 Ideological Congruence in Indonesia

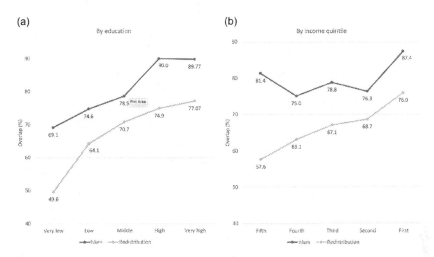

FIGURE 6.4. Ideological overlap between politicians and voters by (a) education and (b) income quintile

socioeconomic status. However, this explanation implies higher levels of political participation by high-income and high-education Indonesians, for which empirical evidence is mixed. Electoral participation is higher in localities where socioeconomic development and educational attainment are lower (Fossati and Martinez i Coma 2020a). Non-electoral forms of participation are about as common among low-income as among high-income individuals. For instance, according to INSP data, the share of respondents who report engaging in informal political participation (such as attending a rally or contacting a politician) is 27.8% for individuals in the lowest income bracket, compared with 24.6% among the wealthiest group. To be sure, addressing this question with survey data alone is insufficient for a conclusive analysis, yet the evidence suggests that inequalities in representation across social classes may be driven by socio-economic differences between the elites and the masses rather than by politicians being more responsive to more affluent social classes.

Finally, the data analyzed in this section offer the opportunity to reflect on how different ideological dimensions interact in shaping political–ideological competition in Indonesia. It is clear from the analysis carried out in Chapter 4 that the two ideological dimensions of political Islam and fiscal redistribution show different dynamics and are largely independent of one another. Economic policy issues lack the salience of state–Islam relations, and political parties do not display the same degree of differentiation for this dimension that they show for the cleavage over

146 *Ideological Representation*

political Islam. However, looking at Figures 6.3 and 6.4, it seems that substantive representation on fiscal issues does intersect with political Islam in a way. Inequalities of representation on fiscal policy exacerbate imbalances of representation along the cleavage over political Islam, resulting in one ideological group, Islamist Indonesians supporting economic redistribution, being dramatically underrepresented compared with the others. The cleavage over political Islam thus intersects, to a certain degree, with divisions in economic policy preferences to create a constituency that may be especially dissatisfied with the quality of representation in Indonesia. As I further discuss in Chapter 8, it remains to be seen if opposition parties will be able to tap into this discontent and channel the demands of this underrepresented group into a coherent programmatic platform.

6.3 POLITICAL PARTIES AND REPRESENTATION

Section 6.2 showed that although some ideological groups are better represented than others, voter and politician preferences on political Islam are generally aligned. This contrasts with the case of support for economic redistribution, for which a large constituency for more assertive policies that would benefit low-income Indonesians is present among the public but lacking among legislators. This section focuses on political parties as institutions that structure political representation. We know from the analysis carried out in the previous two chapters that party positions on political Islam differ and that to a certain degree, voters sort into parties according to their ideological leanings. Based on these findings, we expect a high level of substantive representation on cultural-religious issues and a substantially lower level for economic issues. To test this hypothesis, this section analyzes patterns of ideological congruence between voters and politicians using the measures developed above.

6.3.1 Party–Voter Ideological Linkages

The scatterplot in Figure 6.5 pairs average voter and party positions on state–Islam relations as measured by the PII, and it shows a strong positive relationship between the two. The 45-degree dashed line represents an ideal condition of absolute congruence between parties and voters, and it can be used as a benchmark for an intuitive assessment of ideological congruence based on visual inspection. As the figure shows, most of the dyads are closely clustered along the 45-degree line,

6.3 Political Parties and Representation

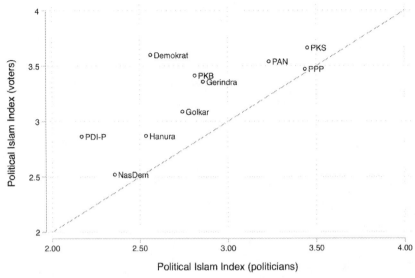

FIGURE 6.5. Average PII values of politicians and voters by party

and the correlation between voter and party positions is strong ($r = 0.75$). This constitutes robust evidence that patterns of substantive representation are well established for this ideological cleavage and that parties play a critical role in structuring political representation in Indonesia. As I mentioned in the analysis of party positions in Chapter 4, the range of policy platforms offered by the Indonesian party system on political Islam is small, especially because of the lack of political parties endorsing unambiguously pluralist positions. Yet this analysis of the PII values of voters and politicians shows a high degree of ideological sorting into parties and ideological alignment between party legislators and party voters. In this respect, Indonesian political parties are satisfactorily performing a basic democratic function, which is to represent a diverse spectrum of voter opinions on the most salient political–ideological issue in this polity. A further observation emerging from the scatterplot is that for all parties, voters appear to be more conservative than politicians on the issue of state–Islam relations. This finding resonates with the data displayed in Figure 6.1, which show that Indonesian political elites have an overall more liberal ideological outlook compared with the public.

The voter–party dyads shown in Figure 6.5 show significant variation in ideological congruence across parties. For some, such as NasDem and PPP, voters and politicians are almost perfectly aligned,

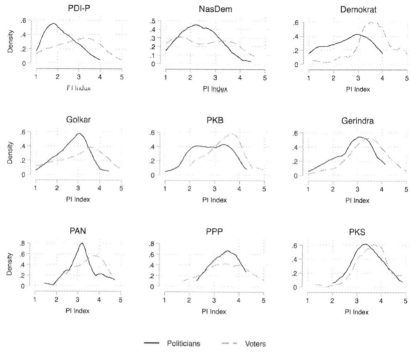

FIGURE 6.6. PII distributions for voters and legislators of nine parties

while for others, such as PDI-P, PKB and Demokrat, the distance from the 45-degree line is greater. As I mentioned, however, analyzing average values on an ideological scale does not provide information on the distribution of such values in the populations of interest. As such, the party dyads based on the PII mean values reported earlier should be analyzed jointly with the full distributions of the PII values for voters and politicians. These are displayed in Figure 6.6, which compares the density plots of politicians' and voters' indexes for the nine largest parties. Visual inspection of the density plots reveals substantial differences across parties in the extent to which the preferences of voters and politicians align. While the overall pattern is one in which the voters of any party are more conservative than legislators, the gap is much more pronounced for some parties than for others. Demokrat is a clear outlier, as voters are preponderantly Islamist and Islamist-leaning while most of its legislators are pluralist-leaning or centrist. Similar but less-extreme patterns of significantly more pluralist legislators are observed for PDI-P, PKB and Golkar, while for parties such as Gerindra and PKS, the density lines of voters and politicians are

6.3 Political Parties and Representation

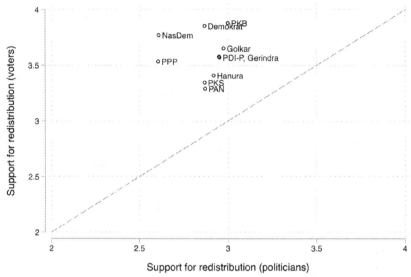

FIGURE 6.7. Politicians' and voters' average support for redistribution by party

remarkably close. These data indicate that party characteristics may be an important driver of ideological congruence between voters and politicians, an idea that I examine in Section 6.3.2.

The descriptive statistics analyzed in Chapter 4 and the results from the factor analysis on party positions leave little doubt that economic policy issues lack salience in Indonesian politics. To illustrate the implications of this marginality for substantive representation on economic issues, Figure 6.7 displays a scatterplot with party dyads of voters and politicians calculated with the mean values of support for economic redistribution as captured by the scale used to generate Figure 6.2. The difference from the previous scatterplot is striking. Whereas for political Islam, the party dyads were spread across the ideological space and proximate to the 45-degree line, all of the observations in Figure 6.7 are closely clustered in the top center of the plot, and the positions of voters and politicians show no correlation ($r = 0.002$). Party positions are barely distinguishable on the issue of economic redistribution, as on average, members of any party seem to support moderate-conservative fiscal policies. For all parties, voters are substantially more progressive on this issue, showing much higher levels of support than politicians for economic redistribution and social insurance programs. This confirms that political parties do not offer differentiated policy platforms on economic issues and that consequently, substantive representation in this area is weak.

6.3.2 Variation in Representation across Parties

The density curves plotted above for politicians and voters of the nine major parties in Indonesia indicate variation across parties in voter–politician ideological congruence. This pattern is somewhat surprising given the prevailing view in the literature that Indonesian political parties have more similarities than differences. Not only are political parties often portrayed as having similar ideological profiles, but it is often argued that they are weak and overall poorly institutionalized, even in the current climate of increased polarization (Aspinall and Mietzner 2019). Yet as Figure 6.6 shows, there may be ideological or organizational differences between Indonesian political parties that might explain why some levels of ideological congruence are higher than others. In this vein, the comparative literature can serve as a reference, as numerous scholars show that ideological congruence across voter–party dyads might vary between parties in accordance with certain features of these parties (Huber and Powell 1994; Wessels 1999; Belchior 2013; Dalton 2017).

The first such feature is intraparty ideological heterogeneity: Parties whose members hold heterogeneous views on key political issues may struggle to maintain an easily identifiable ideological profile, and this lack of clarity may hinder voters' ability to choose a party that supports their views. Second, parties' ideological positions may shape congruence: It may be easier for ideologically extreme parties to send voters clear signals on their ideological position, whereas voters may have difficulty determining the ideologies of parties located in the middle of the spectrum. Third, it may be more difficult for larger parties to maintain a clear ideological profile, as their electoral strategies may involve formulating different and possibly contrasting ideological appeals to reach multiple groups in the electorate. Finally, better-organized and more centralized parties may be more successful in disciplining their members, articulating clear ideological propositions and communicating them to voters.

To explore the extent to which these party characteristics influence ideological distance between parties and voters in Indonesia, I follow a convention in the literature and calculate centrism as the absolute value of the difference between the means of party voters' and elected representatives' positions on their PII scores. Higher values of centrism thus indicate greater distance between voters and politicians and weaker substantive representation. For most of the ten parties covered, centrism values for political Islam are rather modest, ranging from 0.35 for PPP to 0.70 for PDI-P. However, as suggested previously, Demokrat is an

6.3 Political Parties and Representation

outlier with a centrism value of 1.04, almost three times the average value for the remaining nine parties (0.36). In contrast with the other parties, for which substantive representation on political Islam appears to function, the ideological linkage between voters and politicians is broken in this party. This disconnect may be because this party's position in Indonesian politics has changed substantially in recent years. Demokrat occupied a dominant position during the ten-year presidency of party founder Susilo Bambang Yudhoyono, but it has since struggled to preserve its pluralist identity after its electoral defeat in 2014, when it sided with Islamist forces in a losing bid to block Jokowi's rise to the presidency. Regardless of the reasons for this party's status as an outlier in substantive representation, I exclude it from the analysis in the remainder of this section to disentangle the relationship between centrism and the party features mentioned earlier.

Table 6.1 summarizes the operationalization procedures for the four party traits and reports the correlation coefficients between party traits and centrism on political Islam. The correlation coefficients and the scatterplots displayed in Figure 6.8 suggest that all four factors may be associated with ideological distance between voters and politicians. On average, centrism appears to be higher in parties that are more ideologically heterogeneous, larger, more pluralist and less centralized. The high centrism value for PDI-P may thus be ascribed to its internal ideological heterogeneity and its status as Indonesia's largest party, as it has an ideologically pluralist profile but is also engaged in strategic partnerships with Islamic parties such as PKB and PPP. In contrast, a party like PKS can exploit features such as small size, internal cohesion and a more extreme ideological profile to build stronger ideological linkages with its

TABLE 6.1. *Correlation coefficients between centrism on political Islam and party features*

Party trait	Measure	R
Party heterogeneity	Standard deviation of party members' self-assessed party position on political Islam	0.66
Party position	Mean of party members' PII	−0.55
Party size	Share of votes, 2019 legislative elections	0.69
Party structure	Share of elected representatives in the legislator survey saying that candidates for legislative elections are determined exclusively by the central office	−0.46

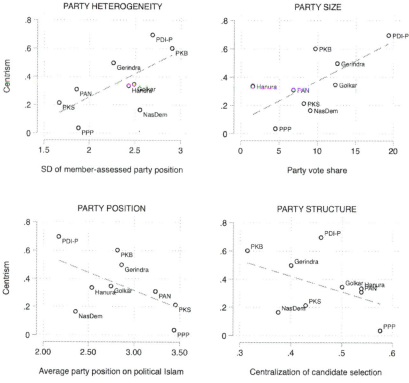

FIGURE 6.8. Party features and ideological distance between politicians and voters

electoral base.[3] Our measure of party structure and centralization suggests that the distance between politicians and voters is shorter for more centralized political parties such as PPP (for which 58% of members say that candidatures are decided by the party's central office with little involvement from local actors) than for more decentralized ones, such as the PKB (for which only 31% report the same practice). Overall, the results reported in this section are based on a limited number of observations, and they should be corroborated by further research and longitudinal studies. However, the data show considerable variation in centrism across parties, and the empirical associations identified here suggest that some of the theoretical frameworks in the comparative literature may be useful in accounting for cross-party variation in representation patterns in Indonesia.

---

[3] This is not to suggest that this party is free from factional politics, however, or that its ideology is as radical as those of extra-parliamentary Islamist groups. See Priohutomo, Kamarudin and Hidayat (2019) and Minardi (2019).

6.3.3 Ideological Linkages and Clientelism

The findings that I have discussed in this section, especially the high degree of party–voter ideological congruence on the cleavage over political Islam, complicate the prevailing characterization of Indonesia as a clientelistic democracy. In political systems where clientelism is predominant, voting based on ideological considerations should be relatively rare. Clientelistic party systems are not usually rooted in consequential ideological cleavages, and voters, having little choice in terms of programmatic differentiation among political parties, often vote based on their own material interests, rewarding politicians who are able to credibly commit to patronage. As previously mentioned, a large body of literature on Indonesian politics (Aspinall and Sukmajati 2016; Aspinall and Berenschot 2019) focuses on clientelism as a key feature of political competition in this country, providing ample evidence of the importance of patronage in shaping voter–politician linkages. The Indonesian electoral system, which features open-list proportional representation, indeed provides strong incentives for candidates to formulate personalistic appeals rather than emphasizing the party line. Yet the data analyzed here suggest that Indonesian voters and politicians *are* sorting into parties along an ideological spectrum. Despite the appeal of clientelistic linkages, the historically rooted cleavage between secular pluralism and political Islam has proven sticky, in much the way that the left–right continuum remains influential in many advanced democracies despite the emergence of new issues that are also important to voters.

How then could such an ideological cleavage be resilient enough to survive decades of stifling authoritarian rule and twenty years of democratic politics marked by transactional politics and ideological moderation? A first point worth discussing is that differences in methodological approach may in part account for why researchers come to different conclusions. Although survey-based studies focus on some pathologies of clientelism, such as vote-buying (Muhtadi 2019), most studies of Indonesian clientelism are based on qualitative and ethnographic studies, where data are collected from observations of (mostly electoral) dynamics at the grassroots level in selected case studies. And at this grassroots level, where candidates and their brokers engage in direct contact with voters, opportunities for vote-buying and distributing material benefits abound. Yet the incidence of these practices in the Indonesian electorate as a whole is not always clear. If only a minority of the population experiences direct contact with candidates and brokers, we cannot exclude the possibility that for a larger and electorally decisive segment of voters, political behavior follows a logic whereby patronage considerations are marginal. Indeed, the data presented in this chapter, based on representative samples of politicians and voters, demonstrate that there is more to citizen–politician linkages in Indonesia than clientelism. Perhaps, rather than asking to what extent Indonesia could be described as a clientelistic democracy, we should allow that in this exceptionally diverse country, different types of voters engage in politics in different ways. While some segments of the electorate may find it more appealing to entrust their vote to a specific candidate rather than a party that they identify with, and they may do so in response to materialistic incentives, other groups may have well-rooted preferences that shape their identity as citizens.

More importantly, however, the analysis above indicates that ideological and materialistic considerations may coexist as drivers of voting behavior in the Indonesian electorate and that Indonesian political parties may rely on multiple strategies to mobilize voters, combining programmatic-ideological and clientelistic appeals. This insight is of course not new, as scholars of clientelism have long argued that clientelism and programmatic politics may be compatible (Shefter 1977). Yet in academic research, we often follow an excessively rigid dichotomy between clientelism and ideology-based politics, assuming that clientelistic linkages preclude the development of other bonds based on shared identities and worldviews. The Indonesian case reminds us that this is simply not true, as the boundary between patronage politics and ideological competition is porous. It is highly plausible that materialistic concerns, ideological factors and candidate traits interact in shaping the political behavior of many Indonesians given the highly competitive land-scape of contemporary Indonesian politics in which, for any ideological camp, voters can choose from multiple parties and candidates. For instance, a voter may have well-defined, stable ideological predispositions, but their final choice may also be influenced by their evaluation of a candidate's ability to channel public funds to their community or their ethnic group. What appears on the surface to be a vote driven by clientelistic concerns is in fact the culmination of a complex process in which ideological consider-ation plays a pivotal role.

6.4 IDEOLOGICAL REPRESENTATION AND PARTISANSHIP: AN EXPERIMENT

Sections 6.2 and 6.3 have shown that the cleavage over political Islam plays an important role in structuring voter–politician linkages in the Indonesian context. In Indonesia, as elsewhere, historical legacies of social

6.4 Ideological Representation and Partisanship

cleavages and ideological competition matter, as they influence contemporary patterns of voting behavior and political representation. While historical knowledge of the Indonesian case indicates that this religious–ideological cleavage precedes and informs partisan preferences, it would be a mistake to conclude that the relationship between the two factors, ideology and partisanship, is one of unidirectional causality moving from the former to the latter. Political elites are of course crucial in determining the salience of historical political cleavages and their contemporary meaning. We should therefore allow the possibility that preferences over political Islam are to an extent malleable, as they are the product of constant interactions between voters, political parties and leaders.

A related issue concerns voters' ability to correctly identify political parties' and leaders' positions on the political Islam ideological spectrum. The aggregate data I have analyzed in this chapter indicate that overall, voters have sufficient knowledge of party platforms, as parties and voters are fairly well aligned in their preferences on religious issues. However, the data also show a high degree of intraparty ideological heterogeneity among both voters and politicians, and such heterogeneity is even greater if we consider preferences for political leaders such as Jokowi or Prabowo, who preside over ideologically heterogeneous coalitions. In other words, Indonesian voters do not appear to be fully "sorted" into political parties or coalitions according to their ideological preferences, and this is plausibly due both to a lack of information about party and candidate positions and often low levels of party (or coalition) ideological cohesion. We can thus hypothesize that some voters, when exposed to information about the ideological positions of parties and candidates, may be inclined to align their own position with those of the politicians they support to avoid cognitive dissonance.

Then, how fluid are voter preferences concerning political Islam? Can they change as a result of exposure to knowledge about where parties and candidates stand on socioreligious issues? To answer this question, I analyze a survey experiment in which respondents are randomly exposed to partisan and leadership cues and then asked about their opinion on an issue that is closely related to the cleavage over political Islam, namely the implementation of Islamic laws in Indonesian local governments.

6.4.1 Experimental Design

To investigate the relationship between ideological preferences and partisan affiliations, I use an experiment embedded in a population-based survey on a representative sample of the Indonesian population. The survey was conducted face-to-face across all of Indonesia's provinces during December 9–14, 2018 in cooperation with *Indikator Politik*, one of Indonesia's most established and well-respected national public opinion polling institutes. At that time, Indonesia was in the early stages of a long campaign period for the simultaneous presidential and legislative elections held in April 2019. Like the INSP, this survey used multistage random sampling techniques based on the 2010 census, in this case to select a probability sample of 1,210 respondents proportionally distributed over the 34 provinces.

The survey experiment is designed to identify and measure the effect of partisan cues on public attitudes concerning the long-standing debate within Indonesia about the legitimacy of local government regulations that reflect religious, most commonly Islamic, precepts. Known locally as *perda agama* or *perda Islam*, Islamic bylaws have been implemented in many Indonesian regions since the entry into force of decentralization reforms in the early 2000s. Most are regulations against what pious Muslims consider to be "moral vices," such as alcohol consumption, gambling and particular styles of dress (mostly for women). While advocates for such regulations are often Islamist organizations and community figures, politicians across the Ideological spectrum have often supported such interventions for electoral gain (Pisani and Buehler 2017; Ikhwan 2018). This issue, which is readily understandable by a large share of the public, has an obvious connection with the cleavage over political Islam, and it is reasonable to expect public preferences about religious bylaws to mirror more general orientations about the role of Islam in politics. While my primary theoretical interest is in general positions along the political Islam spectrum and how they might be affected by partisan cues, asking about a specific policy issue has the advantage of increasing the plausibility of the experimental vignettes, as politicians typically express their positions with reference to specific issues than to more general, abstract principles.

The experimental vignette provides respondents with a short introduction to the issue of religious bylaws and presents two distinct policy positions, between which the respondent is asked to choose. Respondents are randomly assigned to one of three versions of the vignette. In the control condition, the two policy positions are simply read with a brief justification of each, and respondents are not cued about what party or leader supports them. In the first treatment group, each policy is endorsed by one of the two major parties in Indonesian politics,

6.4 Ideological Representation and Partisanship 157

namely PDI-P and Gerindra. In the second treatment group, the cue reveals that the two options are endorsed by the two dominant figures in Indonesian politics, namely Joko Widodo (Jokowi) and Prabowo Subianto. The vignettes are designed to reflect the actual positions of each politician and of elites within their respective parties based on past public statements and actions (i.e., PDI-P and Jokowi are associated with opposition to religious bylaws, while Gerindra and Prabowo with support). In doing so, the vignette ensures that the respondents are not being misled about each side's political preferences.

The experimental vignette was worded as follows:

1. In the lead-up to the 2019 presidential elections, there was debate in the community about local government regulations based on religion. I am now going to read some different opinions concerning this issue:

   A. [Some/PDI-P/Jokowi] believe that Indonesia is a country based on law, not on a particular religion. Regional regulations based on religion may violate the constitution and have the potential to undermine the rights of minorities and women.

   B. In contrast, [some/Gerindra/Prabowo] believe local regulations based on religion are legitimate because Indonesia is a majority Muslim country. Such regulations do not violate the constitution or undermine the rights of minorities and women.

Which of these two opinions is closest to your own?

A. Opinion A
B. Opinion B
C. Don't know/No answer

The dependent variable of interest is thus captured by the responses to this experimental vignette. The main theoretical expectation is that exposure to party and leader cues in the two treatment groups will (a) increase support for Islamic bylaws among supporters of Gerindra and Prabowo; (b) decrease support for such religious legislation among supporters of PDI-P and Jokowi; and (c) have no effect on respondents who report other or no partisan affiliations or are undecided.

6.4.2 Data

To determine partisanship, I classify respondents as supporters of a party or leader based on two questions included in the survey. The first asks,

158   *Ideological Representation*

TABLE 6.2. *Support for religious bylaws across partisan groups*

	Religious bylaws: Agree with implementation?		
	Agree	Disagree	DK/NA
Overall (N = 420)	37.4	39.5	23.1
By partisan preference			
PDI-P (N = 84)	34.5	38.1	27.4
Gerindra (N = 51)	49	39.2	11.8
Other/no preference/no answer (N = 285)	36.1	40	23.9
By leader preference			
Jokowi (N = 228)	36	41.7	22.4
Prabowo (N = 130)	46.9	39.2	13.9
No preference/no answer (N = 62)	22.6	32.3	45.2

"If legislative elections were held today, what party would you vote for?" Based on their answer to this question, respondents are counted as being supporters of PDI-P, Gerindra or other parties, with the latter category also including those who do not answer or say that they would not vote. By the same token, the respondents are divided into three groups (pro-Jokowi, pro-Prabowo and undecided/no answer) according to how they answer a similar election on presidential elections. By these indicators, 21.4% of respondents are PDI-P supporters, 12.3% are Gerindra supporters, 53.1% are Jokowi supporters and 33% are Prabowo supporters.

How, then, are party and leader preferences associated with support for religious bylaws implemented by local governments? Table 6.2 reports the descriptive statistics of responses to the experimental vignette among the 420 respondents assigned to the control group, and it reveals attitudinal differences across partisan groups before exposure to treatment. Overall, respondents are evenly divided between supporters (37.4%) and opposers (39.4%), with a fairly high share of respondents having no opinion on this issue or failing to provide an answer (23.1%). Yet important differences emerge when we compare responses based on party or leader preferences. Support for religious bylaws is much higher among Gerindra (49%) than PDI-P (34%) voters and among Prabowo (46.9%) than Jokowi (36%) supporters. This clear evidence of a partisan divide on this issue is consistent with the data on party positions on state-Islam relations that I previously analyzed. The degree of partisan polarization, however, is perhaps best described as moderate, as any partisan bloc, whether defined by party or leader preference, includes substantial minorities of voters who express a different view from the prevailing one.

6.4 Ideological Representation and Partisanship 159

Interestingly, neither support for nor opposition to Islamic bylaws constitutes a majority position in any partisan group, as a significant number of voters (especially in the PDI-P/Jokowi camp) appear to be undecided. To be sure, the specific issue of religious bylaws is only one of many that concern the ideological cleavage between pluralism and Islamism. To extrapolate from this case to the broader issue of partisan and ideological polarization in Indonesia, the figures reported in the table suggest that political elites have substantial opportunities to further polarize public opinion along partisan lines. In the context of our experiment, these data imply that exposure to partisan cues could significantly affect the structure of popular opinion on issues related to the ideological cleavage over political Islam.

I conduct the data analysis in two steps. First, I analyze the simple differences between the means of support for religious bylaws across the experimental groups to estimate the treatment effects. Second, I specify a full model of support for religious bylaws including treatment assignment and a host of sociodemographic factors,[4] and I use the estimates to predict support for local government Islamic regulations among different partisan groups.

6.4.3 The Effect of Elite Cues on Preferences Regarding Political Islam

Figure 6.9 depicts bar charts that enable visual inspection of the differences between the control and treatment groups for the two experimental treatments, namely party cues (upper two quadrants) and leader cues (lower two quadrants). The graph shows that overall, the treatment effects are very significant and are signed as expected. Exposure to leader cues increases support for Islamic bylaws substantially among supporters of Gerindra (from 49% to 67%, or +18%) and party leader and presidential candidate Prabowo Subianto (from 47% to 72%, or +25%). Conversely, opposition to Islamic bylaws increases significantly among supporters of PDI-P (from 38% to 59%, or +11%) and President Jokowi (from 42% to 61%, or +19%). Partisan cues have a strong effect in polarizing survey respondents' views of religious bylaws, as voters who express support for a specific party or leader are much more likely to align

---

[4] These variables include gender, place of residence (rural/urban), age, religion (Muslim/ non-Muslim), ethnicity (Javanese/non-Javanese), education and income (both of which are measured with ordinal variables). As randomization of the treatment assignment was rigorously implemented, substantial balance is observed in these sociodemographic features and in partisan distributions across the three experimental groups.

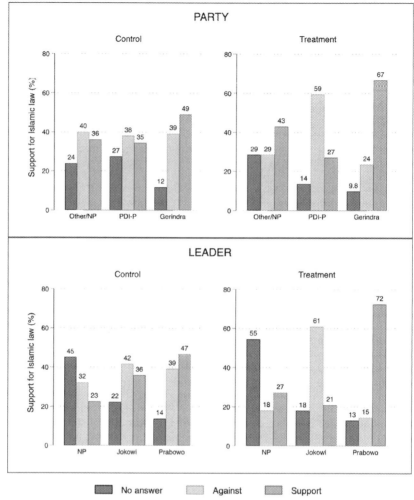

FIGURE 6.9. Average treatment effects for party and leader cues

their views with those of political elites when informed about their positions on this issue. These data therefore suggest that public preferences on political Islam may to some degree be manipulated by political elites, a finding that is not surprising given previous research on the power of partisan and elite cues in various settings.

As the chart shows, the shift observed in the treatment group is not only due to the different behavior of voters who do not have strong opinions regarding Islamic laws (i.e., those who select the "don't know/ no answer" option). With the exception of PDI-P supporters, of whom an

6.4 Ideological Representation and Partisanship   161

exceptionally high 27% in the control group select "no answer," for the remaining three partisan groups (Gerindra, Jokowi, Prabowo), the shares of respondents with no opinion are fairly similar between the control and treatment groups. The bulk of the change therefore appears to take place among voters have an opinion about Islamic bylaws but are open to changing it when prompted that their preferred party or leader holds a different position than their own. This suggests that the effect of exposure to partisan cues is not exclusively due to voters who lack a defined ideological position on the cleavage over political Islam. Unfortunately, the survey does not include a suitable indicator of individual-level ideological positions such as the PII. Nevertheless, it is plausible, for example, that the large swing observed for Gerindra and Prabowo supporters is partially due to pluralist-leaning voters who become supportive of Islamic bylaws when cued about their party/leader stance.

Two findings concerning respondents who do not express a preference for either of the two main parties or leaders are interesting. First, in both experiments, exposure to partisan cues increases the number of respondents who choose "don't know/no answer." Among nonpartisans and voters of other parties, the share of respondents who choose "don't know/no answer" increases by 5 percentage points in the party cue experiment and by 10 percentage points in the leader cue experiment. This contrasts with the treatment effects for the other two partisan groups, for which the shares of "don't know/no answer" responses decline in all of the treatment groups. When cued that parties or leaders they do not support hold different views on Islamic bylaws, nonpartisan voters become less likely to reveal their preferences on this issue. Learning that religious bylaws are a polarized political issue may increase the perceived complexity or sensitivity of issues for this group, which could suppress their response. Second, for both party and leader cues, exposure to treatment increases support for and reduces opposition to Islamic bylaws. In both experiments, opposition to Islamic bylaws prevails among nonpartisans in the control group, but among those exposed to the treatment, support for bylaws is substantially higher than opposition to them. We can speculate that some voters may be "shy" about expressing their support for a policy position associated with radical Islamism. Learning that both views on this issue are legitimately represented in formal politics by ostensibly pluralist parties and leaders might encourage some to be more open about their preferences.

Finally, Figure 6.10 plots support for Islamic bylaws as estimated using a full model that includes various sociodemographic characteristics such as

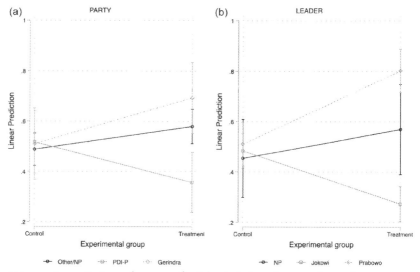

FIGURE 6.10. Estimated support for Islamic bylaws by experimental treatment group

gender, age, religion, education and income and a binary response variable for which 1 indicates support for religious bylaws and 0 indicates opposition to them.[5] By plotting the estimates of average support for each of the three partisan groups for both parties and leaders, we gain a clear picture of the extent of the polarization in respondents' attitudes introduced by the experimental treatment. The two panels of the figure show similar patterns for party (Figure 6.10a) and leader (Figure 6.10b) cues, as the partisan gaps in support for religious bylaws grow substantially in the treatment groups. Opinions in the control group, despite some divergence, are evenly distributed across partisan groups, and the patterns are much more polarized among those included in the treatment groups with party or leader cues. For example, in the case of party cues, estimated support among voters of PDI-P is indistinguishable from support among Gerindra voters in the control group, but the partisan gap is substantial in the treatment group, where support for Islamic bylaws among PDI-P supporters is much lower (37.5%) than among Gerindra supporters (69.3%). Thus, regardless of

---

[5] I thus exclude from the analysis respondents who do not indicate a preference or who say that they do not know, which leaves me with 626 respondents for the party cue experiment and 633 respondents for the leader cue experiment. Although some of the nuance displayed in Figure 6.9 is lost, this strategy enables me to estimate the effect of experimental treatments using a straightforward logistic regression model and an easily interpretable binary variable.

whether respondents are cued by political parties or prominent political figures, exposure to partisan cues polarize mass opinion on this important issue related to the cleavage over political Islam.

This survey experiment provides some intriguing insights into the relationship between partisanship and ideology in Indonesian politics. The results reveal the malleability of popular policy preferences on issues related to the ideological cleavage over political Islam. To be sure, the large swings observed for the experimental groups must contextualized in terms of the limitations of this research design. The extent to which the changes produced by the treatment are applicable to real-world political behavior, as for all experiments, is debatable, and it should be emphasized that Islamic bylaws are only one of the many issues related to the cleavage over political Islam. Yet clearly, a large segment of the Indonesian electorate appears to be quite responsive to elite cues when formulating their opinions on issues related to state–Islam relations, which indicates that popular preferences on the cleavage over political Islam are not rigid. Rather, they result from dynamic interactions between voters and political leaders. Future research could study how individuals with different ideological background respond to elite cues.

The results also indicate an avenue that could deepen partisan divisions on religious issues. As shown throughout this book, Indonesian voters do not appear to be fully sorted into political parties according to their ideological preferences on political Islam. Furthermore, although qualitative studies rightly identify increasing polarization among the elites in party politics and civil society, there is virtually no evidence that Indonesian voters can be characterized as polarized in the way that voters are in countries such as the United States. These experiments suggest that this low-polarization/low-sorting scenario may become increasingly polarized if partisan elites maintain a strategy of appealing to ideology and religious identity, as they have in recent years. The extent to which this will happen, however, is unclear, especially given the recent rapprochement between Prabowo Subianto, formerly the leader of a coalition representing a more Islamist political platform, and the pluralist parties in President Jokowi's coalition.

6.5 CONCLUSION

The overall picture that emerges from the analysis presented in this chapter highlights both the weaknesses and strengths of representation in Indonesia's democracy. In some important ways, the breadth and depth of ideological representation in Indonesia are constrained. Most crucially, representation is virtually nonexistent in a key policy field – fiscal policy – and citizens of modest socioeconomic backgrounds are significantly less well represented than those belonging to affluent classes. Despite these limitations, the cleavage over political Islam is an ideological dimension in which adequate substantive representation is occurring. The survey experiment that I analyzed suggests that significant potential exists for further partisan sorting and polarization on issues related to the cleavage over political Islam. This ideological link between citizens and politicians suggests that the historical ideological cleavage that has long structured Indonesian politics is alive and well despite the pervasiveness of clientelism in the political system. In Chapter 7, I explore some possible implications of this finding by analyzing the relationships between political Islam, conceptions of democracy and evaluations of democracy.

7

Meaning and Evaluation of Democracy

7.1 DEMOCRATIC ATTITUDES IN INDONESIA

Indonesian citizens are highly supportive of democracy, as surveys of public opinion regularly report. For example, 78.8% of the INSP sample agreed or strongly agreed that democracy is the best form of government for their country, while only 4.7% disagreed or strongly disagreed, and the remaining 15.5% expressed a neutral position. For other formulations of the question, which provide a choice of three views of democracy ("democracy is the best form of government"; "an authoritarian government can be preferable under some circumstances"; "for people like me, it doesn't make a difference"), support for democracy appears at least as high, and longitudinal data show a high degree of stability in responses to this question (Aspinall et al. 2020). Compared with other Asian countries, Indonesia shows consistently high levels of support for democracy across different measures and over time (Chu et al. 2016). In this respect, democratic attitudes in Indonesia are typical. Although recent evidence shows weaker support for democracy among younger cohorts (Foa and Mounk 2016), high levels of support for democratic rule are still observed in most countries, regardless of their regime type.

This pervasive support for democracy is perhaps best interpreted as a sign of the strong aspirational and normative appeal of democracy rather than as evidence of high levels of understanding of and support for specific democratic principles, practices and institutions. A more exhaustive analysis of democratic attitudes should focus on at least two areas that have important implications for self-reported support for democracy as a political regime. The first is satisfaction with how democracy is practiced in a specific time and place, as opposed to support for abstract principles of democratic governance. Satisfaction with democracy, or evaluation of democratic performance, is an accurate general measure of the health of a democracy as perceived by citizens, as it encapsulates the gap between public expectations about democratic rule and the performance of democratic institutions in meeting such expectations. As such, it may help us identify issues with democratic practice and pockets of discontent with democratic performance that, in the medium and long term, may affect support for democracy as a political regime and lead to questioning of the legitimacy of democratic institutions (Claassen 2020).

Second, given the overall high levels of public support for democracy, it is crucial to investigate what exactly citizens understand democracy to be about (Huber, Rueschemeyer and Stephens 1997). At a minimum, according to an electoral conception, democracy must entail free and fair elections and feature sufficient levels of competitiveness and participation (Przeworski et al. 2000). Beyond this relatively straightforward requirement, however, the meaning of democracy remains open to academic and political debate. For the majority of analysts, the most important dimension of democracy is a liberal one, as a regime cannot be described as democratic if it does not guarantee civil freedoms and rights for all citizens and does not have a system of government that limits the power of the executive through checks and balances. The distinction between "electoral" and "liberal" democracy, often found in the literature on democratic consolidation, underscores the predominance of these two dimensions in informing empirical research on democracy. In recent years, however, this dichotomy has given way to a more inclusive multidimensional conceptualization of democracy that also includes participatory, egalitarian-social and deliberative dimensions (Lindberg et al. 2014). As citizens may harbor different views and expectations of what democracy is, they may hold democratic practice to different standards and formulate diverging evaluations of whether democracy is "delivering" (Canache, Mondak and Seligson 2001).

As I showed at the beginning of this book, satisfaction with democracy in Indonesia has fluctuated. Surprisingly, it has increased substantially since 2014, when scholars of Indonesian politics began to warn of democratic erosion. In recent months, however, satisfaction has dropped dramatically following the negative repercussions of the COVID-19 pandemic on the economy and public health (Cochrane 2020). These patterns suggest that Indonesian citizens may respond to various events and developments, both in the short and in the medium-long terms, when evaluating democracy, and that analyzing indicators of democratic satisfaction can yield interesting insights into the state of democracy in this country. At the same time, economic and institutional performance, which remain the focus of most research on democratic attitudes (Mujani, Liddle and Ambardi 2018), cannot exhaustively account for these patterns of longitudinal variation. Regarding public conceptions of democracy, studies indicate that most people do not understand democracy in *liberal* terms, as they equate democracy with good governance and policy outcomes rather than a system of checks and balances and limited government (Warburton and Aspinall 2019). These findings point to the importance of investigating the meaning of democracy in a context in which support for democracy is widespread, but what exactly is meant by "democracy" is controversial.

How, then, does the cleavage over political Islam intersect with the study of democratic attitudes? There are two main channels through which views of state-Islam relations can shape how Indonesians evaluate democratic practice. First, political Islam could affect satisfaction with democracy through perceptions of representation, which, as demonstrated in Figure 1.2, are closely associated with satisfaction with democracy. The pluralist camp has traditionally occupied a dominant position in Indonesia's democratic politics by engaging in coalitions with "moderate" Islamic actors and excluding more radical voices, and this legacy of exclusion of radical Islam from formal politics is reflected in the patterns of unequal representation identified in Chapter 6. As Islamist views are underrepresented in democratic institutions, Islamist individuals are likely to be less satisfied with representation and democracy in Indonesia. The data from the survey used to generate Figure 1.2 indicate that this is indeed the case: Islamists are substantially less likely to think that their views are well represented by politicians (23%, compared with 38% for other ideological groups), to believe that elections work well in selecting a political class with views that mirror those of the citizens (26% versus 37%) or to be satisfied with democracy (44% versus 63%). To be sure, as I have argued, the increased prominence of radical Islamic voices in recent years may have substantially improved perceptions of representation among Islamist individuals, which may have helped to increase aggregate scores of satisfaction with democracy. Nevertheless, given the historical legacy of Islamist marginalization in politics, a significant gap in evaluations of democratic performance persists between Islamist and pluralist

Indonesians.[1] The cleavage over political Islam is thus clearly associated with views of substantive representation, which are consequential for evaluations of democratic performance.

The second link between political Islam and democratic attitudes, which is the focus of this chapter, works through popular understandings of democracy. Political Islam can structure conceptions of democracy and thus provide pluralist and Islamist Indonesians with different benchmarks to evaluate democratic performance. As I have shown, the ideological cleavage over the role of Islam in politics intersects with a more general ideological dimension that concerns the role of tradition in social and public life. As such, we can expect Islamist individuals to be less likely to support a liberal understanding of democracy that emphasizes the importance of individual freedoms and rights. The fact that political Islam is also associated with national identity, with Islamists being more likely to endorse an ethnic conception of what it means to be Indonesian, further strengthens this expectation, as the acknowledgment and enforcement of the rights of ethnic and religious minorities are a crucial feature of liberal democracy. As the current process of democratic erosion in Indonesia has primarily threatened the liberal dimension of democracy, we should expect individuals who hold a liberal conception of democracy to be more dissatisfied with how democracy is practiced in contemporary Indonesia.

In the remainder of this chapter, I explore this hypothesis using data from an original web-based survey (N = 2,027) specifically designed to study democratic attitudes in Indonesia and implemented in July and August 2019.[2] I start by outlining the research design and analyzing some descriptive statistics about conceptions of democracy, and I show that two related but distinct conceptions of democracy can be identified in Indonesian public opinion. I then explore using a regression analysis the determinants of these two conceptions of democracy, focusing on the associations between understanding of democracy, political Islam and populist attitudes. Finally, I analyze the implications of conceptions of democracy for satisfaction with and support for democracy. This chapter thus contributes to the argument that I put forward in this book by

---

[1] It should also be noted that the survey was taken at a time (August 2020) in which repression of Islamist movements had significantly intensified compared with previous years. As I discuss further in Chapter 8, these developments have crippled the mobilizational ability of radical Islam.

[2] I designed this survey with Ferran Martinez i Coma. This chapter extends the analysis presented in Fossati and Martinez i Coma (2020b).

7.1 Democratic Attitudes in Indonesia 169

analyzing a crucial ramification of the cleavage over political Islam, which provides further evidence of the importance of this ideological dimension in Indonesia's political culture, as political Islam strongly influences how Indonesian citizens conceptualize democracy and evaluate its performance.

7.1.1 The Meaning of Democracy: Measures and Data

A vast amount of empirical research analyzes aggregate-level data about conceptions of democracy collected by international survey programs. Such data are usually based on large cross-regional samples (Dalton, Sin, and Jou 2007; Norris 2011) or on samples from specific regions such as Europe (Ferrín and Kriesi 2016), East Asia (Chu and Huang 2010), Africa (Mattes and Bratton 2007) or Latin America (Camp 2001). This scholarship reveals the substantial variations in how ordinary citizens understand democracy across different countries and regions and in tracing such variations back to specific historical trajectories of political-cultural development. However, the questions included in these surveys typically suffer from three shortcomings. First, the conceptual frameworks that they rely on do not include the whole range of conceptions of democracy (electoral, liberal, participatory, egalitarian and deliberative). As each dimension is well established in the theoretical literature and could potentially be endorsed by a significant number of citizens, it is important that our measures be derived from an exhaustive typology.

Second, each of the five dimensions discussed previously may entail numerous aspects, and investigating them thoroughly by distilling them into just the handful of questions typically included in such large-scale survey programs may be problematic. Each dimension could instead be disaggregated into a larger number of easy-to-understand attributes or items that can be individually evaluated by survey respondents. Such individual items can then be analyzed to determine the extent to which they are indeed perceived by respondents as belonging to the same dimension of democracy. Finally, survey questions on conceptions of democracy usually ask respondents to choose between different alternatives. In doing so, they may be forcing an artificial choice on respondents that could produce unreliable data, as the various dimensions of democracy, although clearly distinct in theory, may easily overlap in the minds of ordinary citizens.

The analysis presented here is based on a novel instrument to measure public conceptions of democracy based on two premises: First, that democracy can usefully be conceptualized as incorporating the five dimensions of electoral, liberal, participatory, egalitarian and deliberative democracy; and second, that these dimensions are multifaceted and not mutually exclusive. Drawing on the indicators used in the V-Dem project to measure the various dimensions of democracy (Lindberg et al. 2014), we designed thirty-six survey items, each of which can be ascribed to a specific conception of democracy (five to the deliberative conception, eight to the egalitarian conception, ten to the electoral conception, eight to the liberal conception and five to the participatory conception). The survey respondents were prompted that people usually think about different things as being important for a democracy, and they were asked to report their views on how important each of the thirty-six items (presented in random order) were for a political regime to be considered a democracy. This approach allows for a more comprehensive range of possibilities regarding what conceptions of democracy might resonate with the Indonesian public, while at the same time allowing that various dimensions could be closely intertwined in public understandings of what democracies are and should do.

Table 7.1 reports the thirty-six items and their average scores on a scale ranging from 1 (not important at all for being a democracy) to 10 (very important). As shown in the table, there is substantial variation both across items and dimensions. Most of the respondents agreed that certain aspects of various dimensions are crucial for democracy (for instance, "All adult citizens have the right to vote in elections," "Citizens have the right to profess any religion," and "Access to healthcare is guaranteed for all"), while others are less essential (for example, "People participate in politics and civic life beyond elections," "People have the same rights regardless of sexual orientation," and "Decisions are taken on the basis of rational discussion"). Overall, the respondents were most likely to identify egalitarian and liberal statements with democracy (with average scores of 8.01 and 7.98, respectively) and least likely to identify participatory items with democracy (7.29), with the deliberative (7.86) and electoral (7.68) items falling between. As the figures in Table 7.1 indicate, however, there is also some variation across the items within each dimension, indicating that respondents differentiate between aspects that are commonly conceptualized as belonging to the same conception of democracy. For example, in the electoral dimension, the respondents appeared to consider the role of the media or the role of opposition parties to be less important to democracy than universal suffrage or the absence of intimidation during elections.

TABLE 7.1. *Five dimensions of democracy: Measurement and structure*

Dimension	Item	Average score	Factor 1	Factor 2
Electoral	All adult citizens have the right to vote in elections	8.39	0.7892	0.0282
Electoral	Elections are free from intimidation	8.1	0.7334	−0.0026
Electoral	Elections are free from vote-buying	7.97	0.7716	−0.0168
Electoral	Elections are free from fraud	7.95	0.5998	−0.1162
Electoral	Governments are punished in elections when they have done a bad job	7.91	0.8156	0.1319
Electoral	Political parties offer clear policy alternatives	7.63	0.6402	0.2931
Electoral	The media provide citizens with reliable information to judge the government	7.49	0.0996	0.1999
Electoral	People are free to discuss politics in public	7.2	−0.0496	**0.6744**
Electoral	Opposition parties are free to operate, criticize the government and run for elections	7.16	−0.1798	**0.6456**
Electoral	People are free to demonstrate and protest	7.15	0.1347	0.712
Liberal	Citizens have the right to choose and profess any religion	8.38	0.7779	−0.0014
Liberal	Citizens have the same rights regardless of their race and ethnicity	8.31	0.8569	−0.0296
Liberal	Men and women have equal rights	8.23	0.6351	0.1119
Liberal	The parliament keeps the government accountable for what it does	7.94	0.7262	0.1883
Liberal	The courts can stop the government if it acts against the constitution	7.86	0.6065	0.256
Liberal	Laws are applied in the same way for all citizens	7.85	0.2803	−0.0346
Liberal	Citizens have the right to own property	7.84	0.3773	0.178
Liberal	Citizens have the same rights regardless of their sexual orientation	7.54	0.4205	0.2318

(*continued*)

TABLE 7.1. (*continued*)

Dimension	Item	Average score	Factor 1	Factor 2
Egalitarian	Access to healthcare is guaranteed for all	8.27	0.8238	−0.0667
Egalitarian	Access to education is guaranteed for all	8.24	0.7567	−0.0439
Egalitarian	The government ensures law and order for all	8.22	0.8401	−0.0064
Egalitarian	Public goods such as roads and other infrastructure are provided	8.19	0.844	0.0257
Egalitarian	The government protects all citizens against poverty	8.12	0.834	0.0432
Egalitarian	Citizens have the same rights and opportunities in life regardless of the social group they are from	8.01	0.3097	−0.007
Egalitarian	Government policies help reduce the difference between the rich and the poor	7.72	0.4269	0.006
Egalitarian	Employment subsidies are given to those who don't have a job	7.45	0.588	0.3331
Participatory	Women participate in politics as much as men do	7.81	0.3973	0.3186
Participatory	Citizens have the final say on the most important political issues by voting on them directly in referendums	7.61	0.555	0.4471
Participatory	Citizens are interested in political issues	7.07	0.1803	0.7351
Participatory	Voters discuss politics with people they know before deciding how to vote	7.02	−0.0187	0.6437
Participatory	People participate in politics and civic life beyond elections	7	−0.1315	0.5419
Deliberative	When an important decision is made, all points of views are considered	8.12	0.7375	0.0488
Deliberative	Decisions are taken to advance the common good, not to protect special interests	8.04	0.5358	−0.0064
Deliberative	Political adversaries respect each other even when they disagree	8.04	0.6922	−0.0116
Deliberative	The government explains its decisions to voters	7.8	0.6992	0.2572
Deliberative	Decisions are made on the basis of rational discussion	7.34	0.0869	0.2014

7.1 Democratic Attitudes in Indonesia   173

These figures suggest that for Indonesians, as for citizens in other countries, democracy entails more than free and fair elections, as it encompasses issues related to liberalism, social justice, informal participation and deliberation. To better appraise what share of the sample endorses each dimension, and given the average values reported in Table 7.1, we could calculate a simple average of the various items in each dimension and consider 8 as a threshold to determine if a respondent identifies the dimension as being very important for democracy. By this standard, 52% of the sample is classified as "electoral" democrats, 60% as "liberal" democrats, 40% as "participatory" democrats, 61% as "egalitarian" democrats and 57% as "deliberative" democrats. These aggregate figures offer an overview of the complexity of conceptions of democracy in the Indonesian electorate, and they call into question whether there is a prevailing egalitarian understanding of democracy in Indonesia. For example, studies based on data from the Asian Barometer, a survey program implemented in various Asian countries in which notions of democracy are conceptualized as being either "procedural" or "substantive" (Huang 2017), regularly find the predominance of the latter over the former (Warburton and Aspinall 2019; Aspinall et al. 2020). Yet when we conceptualize democracy as a multidimensional rather than a dichotomous concept and refrain from asking respondents to choose one or the other, a more complex picture emerges, as liberal values are about as likely to be mentioned as essential for democracy as egalitarian policy outcomes.

An important caveat regarding the multidimensionality of popular understandings of democracy in the Indonesian context is that individuals differ in their ability to identify the various items reported in Table 7.1 as constitutive traits of democracy. By the measure outlined in the previous paragraph, 34.6% of respondents acknowledge all five dimensions of democracy, 14.8% four dimensions, 6.8% three dimensions, 6.6% two, 5.6% one, and the remaining 31.7% fail to identify any of the five dimensions as being very important for democracy. While some appreciate the complexity and multidimensionality of the idea of democracy, others have a much shallower understanding of the concept, and many others appear unsure as to whether democracy encompasses any of the five dimensions. This variation is related to respondents' level of education, as those with higher education are better able to fully comprehend the various items and reflect on whether they are important for democracy. The share of respondents who endorse no dimensions declines steadily across educational levels, dropping from 55% among those with only elementary education to 24% among college graduates. These data remind us that although most studies focus on aggregate figures and variation across countries, within-country heterogeneity in understandings of democracy is substantial.

Variation in the ability to identify the various conceptions of democracy suggests that some individuals have little knowledge about democracy. This has important implications for support for democracy, as uninformed individuals who lack knowledge of the basic features of democracy may be less likely to support democracy as a political regime (Cho 2014). Data from this survey corroborate this hypothesis, as support for democracy is systematically higher among those who are able to identify more dimensions as crucial for democracy. For example, the share of respondents who believe democracy to be always preferable to any other kind of government decreases from 75.6% of those who identify five dimensions of democracy to 50.4% of respondents who identify no dimensions. Conversely, those who fail to identify any dimension of democracy constitute only 21.2% of respondents who think that democracy is always preferable, but they account for 37.8% of those who believe that authoritarian rule may be justified at times and 40.9% of those who perceive little difference between democratic and authoritarian government. Popular conceptions of democracy may thus be crucial for democratic consolidation in Indonesia. From an analytical standpoint, these findings reassure us of the close connection between conceptions of democracy and other democratic attitudes. From a policy-oriented angle, they suggest that investing in developing and consolidating knowledge about democratic institutions and values may be a fruitful strategy to strengthen public support for democracy.

7.1.2 The Structure of Public Conceptions of Democracy

The data discussed in Section 7.1.1 are a good starting point for appreciating the multidimensionality of conceptions of democracy in Indonesia and the nexus between conceptualizations of and support for democracy. Nevertheless, some important questions cannot be answered with descriptive statistics alone. The average levels of support for each dimension discussed in Section 7.1.1 do not tell us whether the various items within each dimension are perceived as being constitutive of a coherent whole or whether the respondents' answers suggest that they are indeed thinking of each dimension as conceptually distinct from the others. The first question therefore regards the structure of conceptions of democracy: Are the five

7.1 Democratic Attitudes in Indonesia 175

dimensions of democracy indeed distinct in the minds of ordinary Indonesians? Or do popular understandings of democracy merge aspects from different dimensions? Measuring conceptions of democracy with a list of items that can be evaluated independently of one another enables us to address this question, specifically by applying factor analysis to the full set of thirty-six items.

Once again, factor analysis can shed light on this question. In this case, the thirty-six statements on features of democracy are the variables, or items, on which we perform the analysis, and the underlying factors that we are hoping to identify are dimensions of popular conceptions of democracy. By identifying a limited number of underlying factors, we can ascertain the structure of conceptions of democracy in Indonesian public opinion, and we can determine whether only one conception of democracy is present or multiple conceptions of democracy coexist as distinct ideological constructs. Furthermore, by considering the empirical associations between such factors and the thirty-six survey items, we can interpret the "meaning" of the factors and verify whether they correspond to the various dimensions of democracy that we have conceptualized. Finally, we can use the extracted factors in regression analysis to investigate their association with the cleavage over political Islam and their implications for other democratic attitudes, as I do in Sections 7.2 and 7.3.

The results of the factor analysis suggest that there are two distinct conceptions of democracy. The first is the dominant one, accounting for about 60% of the variation in the thirty-six items in the scale, and the factor loading scores reported in Table 7.1 show that this factor is associated with items from the different dimensions that most Indonesians consider very important for democracy. Perhaps the closest association is with egalitarian items, with five of the ten items most closely associated with this factor belonging to this category (both statements about the provision of public goods such as safety and infrastructure and statements on reducing social inequalities and poverty). Yet several liberal statements are also strongly associated with this factor, such as the items on freedom of religion and the statement "Citizens have the same rights regardless of their race and ethnicity," which has the highest loading on this factor. Finally, most of the deliberative items also load on this first factor. Factor 1, the dominant conception of democracy in Indonesia, can thus be described as representing a multilayered conception of democracy that especially blends egalitarian and liberal values. The second factor can be described as "participatory," as three of the five participatory items load strongly on it. ("Citizens are interested in political issues" is the item most strongly associated with Factor 2.) This factor is also closely associated with electoral items that measure informal aspects of participation, such as "People are free to demonstrate and protest" and "People are free to discuss politics in public." A distinct minority participatory conception of democracy can thus also be identified in Indonesian public opinion.

These results indicate that the five-dimensional distinction between electoral, liberal, participatory, deliberative and egalitarian democracy among the Indonesian public has a simpler structure featuring only one dominant conception, blending mostly liberal and egalitarian items, and a second, less-prominent understanding of democracy with a strong participatory character. These findings corroborate prior research on conceptions of democracy in Indonesia and qualify existing knowledge in important ways. In showing that egalitarian conceptions of democracy are widespread and deep-rooted, this study resonates with previous research on Indonesian public opinion. In contrast with prior studies, however, these findings show that liberal and egalitarian views of democracy are intimately related. Although these dimensions are distinct in the thought of political theorists and in the analysis of empirically oriented political scientists, they are not distinct in the minds of Indonesian people, who think of the two as inextricably linked. Concerning the second factor, the existence of a distinct participatory dimension points to the importance of political participation in Indonesian politics. This finding thus resonates with analyses that highlight the importance of civic engagement for the resilience of Indonesian democracy (Lussier and Fish 2012) and indicates the continuing relevance of the legacy of informal progressive politics in the country (Dibley and Ford 2019).

7.2 POLITICAL ISLAM AND CONCEPTIONS OF DEMOCRACY

Conceptions of democracy in Indonesia can therefore be reduced to two main dimensions: liberal–egalitarian and participatory. I next investigate the sociodemographic and attitudinal factors associated with popular understandings of democracy. Do individuals with different conceptions of democracy differ in their socioeconomic backgrounds? Are such different conceptions associated with political preferences and other ideological constructs such as populism, conceptions of national identity and, most importantly, political Islam? The theoretical rationale for investigating these questions is that conceptions of democracy may be systematically linked both to socioeconomic background (especially to education, as

7.2 Political Islam and Conceptions of Democracy 177

previously suggested), and to other political attitudes that equally reflect normative orientations about what is ultimately desirable in a social and political system. We can expect that liberal understandings of democracy, as measured by the first factor, are more likely to be endorsed by individuals with a pluralist political ideology and a civic conception of national identity. In contrast, Islamist individuals and those with an ethnic understanding of national identity should be less likely to endorse liberal notions of democracy. Analyzing the empirical correlates of conceptions of democracy may therefore help us understand how they fit into a broader ideological outlook on social and political values.

To answer these questions, I estimate simple multiple regression models, reported in Table 7.2, in which the two conceptions of democracy result from a range of sociodemographic, attitudinal and political factors that may be associated with political Islam and/or conceptions of democracy. For social and demographic factors, the respondents are grouped into various age groups as reported in the table. Gender, region and religion are measured with binary variables (0 = male, 1 = female; 0 = urban, 1 = rural; 0 = non-Muslim, 1 = Muslim), education with a five-category ordinal indicator, and income with a question grouping respondents into five brackets. For political–ideological indicators, I adopt measures that I have used elsewhere in this book, although in some cases, in simplified form given survey space constraints. Support for the incumbent president is measured with a standard question asking whether respondents are satisfied with how the president is doing his job. For conceptions of national identity, I use the factor analysis technique described in Chapter 5 to obtain indicators of civic and ethnic understandings of national identity. For political Islam, populism and preferences regarding economic redistribution, I analyze the answers to a series of agree/disagree questions.[3] Finally, life satisfaction, or happiness, is measured on a ten-point scale, where higher values denote higher levels of life satisfaction. The estimated models therefore include a wide range of variables that allow me to control for factors that may confound the relationship between political Islam and understandings of democracy.

The estimation results reported in Table 7.2 provide some insights into the factors associated with the two main dimensions. First, two

---

[3] For political Islam: "The government should prioritize Islam over other religions"; for populism: "Politicians always end up agreeing when it comes to protecting their privileges"; for economic redistribution: "The government should spend more to help the poor even if it requires higher taxes."

TABLE 7.2. *Determinants of conceptions of democracy*

Variables	(1) Liberal–egalitarian	(2) Participatory
Age group: 25–34	0.0501 (0.0497)	0.0468 (0.0511)
Age group: 35–44	0.163*** (0.0567)	0.114* (0.0583)
Age group: 45 and older	0.308*** (0.0709)	0.224*** (0.0728)
Gender: Female	0.0753* (0.0416)	−0.0279 (0.0428)
Muslim	0.109* (0.0587)	0.0550 (0.0604)
Rural	−0.100** (0.0455)	−0.0639 (0.0467)
Education: Secondary	0.185* (0.0981)	−0.0924 (0.101)
Education: High school	0.308*** (0.0882)	0.124 (0.0906)
Education: Diploma	0.372*** (0.101)	0.210** (0.104)
Education: College and above	0.356*** (0.105)	0.265** (0.108)
Income: Rp. 2,000,000–3,999,000	0.0118 (0.0611)	−0.103 (0.0628)
Income: Rp. 4,000,000–5,999,000	−0.0835 (0.0599)	−0.179*** (0.0616)
Income: Rp. 6,000,000–7,999,000	−0.101 (0.0773)	−0.0760 (0.0795)
Income: Rp. 8,000,000 or more	−0.0182 (0.0711)	−0.0639 (0.0731)
Political Islam	−0.0862*** (0.0200)	−0.0283 (0.0206)
Support for Jokowi	−0.0127 (0.0252)	0.00118 (0.0259)
Populism	0.0246 (0.0212)	0.0919*** (0.0218)
Support for redistribution	−0.0146 (0.0196)	0.0616*** (0.0202)
Ethnic national ID	−0.0968*** (0.0252)	0.0679*** (0.0259)
Civic national ID	0.173*** (0.0238)	0.105*** (0.0245)
Happiness	0.166*** (0.00943)	0.147*** (0.00969)

7.2 Political Islam and Conceptions of Democracy 179

TABLE 7.2. (*continued*)

Variables	(1) Liberal–egalitarian	(2) Participatory
Constant	-1.433^{***} (0.175)	-1.626^{***} (0.179)
Observations	2,027	2,027
R-squared	0.23	0.187

Standard errors in parentheses. *** p $<$ 0.01, ** p $<$ 0.05, * p $<$ 0.10. All models include fixed effects for regions, which are not reported.

demographic covariates, education and age, are positively associated with both conceptions of democracy, as respondents who are better educated and older are more likely to have a clearly defined conception of democracy, be it liberal–egalitarian or participatory. For education, respondents who have attained an education level higher than high school (i.e., diploma, college or postgraduate) are significantly more likely to have a strong conception of democracy of either type, which confirms the correlations presented in Section 7.1. The association with education suggests that conceptions of democracy are related to political sophistication, or knowledge about politics, as highly educated individuals may be better able to fully understand the thirty-six items and evaluate them coherently. Regarding age, both liberal–egalitarian and participatory conceptions of democracy appear to be more deeply rooted in respondents aged forty-five and above than in younger respondents (eighteen to twenty-four). This finding may indicate that conceptions of democracy, like other political attitudes, develop and consolidate over time as part of a person's political socialization. Sociodemographic factors therefore have important effects on conceptions of democracy, as they determine whether a person has a coherent idea of what democracy entails, but they alone do not tell us *which* conception a person might have.

Second, the estimation results are consistent with expectations regarding to the ideological factors associated with the predominant liberal–egalitarian conception of democracy. As expected, the estimated coefficient for political Islam is negatively signed and significant at the 0.05 level, which shows that Islamist individuals (i.e., respondents who strongly agreed that the Indonesian government should prioritize Islam over other religions) are less likely than are pluralists to hold a liberal–egalitarian conception of democracy. Furthermore, ethnonationalist individuals are significantly less likely to understand democracy in liberal terms, while civic nationalists are more likely do so. These associations corroborate the hypothesis that liberal conceptions of democracy are associated with inclusive ideas of who should belong to the Indonesian nation, whereas liberal democrats are less likely to be found among those who define membership of the Indonesian nation along ethnic lines. Overall, these results concerning the nexus between political Islam, national identity and conceptions of democracy reassure us that indeed, the predominant conception of democracy in Indonesia should be described as *liberal–egalitarian* rather than exclusively or predominantly egalitarian. If egalitarian, social or "substantive" understandings of democracy clearly prevailed in this multifaceted conception of democracy identified by factor analysis, we would likely not observe such a strong relationship between political Islam and conceptions of national identity.

Finally, with regard to the participatory conception of democracy, the estimation results suggest some interesting associations with political ideology, although this second factor is not significantly associated with political Islam. Rather, it is populism, understood as described in Chapter 5 (i.e., a "thin ideology" in which virtuous masses are in opposition to corrupt elites), that shows a strong positive association with participatory understandings of democracy. Respondents who view the sociopolitical world as being divided into two homogenous camps of elites and masses and who have a negative view of political elites in general are thus more likely to have a strong participatory conception of democracy. The estimation results also indicate that participatory conceptions of democracy are systematically stronger among respondents who support economic redistribution, which indicates a close relationship between participatory notions of democracy, populist views and concerns about economic inequality.

These results further corroborate the idea of a dualistic structure of popular understandings of democracy in Indonesia. On the one hand, the dominant factor, liberal–egalitarian, is associated with the primary dimension of ideological competition in Indonesian politics, namely political Islam. On the other hand, the participatory conception of democracy, empirically distinct from the first factor but less common among the Indonesian public, is linked with support for progressive fiscal policies and populist attitudes. The correlation between this second factor and economic policy preferences is somewhat surprising, given that the first factor is more closely associated with egalitarian items.[4] Yet the

---

[4] Most of them, however, do not explicitly suggest the desirability of economic redistribution.

7.3 Democracy and Evaluations of Democratic Performance 181

association between populism and support for more economic redistribution resonates with the findings reported in Chapter 5 showing that populist individuals are more likely to harbor economic grievances.

7.3 THE MEANING OF DEMOCRACY AND EVALUATIONS OF DEMOCRATIC PERFORMANCE

The final part of my analysis of the correlations and implications of popular conceptions of democracy explores the intersection between conceptions and evaluations of democracy. As mentioned, the logic behind this undertaking is that different conceptions of democracy are plausibly associated with the use of different standards to evaluate democratic performance, which could lead to diverging perceptions of the state of democracy in Indonesia or to different degrees of satisfaction with how democracy is implemented. To perform this analysis, I rely again on multiple regression techniques, and I focus on three questions in the survey instrument. The first asked whether the respondents believed Indonesia to be a democracy. Four choices were provided as to what degree Indonesian could be considered a democratic regime. (1) Not a democracy; (2) a democracy with major problems; (3) a democracy with minor problems; and (4) a full democracy. Most of the respondents in the sample were quite critical of the state of democracy in contemporary Indonesia, as more than half of them described their country either as not being a democracy (5.3%) or as being a democracy with serious flaws (45%). Only a minority considered Indonesia to be a full democracy (15%); the remaining 34.7% considered Indonesia to be a democracy with minor problems.

The second question asked whether the respondents were satisfied with how democracy is working in Indonesia. Again, four choices were provided, ranging from "very dissatisfied" to "very satisfied," but the answers to this question overlapped only partially with the previous question. A clear majority, 61% of the sample, were satisfied or very satisfied with how democracy is working in their country, while a smaller share of respondents were either somewhat dissatisfied (39%) or very dissatisfied (9%). Finally, we asked about support for democracy as a political regime with the question, "Do you agree or disagree with the following statement: Democracy may have its problems, but it is still the best form of government for Indonesia." This is a typical "Churchill" question often analyzed in surveys of democratic attitudes in public opinion, and our sample aligns with the consensus of generally high levels of support for democracy in Indonesia: While 14.3% of the respondents disagreed or strongly disagreed with this statement, 61% agreed, and 24.7% strongly agreed.

Table 7.3 reports the estimates for a series of ordered logit models that enable us to analyze the effect of conceptions of democracy on these three outcomes. The first two columns (assessments of whether Indonesia is a democracy and satisfaction with democracy in Indonesia) show strong effects of conceptions of democracy on democratic performance and satisfaction with democracy. Most crucially, however, the two conceptions of democracy – liberal–egalitarian and participatory – have opposite effects on evaluations of democratic performance. Respondents with a strong liberal–egalitarian conception of democracy are more critical in assessing the state of democracy in Indonesia than those who lack this conception, as they are less likely to believe that Indonesia is a democracy or to be satisfied with how democracy is working in Indonesia. In contrast, the participatory conception of democracy is significantly and positively associated with the two outcome variables: "participatory democrats" are more likely to describe the current political system in Indonesia as a democracy and to be satisfied with it. In all of the cases, the estimated coefficients are sizable in magnitude and significant at conventional levels, which shows how strongly ideas about the meaning of democracy are associated with other democratic attitudes.

These strong empirical associations suggest that conceptions of democracy are crucial in shaping public satisfaction with democracy. When we control for a wide range of sociodemographic variables, Indonesians with a strong liberal–egalitarian conception of democracy are more likely to be dissatisfied with the state of democracy in their country, and those who appreciate the value of participation as a constitutive element of democracy are more likely be satisfied. While the finding about the dominant conception of democracy conforms to expectations, given the current debate about democratic erosion in Indonesia, the positive connection between participatory understandings of democracy and evaluations of democracy is somewhat puzzling. Data from the V-Dem project show that experts on Indonesian politics identify the participatory dimension as the most poorly consolidated of those various measured (Hicken 2020), and many still see Indonesian democracy as dominated by predatory elites (Winters 2011; Hadiz and Robison 2013). Yet this finding is robust, and the estimated coefficient is even larger than that for the liberal–egalitarian conception: Those who see democracy primarily as a matter of public participation are actually *more* satisfied with democracy. As I further discuss in the concluding chapter (Chapter 8), to account for

7.3 Democracy and Evaluations of Democratic Performance   183

TABLE 7.3. *Conceptions of democracy, evaluations of democratic performance and support for democracy*

Variables	(1) Indonesia a democracy?	(2) Satisfied with democracy?	(3) Support democracy?
Liberal–egalitarian conception of democracy	−0.136** (0.0564)	−0.151*** (0.0562)	0.205*** (0.0603)
Participatory conception of democracy	0.330*** (0.0567)	0.426*** (0.0571)	0.324*** (0.0602)
Age group: 25–34	−4.74e-05 (0.109)	0.0160 (0.109)	−0.0987 (0.117)
Age group: 35–44	−0.175 (0.124)	−0.168 (0.124)	−0.0862 (0.134)
Age group: 45 and older	−0.0620 (0.155)	0.00973 (0.156)	−0.142 (0.167)
Gender: Female	−0.323*** (0.0916)	−0.170* (0.0911)	0.0443 (0.0980)
Muslim	−0.102 (0.113)	−0.577*** (0.116)	−0.777*** (0.123)
Rural	0.0984 (0.0991)	−0.0852 (0.0997)	−0.103 (0.108)
Education: Secondary	0.0105 (0.222)	−0.0137 (0.223)	0.253 (0.235)
Education: High school	−0.141 (0.200)	−0.472** (0.202)	0.111 (0.212)
Education: Diploma	−0.0974 (0.228)	−0.478** (0.229)	−0.140 (0.242)
Education: College and above	−0.490** (0.237)	−0.468* (0.239)	0.225 (0.252)
Income: Rp. 2,000,000–3,999,000	−0.158 (0.133)	0.0199 (0.134)	0.177 (0.144)
Income: Rp. 4,000,000–5,999,000	−0.429*** (0.131)	−0.0104 (0.131)	0.158 (0.142)
Income: Rp. 6,000,000–7,999,000	−0.193 (0.169)	−0.126 (0.168)	0.394** (0.183)
Income: Rp. 8,000,000 or more	−0.208 (0.153)	−0.103 (0.155)	0.557*** (0.167)
/cut1	−3.649*** (0.267)	−3.597*** (0.263)	−4.011*** (0.290)
/cut2	−0.485** (0.247)	−1.692*** (0.252)	−2.498*** (0.270)
/cut3	1.234*** (0.249)	1.015*** (0.250)	0.809*** (0.263)
Observations	2,027	2,027	2,027
Log-likelihood	−2270	−2284	−1879

Standard errors in parentheses. *** $p < 0.01$, ** $p < 0.05$, * $p < 0.10$. All models include fixed effects for regions, which are not reported.

this finding, we need to acknowledge that Indonesia's democratic backsliding has been coupled with a genuine surge in popular participation in politics. As I have argued in this book, this development may have been unfolding against the background of the erosion of democratic checks and balances, but it has had positive implications for democratic legitimacy. The tension between these two dimensions of democracy is therefore a crucial, although so far neglected, feature of democratic backsliding in Indonesia.

One last important observation emerging from the results reported in Table 7.3 concerns the determinants of support for democracy as a political regime, as opposed to satisfaction with the practice of democracy in Indonesia. While the two conceptions of democracy have opposite effects on satisfaction with democracy, the results for the third model show that this bifurcation does not extend to support for democracy. Both conceptions of democracy are positively associated with the belief that democracy, while imperfect, is the best form of government for Indonesia. Having strong, clearly defined ideas of what it means to be a democracy is therefore conducive to higher levels of public support for democracy as a suitable political regime for Indonesia regardless of the specific conception of democracy.

These findings remind us that it is useful to draw a clear analytical distinction between the determinants of satisfaction with democracy and those of support for democracy. First, these two constructs are conceptually and empirically distinct. Indonesians are aware of the many flaws of democracy in their country, and they are thus often dissatisfied with how democracy is being practiced. However, when they are asked whether other regimes would be preferable to a democratic one, for most individuals, appreciation for the progress made so far trumps frustration about the work that still needs to be done. Second, satisfaction with and support for democracy are distinct in their determinants, although both are attitudinal, as shown by the different relationships with conceptions of democracy, and sociodemographic characteristics, as shown by educational attainment. The charts in Figure 7.1 display these differences by plotting the estimated probabilities of satisfaction with and support for democracy at different levels (and for different types) of conceptions of democracy. The contrast between the top two (satisfaction with democracy) and the bottom two (support for democracy) quadrants are clear, and they underscore the difference between the two conceptions.

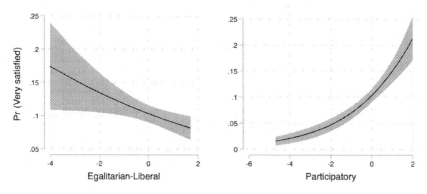

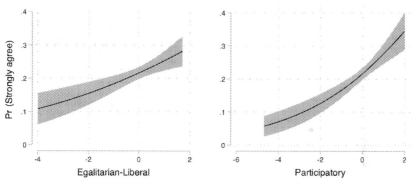

FIGURE 7.1. Predicted probability of satisfaction with and support for democracy by conception of democracy

7.4 CONCLUSION

The analysis carried out in this chapter advances our understanding of democratic attitudes in Indonesia and unveils an important path by which political Islam can shape democratic satisfaction. In contrast with prior studies that focus on the prevalence of egalitarian–substantive understandings of democracy, the various empirical associations discussed in this chapter suggest that liberal values are at least as important as substantive outcomes to inform the prevailing conception of democracy among the Indonesian public. Furthermore, this analysis shows that there is more diversity in conceptions of democracy than commonly thought, as a segment of the public acknowledges a different conception of democracy, which we have defined as participatory. To understand democratic attitudes and evaluations of democratic performance in this group, it is essential to conceptualize democratic performance in terms of inputs such as representation and participation rather than in terms of outputs such as economic development and the provision of public goods. Finally, Islamist and pluralist Indonesians differ in their understandings of democracy, and this divide results in different expectations about democratic practice and diverging evaluations of democratic performance. This is further evidence of the pervasiveness of the cleavage over political Islam in shaping political attitudes and political behavior, and it concludes the empirical analysis carried out in this book.

8

Conclusions

8.1 A RESILIENT DEMOCRACY

In the aftermath of authoritarian breakdown, Indonesia appeared to be an unlikely case for democratic transition, as it was characterized by economic, social and cultural factors that are usually considered detrimental to democratic advancement. While Indonesia had experienced decades of sustained economic development during the New Order, poverty was still widespread, educational attainment levels were very low and millions of people's livelihoods were severely disrupted by a deep economic recession. The military was still an influential actor, and numerous factions were willing to seize power and capitalize on the chaos produced by widespread social unrest. Furthermore, Indonesia's outlook presented a range of factors that are sometimes argued to be detrimental to democratic consolidation, such as a Muslim-majority society, exceptionally diverse ethnic and religious compositions, an economy in which rents from oil and natural resources played a key role in economic development, a recent history of mass violence and a poorly consolidated liberal–democratic political culture. It is thus no surprise that in the years immediately following authoritarian breakdown, it was common for observers of Indonesian politics to ask not only whether Indonesia would survive as a democracy, but even whether it would survive as a unified country. Yet democracy did survive despite its well-known limitations and some recent setbacks.

This book has been written against this background: the case of a young democracy that has surprised analysts by surviving and, in some respects, thriving despite tough odds. In seeking to contribute to our

187

understanding of this development, I build on the work of numerous scholars. Some of them focus on the process of democratic transition. Many study political elites, showing how their fragmentation forced them into inclusive power-sharing agreements that motivated the establishment of democratic institutions (Crouch 2010; Horowitz 2013). Others explain why the military did not seize power, focusing on factors such as internal divisions in the army and the increasing assertiveness of civilian elites (Mietzner 2006; Honna 2013). Some emphasize the role of ordinary people and the many activists that have opposed authoritarian rule in the late New Order (Aspinall 2005). Yet others focus on specific institutions such as elections or political parties (King 2003; Tomsa 2008), or dissect how economic collapse led to authoritarian breakdown (Pepinsky 2009). By focusing on the process of regime change, this research enhances understanding of why, despite the odds, Indonesia was able to democratize smoothly and successfully.

Looking beyond the process of democratic transition, many scholars ask why, despite various challenges, democracy has remained the dominant political regime in Indonesia. Edward Aspinall, for example, argues that the clientelistic nature of Indonesian politics is intimately linked to Indonesia's success as a durable democracy (Aspinall 2010, 2013). Indonesia's democratic regime has been essentially accommodative, as political elites have forged large coalitions that have tended to incorporate all key political forces, including those with close ties to the New Order. This inclusive style has stymied further political reform and ensured that illiberal forces have possessed veto power. However, the same "absorptive capacity" has also contributed to the stability and durability of the new regime, as a range of potentially antidemocratic actors have obtained stakes in democratic governance. Indonesia's political regime has been held together by such generous accommodative arrangements, whose validity is daily reasserted through the widespread practices of corruption and patronage.

A strong emphasis on historical legacies also features in Dan Slater's analysis of the successes and failures of democratic consolidation in Indonesia (Slater 2020). First, many of the key social and political forces in post-Suharto Indonesia can trace their origins back to the nationalist struggle and continue to represent its egalitarian, inclusionary and pluralistic values. The fragmentation of Indonesia's political landscape has ensured that none of these actors is in a position to turn Indonesia's democracy into an authoritarian regime. Second, the strong institutions

8.1 A Resilient Democracy

inherited from the New Order, most notably the Golkar party and a fairly professional military, were key in avoiding the breakdown of the Indonesian state during the tremendous security challenges of the late 1990s and early 2000s. While these two assets alone may not have been sufficient for Indonesia to accomplish a transition to full liberal democracy, they have been instrumental in ensuring that democracy has indeed flourished in a "hard place."

The argument that I put forward in this book resonates with these two prominent explanations of democratic development in Indonesia. First, I emphasize historical legacies to account for modern developments in Indonesian democracy, as I focus on the ideological division over the role of Islam in politics, whose emergence dates back to the nationalist movement. Second, I suggest that the liabilities preventing Indonesia from evolving into a full liberal democracy can to some degree also be considered as assets. The ideological division over political Islam, which underpins partisan polarization, can also strengthen the legitimacy of democracy by allowing for meaningful participation and representation. Indeed, in focusing on ideological contestation, the analysis that I present here is immediately relevant to understanding Indonesia's democratic erosion.

Over the last several years, perhaps starting with the 2014 election, democracy in Indonesia has changed substantially; by most accounts, it has deteriorated. A development that is particularly significant for my analysis is the resurgence of radical Islam, which features prominently in studies of democratic backsliding (Arjon 2018; Sebastian, Hasyim and Arifianto 2020; Muharam, Marijan and Kusman 2021). Understandably, the rise of Islamist movements and groups has been viewed as a concerning trend, as it has been coupled with undesirable changes in Indonesian politics: Attacks on religious minorities have become more common, political debate has become more acrimonious and polarized, and nativism and populist rhetoric have dented the image of Indonesia's democracy as a model of inclusiveness and moderation (Haq 2021; Jamhari and Nisa 2021; Masykuri and Ramadlan 2021). However, the rise of Islamism can also be assessed in a more positive light. The emergence of a strong illiberal Islamist movement could be interpreted as a sign of the success, not the failure, of Indonesia's democracy. As in the case of far-right movements and parties in other contexts, the growing political fortunes of illiberal groups can be considered a "cultural backlash" against increasingly pluralistic and liberal societies (Inglehart and Norris 2016). Indeed, Indonesian society has become more religiously tolerant over its twenty years of democracy (Mietzner, Muhtadi, and Halida 2018).[1] Second, as I discuss in Section 8.2, the resurgence of the division over political Islam has important and potentially beneficial implications for crucial aspects of Indonesia's democracy, namely representation, participation and accountability.

8.2 INDONESIA: A DEMOCRACY IN DECLINE?

This book studies how political Islam shapes the attitudinal and behavioral orientations of Indonesian citizens. This strong analytical focus on public opinion reflects a belief in the importance of ordinary people in democratic practice and in the usefulness of studying mass attitudes in understanding how democracy works. However, in bringing ordinary people to the fore and analyzing the degree to which political elites channel and represent their preferences, I do not equate democracy with merely following the "will of the people." Rather, I simply acknowledge that any modern democracy is representative. A key task in assessing democratic performance is therefore to evaluate to what extent politicians are fulfilling their duty to represent their constituents. Of course, this is only one of many important aspects of democratic performance. As discussed previously, democracy can be conceptualized in many ways and therefore evaluated from different perspectives. In any case, if we accept that democracy is a complex multidimensional construct, we need to allow that the same political developments may have contrasting implications for democratic advancement, as the case of rising Islamism in Indonesia demonstrates. The resurgence of illiberal forms of political Islam has eroded the possibility of protecting liberal freedoms, but it has also strengthened political representation and responsiveness. In the long term, this may have beneficial implications for the legitimacy of democratic institutions in Indonesia.

Beyond the Indonesian context, studying the roles of public opinion and ordinary citizens in democratic practice is especially important given the current wave of global democratic backsliding, in which autocrats are increasingly likely to be democratically elected and to invest considerable effort in fostering public support for their attacks on democracy (Curato and Fossati 2020). In this respect, the theoretical and methodological approach that I follow here, with its emphasis on understanding public

---

[1] See also Mujani (2019, 2020).

8.2 Indonesia: A Democracy in Decline? 191

opinion formation and democratic attitudes, is applicable to other cases in which democratic institutions have suffered from the same trends observed in Indonesia, such as increasing illiberalism and executive aggrandizement. Furthermore, focusing on deep-rooted social and political cleavages can help us understand how leaders seek to exploit these partisan and ideological legacies to mobilize consensus for their authoritarian agendas. More broadly, my analysis offers a reminder of the resilience and significance of historical and cultural divisions in shaping the dynamics of political competition and linkages between politicians and voters – a subject that is receiving renewed attention in comparative political research (Gethin, Martínez-Toledano and Piketty 2021).

While the analytical approach that I follow may be fruitfully applied elsewhere, the most immediate implications of the findings concern the study of Indonesian politics. I do not aim to offer an exhaustive assessment of the state of democracy in modern Indonesia, as many areas of democratic practice in this country are beyond the scope of this book. Nevertheless, in focusing on democratic representation and ideological competition, my argument directly relates to the current discussion on democratic backsliding and has implications for the assessment of Indonesia's democratic development.

8.2.1 Representation and Participation

The first contribution made by this study to debate on the current state of democracy in Indonesia comes from the main analytical focus on substantive representation, which is neglected in studies of Indonesian democracy. Representation, broadly understood, is of course a central concern for scholars of Indonesian politics, many of whom lament the shortcomings of representative democracy in this country, such as by emphasizing the pernicious effects of economic inequality and the dominant position of economic elites. Yet because of a lack of suitable data, studies of substantive representation in Indonesia are lacking, as the degree of ideological congruence between Indonesian politicians and citizens is not accurately studied. This book addresses this void by drawing on original surveys of elites and ordinary citizens that were designed specifically to study substantive representation, and it identifies both important weaknesses and strengths in patterns of citizen–politician linkages. While substantive representation is lacking in the crucial sphere of economic issues in Indonesia, it is well established in the most salient ideological axis of political competition, the division over political Islam.

Longitudinal data are not available to measure changes in patterns of substantive representation in Indonesia over time, but the available evidence suggests that this area of democratic governance has not witnessed significant deterioration in recent years. On the one hand, the lack of substantive representation on economic policy issues is hardly novel, as a lack of programmatic differentiation between political parties is a long-standing feature of Indonesia's democracy. On the other hand, the recent conservative turn toward a more influential role for Islam in politics suggests that politicians may have become *more* aligned with ordinary citizens on social issues, as the masses appear to be substantially less liberal than the elites in their political orientations. To be sure, the extent to which the Indonesian public could be considered more conservative than political elites needs to be contextualized against the background of successful Islamist mobilization, which may have increased public support for an Islamist agenda in the short term (Septiana, Al-Hamdi and Gusmi 2020). Yet political institutions have responded to growing Islamist demands – as indicated, for example, by the ascent of Ma'ruf Amin to the vice presidency. As evaluations of the quality of substantive representation are associated with satisfaction with democracy, increased responsiveness to conservative preferences may have increased the legitimacy of democratic institutions in the eyes of many Indonesian citizens.

Evidence of these relatively positive developments in representation supplement dominant accounts of Indonesian politics, which see this country's political system as an oligarchy dominated by predatory elites who leave little or no room for meaningful participation by ordinary people (Hadiz and Robison 2013). This framework does raise the crucial question of how much choice and control ordinary Indonesians have in shaping the trajectory of their democracy. Do ordinary people really have a say on important matters, or do elites make decisions without substantial constraints from public opinion? My analysis presents mixed findings in response to the critical view of Indonesian democracy put forward by this school of thought. Indonesian voters do not seem to have much of a choice when it comes to economic policy, a crucial policy area with substantial distributional implications. Politicians of all parties express the same views on economic issues, which are presumably the only issues that oligarchs really care about: They reject substantial economic redistribution and the progressive taxation needed to finance it, and they endorse a highly interventionist role for the state in the economy, which in the context of Indonesia is coupled with high levels of corruption and market

8.2 Indonesia: A Democracy in Decline? 193

distortions that disproportionally benefit established elites. There are powerful latent demands for economic redistribution by the public, but because of the lack of programmatic differentiation between political parties, these demands remain unarticulated and unaddressed. From this angle, Indonesia's democracy indeed looks like a political system that deprives ordinary citizens of sovereignty in a key policy domain.

However, a high degree of diversification exists between political parties on social and religious issues, and such ideological differences represent real, meaningful choices for many ordinary Indonesians. Although debates on the role of Islam in politics do not present distributional implications as clear and as substantial as those of economic policy choices, the dimension of ideological competition should not be considered less consequential. Furthermore, there is evidence of an incipient, albeit tenuous, link between political Islam and economic policy preferences, as Islamist Indonesians are more likely to consider certain economic issues salient and to support economic redistribution. To speculate, this association might foreshadow a future in which the religious–cultural cleavage over Islam is reinforced and broadened to include an economic dimension, with a contraposition between pluralist, fiscally conservative and Islamist, fiscally redistributive poles. Indonesia's political system thus appears to be one in which the choices of ordinary citizens and the influence that they have on the policy-making process are limited in many important ways; nevertheless, in contrast with many other young democracies, it also offers meaningful choices on issues that are important to many.

Against this background, the current repression of radical Islam is concerning. As many scholars observe, the Indonesian state has responded to the challenge presented by illiberal Islamist forces with equally illiberal measures (Mietzner 2018; Power 2018). Especially since the outbreak of the COVID-19 pandemic in early 2020, political repression of hardline Islamists has intensified to the extent that scholars of Indonesian politics now view executive aggrandizement by the Jokowi administration as the main threat to Indonesia's democracy (Mujani and Liddle 2021). Repressing radical Islam has curbed the mobilizational capacity of illiberal actors, and it may well have been welcomed by many Indonesian citizens (Fealy and White 2021). However, as is the case in other democracies that are being challenged by illiberal forces, repressive strategies could deepen polarization and feelings of exclusion (Lührmann 2021). In the case of political Islam in Indonesia, harsh, repressive measures risk pushing targeted groups toward violent radicalization

(Nuraniyah 2021). My argument suggests that repressing radical Islam is also dangerous from the perspective of democratic representation and legitimacy. To deprive radical Islamist groups of their ability to mobilize is also to deprive a substantial number of Indonesian citizens of their voice. To marginalize the most conservative views on state–Islam relations means further truncating ideological representation on the political Islam continuum. Thus, substantive debates about the most important ideological dimension of political competition in this country will become less meaningful and less salient, and ideological–programmatic differentiation between political parties will become more difficult. A crucial dimension of democratic development and citizen–politician linkage will therefore be seriously compromised.

A related issue concerns political participation, a crucial bellwether of the functioning of any democracy. Here, too, observers of Indonesian politics are critical of the current state of participatory politics, which appears to have declined in recent years, as measured by key indicators used in comparative analysis (Hicken 2020). The implementation of new restrictions on the freedom of association and the government's use of force in response to peaceful demonstrations in recent years are especially important factors of concern. In formal politics, political parties have sought to constrain participation by tightening electoral rules; in informal politics, the government is seen as having attacked the freedom of association with harsh repression of public demonstrations and initiatives such as the 2017 government decree on civil society organizations,[2] which empowered the executive to disband nongovernment organizations deemed to pose a security threat. However, the positive association between participatory understandings of democracy and evaluations of democratic performance uncovered in Chapter 7 indicates that citizens may disagree with experts on this point. While liberal democrats appear to share expert concerns about declining liberalism in Indonesian politics, participatory democrats do not seem to perceive a shrinking of possibilities for political participation.

Indeed, despite the recent erosion of civil freedoms, Indonesia's democracy is characterized by high levels of popular participation. We can witness this not only in the unique legacy of this country's vibrant associational life and in the high electoral participation figures, but also in some of the developments that have unfolded during democratic

---

[2] Government Regulation in Lieu of Law no. 2/2017 regarding Social Organizations (commonly known as PERPPU Ormas).

8.2 Indonesia: A Democracy in Decline?

backsliding, such as a resurgence of student movements and protests on various issues such as transparency, racism in Papua and workers' rights. To be sure, in these cases as well, the government has shown a repressive streak, and many of the appeals of civil society organizations have remained unheard, such as in the case of the labor movement (Caraway 2021). Yet this also indicates that, as elsewhere in the world, to the extent that democratic backsliding is occurring, many in Indonesia have been pushing back (Maerz et al. 2020). Overall, over the last five years, Indonesian citizens have become more engaged in politics, not less; despite the government's repeated refusal to engage with protesters, we have seen more people demonstrating, not fewer, about a broad range of issues; and electoral turnout in national elections has increased, not decreased.

This book has studied the role of ideological divisions in sustaining formal and informal political participation, and it has documented a close relationship between the two in the Indonesian context. As much as ideological polarization may be divisive, we should not forget that substantive disagreement over important issues is also a *conditio sine qua non* for civic and political engagement. The surge in Islam-based mobilization during Indonesia's democratic backsliding, while very different from the "civil Islam" whose contributions to civic engagements and democracy are often celebrated in the literature (Hefner 2011), has highlighted a new vibrancy of informal participation and associational life in Indonesia. By increasing the salience of the cleavage over political Islam, these developments may have strengthened perceptions (among citizens of any ideological orientation) that democracy in Indonesia entails meaningful, substantive political debates and allows for ideological representation on the crucial issue of state–Islam relations. When we focus on the historical legacy of the cleavage over political Islam as a source of meaning and democratic legitimacy, we are thus better able to appreciate why Indonesian democracy, despite its many limitations, continues to witness higher levels of participation than many other young democracies.

8.2.2 Accountability

My argument also has implications for another prevailing account of Indonesian politics, which portrays this polity as characterized by clientelism as the main form of citizen–politician linkages (Aspinall and Sukmajati 2016; Aspinall and Berenschot 2019). Short-term materialistic considerations are the main driver of political behavior according to this analytical framework, which tends to downplay the role of ideological and programmatic factors. My analysis does not aim to challenge the argument that clientelism is a powerful force in Indonesian politics, a hypothesis that is well corroborated in qualitative and quantitative research, but I do aim to show that clientelism is only one of the modes through which voters and politicians interact in this large and diverse democracy, and not necessarily the predominant one. Throughout the book, I have analyzed evidence of the various channels through which ideology matters in Indonesian politics, and I have demonstrated that voters and politicians are fairly well aligned in their views of political Islam, the salient ideological cleavage in Indonesian politics. These findings do not run counter to the hypothesis that clientelism looms large in Indonesia, but complement it. Ideology-based linkages between citizens and politicians are compatible with clientelistic linkages, as voters can choose parties and candidates according to a wide range of differing and sometimes contradicting criteria. My findings also reveal patterns of political participation and accountability that have received much less attention in the literature, which emphasizes the marginality of ideological and programmatic considerations in shaping voting behavior. I thus underscore the importance of an additional layer of representation and accountability that has a similar role to clientelism in ensuring sufficient levels of inclusion and legitimacy for the Indonesian political system. Indonesia is being kept together not only by clientelism and short-term transactional politics but also by a binding deep-seated cleavage, an axis of ideological contestation where Indonesians of various political orientations find meaning and purpose.

Another well-established view of voting behavior in Indonesia based on quantitative studies of survey data (Mujani, Liddle and Ambardi 2018) also tends to downplay the role of ideological and religious factors in shaping voting choices. In contrast with studies of clientelism, however, this literature indicates that Indonesians vote according to evaluations of economic and institutional performance rather than based on the selective and targeted benefits typically involved in clientelistic exchanges. My analysis complements this approach by showing first, that ideology should be taken seriously as one of the key drivers of voting behavior in the Indonesian electorate. As I have shown elsewhere with reference to local politics, Indonesian do vote retrospectively based on their evaluation of government performance (Fossati 2018), but this is only part of the picture, especially pertaining to voting in legislative elections, where partisan and ideological factors may be more salient than in local

8.2 Indonesia: A Democracy in Decline?

electoral races. The cleavage over political Islam structures public attitudes on a number of consequential issues, and voters are, to a degree, sorted into political parties according to their ideological beliefs. We should therefore pay more attention to ideology and systematically include this factor in studies of voting behavior to fully understand the various facets of its impact on voting choices and its interactions with other factors such evaluations of economic performance and candidate traits. Second, my approach calls for a broader conceptualization of democratic performance, as I suggest that voters may evaluate democracy according to various benchmarks. While economic and institutional factors feature prominently among the various yardsticks used to evaluate democracy, we should not underestimate the importance of more "political" goods such as the availability of meaningful avenues for representation and participation. From this perspective, Indonesia has performed better than other democracies in offering such opportunities, and it may therefore be better equipped to weather crises of legitimacy arising from economic crises or low levels of institutional capacity.

The question remains open as to which of the various types of linkages (clientelism, retrospective voting, cleavage-based politics) is most prevalent in shaping patterns of voter mobilization and accountability in contemporary Indonesia. Some of the data that I have analyzed in this book suggest that the importance of the cleavage over political Islam may have increased in recent years. For example, I have shown that electoral participation has risen substantially following the emergence of more polarized politics and the renewed prominence of hardline Islamism, and aggregate levels of satisfaction with democracy have followed a similar trend.[3] Yet the recent repressive campaigns against radical Islam have seriously crippled the Islamist camp's ability to participate in politics, and they may have paved the way to a post-polarization phase of Indonesian democracy in which ideological competition may again become less salient. In either case, a fruitful way to study patterns of voting behavior and accountability is to acknowledge the high degree of diversity among Indonesian voters, who differ substantially in ideological orientation, political knowledge, education, socioeconomic background, place of residence, ethnicity and religion. While some voters may be highly responsive to and easily mobilized by material incentives, others will have strong ideological predispositions and yet others may be only

---

[3] See also Ahyar (2017) on rising Islamism and participation in online media in Indonesia.

marginally interested in politics or informed about it. In a large, diverse democracy such as Indonesia, multiple arenas of accountability, sustained by different logics and dynamics, may therefore coexist and overlap.

Partisan polarization, an issue closely related to democratic accountability, is also typically discussed as a driver of democratic decline in Indonesia, to the extent that the current era of democratic erosion is also described as an era of polarization (Davidson 2018). It is hard to overemphasize the corrosive effect of polarization for democracy. Yet for the Indonesian case, the empirical record is more mixed than is often assumed (Warburton 2019). While qualitative studies convincingly show increasing animosity in political discourse, there is no evidence that Indonesian voters are indeed polarized in a way in which a strong affective attachment to a party or leader is coupled with strong antipathy for the opposing camp. By this measure, Indonesians are not nearly as polarized as voters in many democracies that suffer from the same ailment. Throughout this book, I have presented evidence that Indonesians do vote, in part, according to ideological considerations and that they do rely on political parties and leaders when forming political opinions. However, these are not necessarily signs of increasing polarization, as voters may have recently become more likely to vote according to ideological considerations, and as a result, they may now be better "sorted" into political parties than they used to be. Focusing on the division over political Islam reminds us that voting according to one's own ideological leanings is hardly a malady of democracy, and it does not imply affective polarization. On the contrary, it is a prerequisite for democratic accountability. While this development is disruptive in the context of Indonesian politics, its implications are not necessarily negative; it might also entail a healthy resurgence of traditional, stable partisan identities, which are typically considered conducive to the consolidation of democratic institutions.

A final point of reflection on the nexus between rising Islamism and accountability regards a well-known feature of the Indonesian political system: the lack of a genuine cohesive opposition that could function as a check on executive powers, as parties tend to form ideologically promiscuous coalitions once in power (Slater 2018). During the era of democratic backsliding, Indonesian politics have shown an interesting tension between two powerful historical legacies. Islamism has resurfaced at the center of political debate, a reminder of the enduring nature and relevance of the division over political Islam and the tensions and polarization that it implies and entails. Yet this resurgence of ideology has taken place

8.3 Practical Implications

within the institutional boundaries of a tradition of accommodating, including and co-opting oppositional forces that is a key feature of post-Suharto politics. Since Prabowo Subianto joined the Jokowi administration after the 2019 elections, "cartelization" practices seem to have prevailed and political polarization has considerably decreased. Yet as the Islamist camp mounted a powerful challenge to the Indonesian state, it gave us a glimpse of what more "normal" (i.e., featuring clearly demarcated opposing camps with differentiated political agendas) Indonesian politics could look like. Given the current landscape of Indonesian politics, a cohesive opposition could only take the form of an assertive Islamist camp, and a more prominent role for radical political Islam is a necessary condition for the emergence of this political bloc. There is therefore a trade-off between consolidating liberal values, which requires a clearer separation between religion and politics, and strengthening democratic representation and accountability, which requires ideological congruence between citizens and politicians and transitions of power between clearly identifiable opposing partisan camps. In short, the implications of rising Islamism could again be either negative or positive, depending on what specific dimension of democratic practice is being prioritized.

This book thus contributes to the literature on Indonesian politics by emphasizing relatively underexplored issues. While the literature on Indonesian politics is diverse, its discussion of Indonesia's democratic development in recent years overwhelmingly focuses on negative trends. This book seeks to correct this bias by focusing on ideology and representation. While I do not suggest that these topics are entirely absent from previous studies, I contend that they are not sufficiently analyzed in studies to date, which largely overlook their implications in terms of representation and legitimacy. Democracy in Indonesia, as in any other country, may be more fragile than it appears, but if democratic politics continue to allow for substantive debates and representation rooted in social and ideological identities, we have reason to be confident in the ability of Indonesia's democracy to overcome present and future authoritarian challenges.

8.3 PRACTICAL IMPLICATIONS

The analysis in this book provides new insights into the nature of Indonesian democracy and the challenges that the country's democratic institutions are currently facing. As such, this book also speaks to more policy-oriented debates on how to contain and counter processes of democratic erosion (Lührmann 2021). Venturing into the field of policy prescription is beyond the scope of this work, but we can speculate on the pathways through which Indonesia's democracy could overcome the most pressing challenges that it now faces and, in the medium to long term, become ever stronger.

The first reflection is that the deep-seated ideological division between pluralism and Islamism in Indonesia should be conceived more as a resource than as a limitation. In a polarized political climate, ideological conflict is often discussed as a source of conflict and animosity, but this view should be revised in light of the importance of social divisions to political representation and participation. Disruptive as Indonesia's polarization may appear, such ideological debates matter to many citizens, as they pertain to Indonesia's very essence as a national and civic community. We should welcome the fact that Indonesian politics feature public discussion on such consequential questions. Of course, the most deleterious forms of polarized politics should be avoided in favor of respectful debate and a commitment to compromise between different positions. However, a premise for constructive dialogue is to acknowledge ideological and partisan differences as serious and substantial rather than to denounce the influence of religious, historical or partisan factors as signs of "irrationality" in voting behavior. The division over political Islam is not exclusively a matter of identity politics, as it entails a very important ideological dimension that varies substantially among Muslims (Maksum 2017; Maksum, Febrianto and Wahyuni 2019; Munabari et al. 2020). To the extent that this division *is* identity politics, as it harkens back to historical partisan identities that have survived generations, it is important to remember that such a division, although potentially a source of polarization and conflict, is also a powerful driver of democratic legitimacy and mobilization.

Regarding the rise of radical Islamism, the social and political profile of Islamist Indonesians that emerges from my analysis is one of a marginalized and illiberal group. Indonesian Islamists are markedly less educated and poorer than pluralists, and they present overall lower levels of political sophistication and participation. Because of this unprivileged position and a legacy of exclusion of radical Islam from mainstream Indonesian politics, Islamists tend to hold stronger economic and political grievances, which are often reinforced by a populist worldview. Indonesian Islamists are supportive of electoral democracy but relatively unlikely to hold a liberal understanding of democracy as characterized by checks and balances on executive powers and respect for the rights of ethnic and

8.3 Practical Implications

religious minorities. The increasing influence of Islamist ideals therefore presents a conundrum for Indonesia's democracy. While it could be seen as a step forward in terms of the representation and inclusion of a substantial group of Indonesians whose voices and participation have long been marginalized, it is also clear that this group supports an illiberal agenda that may be even more destructive than inequalities in political representation and inclusion. As in the case of polarization, given this tension between the need to build inclusionary institutions and to ensure that liberal principles are respected, it is difficult to determine at what point the costs outweigh the benefits. However, allowing for a more inclusive and representative political system may be crucial to contain the fallout of this threat to Indonesia's democracy.

Beyond this dilemma between representation and liberalism, the data analyzed in this book give us a better appreciation of the ideological profile of Islamist Indonesians, which could help calibrate policies that address their grievances. In terms of their views on economic policy, Islamists are more supportive of redistribution than any other ideological group, and they ascribe greater salience to economic issues such as inflation and unemployment. This suggests that serious social policies addressing the needs of the less affluent and a taxation regime that promotes a more equitable distribution of resources may be powerful tools to contain the advancement of radical Islam without repressing it. As some scholars argue in other contexts, protecting liberalism requires catering to the preferences of voters drawn to illiberal forces, especially their economic preferences (Diamond 2022). However, given the legacy of fiscally conservative policies and the absence of an economic left in Indonesia's political landscape, it is unlikely that such a policy shift will occur any time soon. In any case, it is important to emphasize that cultural–religious issues are not merely epiphenomenal to economic issues. For this reason, relying on an economic strategy alone to accommodate radical Islamism would probably be insufficient.

A final point regards the pluralist ideological camp and the prospects for a more stable democratic Indonesia. While debates on democratic dissatisfaction tend to focus on Islamist Indonesians, their economic grievances and their populist rhetoric, pluralist Indonesians may also harbor substantial discontent with democratic practice. As I have shown, pluralists are much more likely to endorse liberal notions of democracy, and when liberalism is used as a yardstick to evaluate democracy, perceptions of democratic performance tend to be more negative. To avert legitimacy crises, Indonesia's democracy will thus have to serve two masters, namely the two constituencies at the extremes of the political Islam spectrum: an Islamist one that has forcefully brought to the fore issues of economic inequality and uneven representation, and a pluralist one that is increasingly frustrated with the lack of progress on liberal issues and concerned about the prospect of an even more influential Islamist–illiberal bloc. Preferences and expectations diverge between these two groups, and either may turn its back on democracy if it fails to deliver according to their expectations. The future of democracy in Indonesia will thus hinge upon the willingness and ability of democratic institutions to address and reconcile the wide range of social, economic and political demands of the ordinary citizens of this very diverse nation.

References

Ahyar, Muzayyin. 2017. "Islamic clicktivism: Internet, democracy and contemporary Islamist activism in Surakarta." *Studia Islamika* 24 (3):435–468.

Albright, Jeremy J. 2010. "The multidimensional nature of party competition." *Party Politics* 16 (6):699–719.

Alesina, Alberto, Reza Baqir, and William Easterly. 1999. "Public goods and ethnic divisions." *Quarterly Journal of Economics* 114 (4):1243–1284.

Allen, Nathan W. 2015. "Clientelism and the personal vote in Indonesia." *Electoral Studies* 37:73–85.

Allen, Nathan W., and Shane J. Barter. 2017. "Ummah or tribe? Islamic practice, political ethnocentrism, and political attitudes in Indonesia." *Asian Journal of Political Science* 25 (1):45–67.

Alonso, Sonia, John Keane, and Wolfgang Merkel. 2011. *The Future of Representative Democracy*. New York: Cambridge University Press.

Ambardi, Kuskridho. 2008. "The making of the Indonesian multiparty system: A cartelized party system and its origin." Doctoral dissertation, Political Science, The Ohio State University.

Anderson, Benedict. 1972. *Java in a Time of Revolution*. Ithaca, NY: Cornell University Press.

Andeweg, Rudy B. 2011. "Approaching perfect policy congruence: Measurement, development, and relevance for political representation." In *How Democracy Works: Political Representation and Policy Congruence in Modern Societies*, edited by Martin Rosema, Bas Denters and Kees Aarts, 39–52. Amsterdam: Amsterdam University Press.

Anduiza, Eva, Marc Guinjoan, and Guillem Rico. 2019. "Populism, participation, and political equality." *European Political Science Review* 11 (1):109–124.

Arbatli, Ekim, and Dina Rosenberg. 2021. "United we stand, divided we rule: How political polarization erodes democracy." *Democratization* 28 (2):285–307.

Ariely, Gal. 2013. "Public administration and citizen satisfaction with democracy: Cross-national evidence." *International Review of Administrative Sciences* 79 (4):747–766.

References

Arjon, Sugit Sanjaya. 2018. "Religious sentiments in local politics." *Jurnal Politik* 3 (2):171–198.

Aspinall, Edward. 1996. "The broadening base of political opposition in Indonesia." In *Political Oppositions in Industrializing Asia*, edited by Garry Rodan, 215–240. New York: Routledge.

2005. *Opposing Suharto: Compromise, Resistance, and Regime Change in Indonesia*. Stanford, CA: Stanford University Press.

2010. "Indonesia: The irony of success." *Journal of Democracy* 21 (2):20–34.

2013. "A nation in fragments: Patronage and neoliberalism in contemporary Indonesia." *Critical Asian Studies* 45 (1):27–54.

2015. "Oligarchic populism: Prabowo Subianto's challenge to Indonesian democracy." *Indonesia* 99 (1):1–28.

Aspinall, Edward, and Ward Berenschot. 2019. *Democracy for Sale: Elections, Clientelism, and the State in Indonesia*. Ithaca, NY: Cornell University Press.

Aspinall, Edward, Diego Fossati, Burhanuddin Muhtadi, and Eve Warburton. 2020. "Elite, masses and democratic decline in Indonesia." *Democratisation* 27 (4):505–526.

Aspinall, Edward, and Marcus Mietzner. 2010. *Problems of Democratisation in Indonesia: Elections, Institutions and Society*. Singapore: Institute of Southeast Asian Studies.

2019. "Indonesia's democratic paradox: Competitive elections amidst rising illiberalism." *Bulletin of Indonesian Economic Studies* 55 (3):295–317.

Aspinall, Edward, Marcus Mietzner, and Dirk Tomsa. 2015. *The Yudhoyono Presidency: Indonesia's Decade of Stability and Stagnation*. Singapore: Institute of Southeast Asian Studies.

Aspinall, Edward, and Mada Sukmajati. 2016. *Electoral Dynamics in Indonesia: Money Politics, Patronage and Clientelism at the Grassroots*. Singapore: National University of Singapore Press.

Baker, Reg, J. Michael Brick, Nancy A. Bates, Mike Battaglia, Mick P. Couper, Jill A. Dever, Krista J. Gile, and Roger Tourangeau. 2013. "Summary report of the AAPOR task force on non-probability sampling." *Journal of Survey Statistics and Methodology* 1 (2):90–143.

Bakker, Ryan, Seth Jolly, and Jonathan Polk. 2020. "Multidimensional incongruence, political disaffection, and support for anti-establishment parties." *Journal of European Public Policy* 27 (2):292–309.

Banducci, Susan A., Todd Donovan, and Jeffrey A. Karp. 2004. "Minority representation, empowerment, and participation." *Journal of Politics* 66 (2):534–556.

Barber, Benjamin. 2003. *Strong Democracy: Participatory Politics for a New Age*. Berkeley, CA: University of California Press.

Bartolini, Stefano, and Peter Mair. 2007. *Identity, Competition and Electoral Availability: The Stabilisation of European Electorates 1885–1985*. Colchester: ECPR Press.

Baswedan, Anies Rasyid. 2004. "Political Islam in Indonesia: Present and future trajectory." *Asian Survey* 44 (5):669–690.

Belchior, Ana Maria. 2013. "Explaining left–right party congruence across European party systems: A test of micro-, meso-, and macro-level models." *Comparative Political Studies* 46 (3):352–386.

References

Benda, Harry J. 1964. "Democracy in Indonesia." *Journal of Asian Studies* 23 (3):449–456.

Bermeo, Nancy. 2016. "On democratic backsliding." *Journal of Democracy* 27 (1):5–19.

Birch, Anthony H. 2007. *Concepts and Theories of Modern Democracy*. New York: Routledge.

Blaydes, Lisa, and Drew A. Linzer. 2008. "The political economy of women's support for fundamentalist Islam." *World Politics* 60 (4):576–609.

Bleck, Jaimie, and Nicolas Van de Walle. 2013. "Valence issues in African elections: Navigating uncertainty and the weight of the past." *Comparative Political Studies* 46 (11):1394–1421.

Bone, Robert C. 1955. "Organization of the Indonesian elections." *American Political Science Review* 49 (4):1067–1084.

Bourchier, David. 2014. *Illiberal Democracy in Indonesia: The Ideology of the Family State*. New York: Routledge.

2019. "Two decades of ideological contestation in Indonesia: From democratic cosmopolitanism to religious nationalism." *Journal of Contemporary Asia* 49 (5):713–733.

Bowler, Shaun, David Denemark, Todd Donovan, and Duncan McDonnell. 2017. "Right-wing populist party supporters: Dissatisfied but not direct democrats." *European Journal of Political Research* 56 (1):70–91.

Brady, Henry E., Sidney Verba, and Kay Lehman Schlozman. 1995. "Beyond SES: A resource model of political participation." *American Political Science Review* 89 (2):271–294.

Buehler, Michael. 2016. *The Politics of Shari'a Law: Islamist Activists and the State in Democratizing Indonesia*. Cambridge: Cambridge University Press.

Bush, Robin. 2009. *Nahdlatul Ulama and the Struggle for Power within Islam and Politics in Indonesia*. Singapore: Institute of Southeast Asian Studies.

Camp, Roderic Ai. 2001. *Citizen Views of Democracy in Latin America*. Pittsburgh: University of Pittsburgh Press.

Canache, Damarys, Jeffery J Mondak, and Mitchell A Seligson. 2001. "Meaning and measurement in cross-national research on satisfaction with democracy." *Public Opinion Quarterly* 65 (4):506–528.

Caraway, Teri L. 2021. "Labor's reversal of fortune: Contentious politics and executive aggrandizement in Indonesia." *Social Movement Studies* 1–17.

Caraway, Teri L., and Michele Ford. 2020. *Labor and Politics in Indonesia*. Cambridge: Cambridge University Press.

Carnes, Nicholas. 2012. "Does the numerical underrepresentation of the working class in Congress matter?" *Legislative Studies Quarterly* 37 (1):5–34.

Cho, Youngho. 2014. "To know democracy is to love it: A cross-national analysis of democratic understanding and political support for democracy." *Political Research Quarterly* 67 (3):478–488.

Chu, Yun-han, Yu-Tzung Chang, Min-hua Huang, and Mark Weatherall. 2016. *Re-Assessing the Popular Foundations of Asian Democracies: Findings from Four Waves of the Asian Barometer Survey*. Taipei: National Taiwan University.

Chu, Yun-han, and Min-hua Huang. 2010. "The meanings of democracy: Solving an Asian puzzle." *Journal of Democracy* 21 (4):114–122.

Chua, Christian. 2004. "Defining Indonesian Chineseness under the new order." *Journal of Contemporary Asia* 34 (4):465–479.

Claassen, Christopher. 2020. "Does public support help democracy survive?" *American Journal of Political Science* 64 (1):118–134.

Clifford, Scott, Ryan M. Jewell, and Philip D. Waggoner. 2015. "Are samples drawn from Mechanical Turk valid for research on political ideology?" *Research & Politics* 2 (4). https://doi.org/10.1177/2053168015622072.

Cochrane, Joe. 2020. "Indonesia sours on democracy as coronavirus ravages economy, survey finds." *South China Morning Post*, June 11.

Cohen, Joshua. 1997. "Procedure and substance in deliberative democracy." In *Deliberative Democracy: Essays on Reason and Politics*, edited by James Bohman and William Rehg, 407–438. Cambridge, MA: MIT Press.

Cordero, Guillermo, and Pablo Simón. 2016. "Economic crisis and support for democracy in Europe." *West European Politics* 39 (2):305–325.

Costello, Rory, Jacques Thomassen, and Martin Rosema. 2012. "European parliament elections and political representation: Policy congruence between voters and parties." *West European Politics* 35 (6):1226–1248.

Croissant, Aurel, and Philip Völkel. 2012. "Party system types and party system institutionalization: Comparing new democracies in East and Southeast Asia." *Party Politics* 18 (2):235–265.

Crouch, Harold. 2010. *Political Reform in Indonesia after Soeharto*. Singapore: Institute of Southeast Asian Studies.

Cunningham, Frank. 2002. *Theories of Democracy: A Critical Introduction*. New York: Routledge.

Curato, Nicole, and Diego Fossati. 2020. "Authoritarian innovations." *Democratisation* 27 (6):1006–1020.

Dahlberg, Stefan, Jonas Linde, and Sören Holmberg. 2015. "Democratic discontent in old and new democracies: Assessing the importance of democratic input and governmental output." *Political Studies* 63:18–37.

Dalton, Russell J. 1985. "Political parties and political representation: Party supporters and party elites in nine nations." *Comparative Political Studies* 18 (3):267–299.

2006. "Social modernization and the end of ideology debate: Patterns of ideological polarization." *Japanese Journal of Political Science* 7 (1):1–22.

2008. "The quantity and the quality of party systems: Party system polarization, its measurement, and its consequences." *Comparative Political Studies* 41 (7):899–920.

2017. "Party representation across multiple issue dimensions." *Party Politics* 23 (6):609–622.

Dalton, Russell J., To-ch'öl Sin, and Willy Jou. 2007. "Understanding democracy: Data from unlikely places." *Journal of Democracy* 18 (4):142–156.

Dalton, Russell J., and Steven Weldon. 2007. "Partisanship and party system institutionalization." *Party politics* 13 (2):179–196.

Davidson, Jamie S. 2018. *Indonesia: Twenty Years of Democracy*. Cambridge: Cambridge University Press.

De Vries, Catherine E., Armen Hakhverdian, and Bram Lancee. 2013. "The dynamics of voters' left/right identification: The role of economic and cultural attitudes." *Political Science Research and Methods* 1 (2):223–238.

References

Diamond, Larry. 2022. "January 6 and the paradoxes of America's democracy agenda: Why protecting liberalism will require a dose of populism." *Foreign Affairs*, January 6.

Dibley, Thushara, and Michele Ford. 2019. *Activists in Transition: Progressive Politics in Democratic Indonesia*. Ithaca, NY: Cornell University Press.

Diprose, Rachael, Dave McRae, and Vedi R. Hadiz. 2019. "Two decades of Reformasi in Indonesia: Its illiberal turn." *Journal of Contemporary Asia* 49 (5):691–712.

Easton, David. 1975. "A re-assessment of the concept of political support." *British Journal of Political Science* 5 (4):435–457.

Ekiert, Grzegorz, and Daniel Ziblatt. 2013. "Democracy in Central and Eastern Europe one hundred years on." *East European Politics and Societies* 27 (1):90–107.

Evans, Geoffrey. 2006. "The social bases of political divisions in post-communist Eastern Europe." *Annual Review of Sociology* 32:245–270.

Evans, Geoffrey, and Stephen Whitefield. 1995. "The politics and economics of democratic commitment: Support for democracy in transition societies." *British Journal of Political Science* 25 (4):485–514.

Fails, Matthew D., and Heather Nicole Pierce. 2010. "Changing mass attitudes and democratic deepening." *Political Research Quarterly* 63 (1): 174–187.

Fair, C. Christine, Rebecca Littman, and Elizabeth R. Nugent. 2018. "Conceptions of Sharia and support for militancy and democratic values: Evidence from Pakistan." *Political Science Research and Methods* 6 (3):429–448.

Fawcett, Edmund. 2018. *Liberalism: The Life of an Idea*. Princeton, NJ: Princeton University Press.

Fealy, Greg, and Sally White. 2008. *Expressing Islam: Religious Life and Politics in Indonesia*: Institute of Southeast Asian Studies.

2021. "The politics of banning FPI." *New Mandala*, June 18.

Fearon, James D. 1999. "Why ethnic politics and 'pork' tend to go together." In *SSRC-MacArthur Sponsored Conference on "Ethnic Politics and Democratic Stability*," University of Chicago.

Feith, Herbert. 1962. *The Decline of Constitutional Democracy in Indonesia*. Ithaca, NY: Cornell University Press.

Fernandez, Kenneth E., and Michele Kuenzi. 2010. "Crime and support for democracy in Africa and Latin America." *Political Studies* 58 (3):450–471.

Ferrín, Mónica, and Hanspeter Kriesi. 2016. *How Europeans View and Evaluate Democracy*. Oxford: Oxford University Press.

Fishkin, James S. 1991. *Democracy and Deliberation: New Directions for Democratic Reform*. New Haven, CT: Yale University Press

Foa, Roberto Stefan, and Yascha Mounk. 2016. "The danger of deconsolidation: The democratic disconnect." *Journal of Democracy* 27 (3):5–17.

2017. "The signs of deconsolidation." *Journal of Democracy* 28 (1):5–15.

Fogg, Kevin William. 2012. *The Fate of Muslim Nationalism in Independent Indonesia*. New Haven, CT: Yale University.

Fossati, Diego. 2016. "Is Indonesian local government accountable to the poor? Evidence from health policy implementation." *Journal of East Asian Studies* 16 (3):307–330.

2018. "A tale of three cities: Electoral accountability in Indonesian local politics." *Journal of Contemporary Asia* 48 (1):23–49.

forthcoming. "When conservatives support decentralization: The case of political Islam in Indonesia." *Regional & Federal Studies* 1–25.

Fossati, Diego, Edward Aspinall, Burhan Muhtadi, and Eve Warburton. 2020. "Ideological representation in clientelistic democracies: The Indonesian case." *Electoral Studies* 63.

Fossati, Diego, and Ferran Martinez i Coma. 2020a. "Exploring citizen turnout and invalid voting in Indonesia: Two sides of the same coin?" *Contemporary Politics* 26 (2):125–146.

2020b. "How popular conceptions of democracy shape democratic support in Indonesia." In *Democracy in Indonesia: From Stagnation to Regression?* edited by Thomas Power and Eve Warburton, 166–188. Singapore: ISEAS.

Fossati, Diego, and Marcus Mietzner. 2019. "Analyzing Indonesia's populist electorate: Demographic, ideological and attitudinal trends." *Asian Survey* 59 (5):769–794.

Fossati, Diego, Burhanuddin Muhtadi, and Eve Warburton. 2022. "Why democrats abandon democracy: Evidence from four survey experiments." *Party Politics* 28 (3):554–566.

Geertz, Clifford. 1960. *The Religion of Java.* Chicago: University of Chicago Press.

Gethin, Amory, Clara Martínez-Toledano, and Thomas Piketty. 2021. *Political Cleavages and Social Inequalities: A Study of Fifty Democracies, 1948–2020.* Cambridge, MA: Harvard University Press.

Gilley, Bruce. 2006. "The determinants of state legitimacy: Results for 72 countries." *International Political Science Review* 27 (1):47–71.

Glasius, Marlies. 2018. "What authoritarianism is… and is not: A practice perspective." *International Affairs* 94 (3):515–533.

Golder, Matt, and Jacek Stramski. 2010. "Ideological congruence and electoral institutions." *American Journal of Political Science* 54 (1):90–106.

Graham, Matthew, and Milan W. Svolik. 2020. "Democracy in America? Partisanship, polarization, and the robustness of support for democracy in the United States." *American Political Science Review* 114 (2):392–409.

Hadiz, Vedi R. 2002. "The Indonesian labour movement: Resurgent or constrained?" *Southeast Asian Affairs* 130–142.

Hadiz, Vedi R., and Richard Robison. 2017. "Competing populisms in post-authoritarian Indonesia." *International Political Science Review* 38 (4): 488–502.

Hadiz, Vedi R. 2018. "Imagine all the people? Mobilising Islamic populism for right-wing politics in Indonesia." *Journal of Contemporary Asia* 48 (4): 566–583.

Hadiz, Vedi R., and Richard Robison. 2013. "The political economy of oligarchy and the reorganization of power in Indonesia." *Indonesia* 96 (1):35–57.

Hamayotsu, Kikue. 2002. "Islam and nation building in Southeast Asia: Malaysia and Indonesia in comparative perspective." *Pacific Affairs* 75 (3):353–375.

Haq, Muhammad Naziful. 2021. "Patronizing the mass: How middle-agents deepened populism and post-truth in Indonesia 2019 presidential election." *Jurnal Politik* 7 (1):75–104.

References

He, Baogang, and Hendrik Wagenaar. 2018. "Authoritarian deliberation revisited." *Japanese Journal of Political Science* 19 (4):622–629.

Hefner, Robert W. 2011. *Civil Islam: Muslims and Democratization in Indonesia*. Vol. 40. Princeton, NJ: Princeton University Press.

Helmke, Gretchen, and Steven Levitsky. 2006. *Informal Institutions and Democracy: Lessons from Latin America*. Baltimore: The John Hopkins University Press.

Hicken, A. 2011. "Clientelism." *Annual Review of Political Science* 14:289–310.

Hicken, Allen. 2020. "Indonesia's democracy in comparative perspective." In *Democracy in Indonesia: From Stagnation to Regression?* edited by Thomas Power and Eve Warburton, 23–44. Singapore: ISEAS.

Hicks, Jacqueline. 2012. "The missing link: Explaining the political mobilisation of Islam in Indonesia." *Journal of Contemporary Asia* 42 (1):39–66.

Hidayat, Budi, Hasbullah Thabrany, Hengjin Dong, and Rainer Sauerborn. 2004. "The effects of mandatory health insurance on equity in access to outpatient care in Indonesia." *Health Policy and Planning* 19 (5):322–335.

Hindley, Donald. 1970. "Alirans and the Fall of the Old Order." *Indonesia* (9):23–66.

Honna, Jun. 2013. *Military Politics and Democratization in Indonesia*. New York: Routledge.

Horowitz, Donald L. 2013. *Constitutional Change and Democracy in Indonesia*. Cambridge: Cambridge University Press.

Huang, Min-hua. 2017. "Congnitive involvement and democratic understanding." In *Routledge Handbook of Democratization in East Asia*, edited by Tun-jen Cheng and Yun-han Chu, 297–313. London: Routledge.

Huang, Min-hua, Yu-tzung Chang, and Yun-han Chu. 2008. "Identifying sources of democratic legitimacy: A multilevel analysis." *Electoral Studies* 27 (1): 45–62.

Huber, Evelyne, Dietrich Rueschemeyer, and John D. Stephens. 1997. "The paradoxes of contemporary democracy: Formal, participatory, and social dimensions." *Comparative Politics* 29 (3):323–342.

Huber, John D., and G. Bingham Powell. 1994. "Congruence between citizens and policymakers in two visions of liberal democracy." *World Politics* 46 (3):291–326.

Huber, Robert A., and Saskia P. Ruth. 2017. "Mind the gap! Populism, participation and representation in Europe." *Swiss Political Science Review* 23 (4): 462–484.

Ikhwan, Hakimul. 2018. "Fitted sharia in democratizing Indonesia." *Journal of Indonesian Islam* 12:17–44.

Inglehart, Ronald. 1997. *Modernization and Postmodernization: Cultural, Economic, and Political Change in 43 Societies*. Princeton, NJ: Princeton University Press.

Inglehart, Ronald, and Pippa Norris. 2016. "Trump, Brexit, and the rise of populism: Economic have-nots and cultural backlash." *HKS Working Paper* (RWP16–026).

Jamal, Amaney, and Mark Tessler. 2008. "The democracy barometers (Part II): Attitudes in the Arab world." *Journal of Democracy* 19 (1):97–111.

Jamhari, Jamhari, and Yunita Faela Nisa. 2021. "Voices from Indonesian legislative on religious education policy." *Studia Islamika* 28 (1):245–252.

Jones, Frank L., and Philip Smith. 2001. "Diversity and commonality in national identities: An exploratory analysis of cross-national patterns." *Journal of Sociology* 37 (1):45–63.

Jou, Willy, and Russell J. Dalton. 2017. *Left-Right Orientations and Voting Behavior*. Oxford: Oxford University Press.

Kaltwasser, Cristóbal Rovira. 2012. "The ambivalence of populism: Threat and corrective for democracy." *Democratization* 19 (2):184–208.

Keefer, Philip. 2007. "Clientelism, credibility, and the policy choices of young democracies." *American Journal of Political Science* 51 (4):804–821.

King, Dwight Y. 2003. *Half-Hearted Reform: Electoral Institutions and the Struggle for Democracy in Indonesia*. Santa Barbara, CA: Greenwood Publishing Group.

Klein, Ezra. 2020. *Why We're Polarized*. New York: Simon and Schuster.

Kohn, Hans. 1944. *The Idea of Nationalism: A Study in Its Origin and Background*. London: Transaction.

Kriesi, Hanspeter. 2018. "The implications of the euro crisis for democracy." *Journal of European Public Policy* 25 (1):59–82.

Kriesi, Hanspeter, Edgar Grande, Romain Lachat, Martin Dolezal, Simon Bornschier, and Timotheos Frey. 2008. *West European politics in the age of globalization*. Vol. 6. Cambridge: Cambridge University Press.

Kuipers, Nick. 2019. "Who's running on political Islam in Indonesia?" *New Mandala*, March 26.

Kusumo, Rangga, and Hurriyah Hurriyah. 2018. "Populisme Islam di Indonesia: Studi Kasus Aksi Bela Islam oleh GNPF-MUI Tahun 2016–2017." *Jurnal Politik* 4 (1):87–114.

Laffan, Michael Francis. 2003. *Islamic nationhood and colonial Indonesia: The umma below the winds*. New York: Routledge.

Latif, Yudi. 2018. "The religiosity, nationality, and sociality of Pancasila: Toward Pancasila through Soekarno's way." *Studia Islamika* 25 (2): 207–245.

Laver, Michael. 2014. "Measuring policy positions in political space." *Annual Review of Political Science* 17:207–223.

LeBas, Adrienne. 2018. "Can polarization be positive? Conflict and institutional development in Africa." *American Behavioral Scientist* 62 (1):59–74.

Lefkofridi, Zoe, Nathalie Giger, and Aina Gallego. 2014. "Electoral participation in pursuit of policy representation: Ideological congruence and voter turnout." *Journal of Elections, Public Opinion and Parties* 24 (3):291–311.

Levitsky, Steven, and Daniel Ziblatt. 2018. *How Democracies Die*. New York: Broadway Books.

Liddle, R. Willam. 1978. "Participation and the political parties." In *Political power and communications in Indonesia*, edited by Karl D. Jackson and Lucian W. Pye. Berkeley: University of California Press.

Lindberg, Staffan I., Michael Coppedge, John Gerring, and Jan Teorell. 2014. "V-Dem: A new way to measure democracy." *Journal of Democracy* 25 (3): 159–169.

References

Lipset, Seymour M., and Stein Rokkan. 1967. "Cleavage structures, party systems, and voter alignments: An introduction." In *Party Systems and Voter Alignments: Cross-National Perspectives*, edited by Seymour M. Lipset and Stein Rokkan, 1–64. Toronto: The Free Press.

Lührmann, Anna. 2021. "Disrupting the autocratization sequence: Towards democratic resilience." *Democratization* 28 (5):1017–1039.

Lührmann, Anna, and Staffan I. Lindberg. 2019. "A third wave of autocratization is here: What is new about it?" *Democratization* 27 (7):1095–1113.

Luna, Juan P., and Elizabeth J. Zechmeister. 2005. "Political representation in Latin America: A study of elite-mass congruence in nine countries." *Comparative Political Studies* 38 (4):388–416.

Lupu, Noam. 2015. "Party polarization and mass partisanship: A comparative perspective." *Political Behavior* 37 (2):331–356.

Lussier, Danielle N. 2016. *Constraining Elites in Russia and Indonesia: Political Participation and Regime Survival*. New York: Cambridge University Press.

Lussier, Danielle N., and M. Steven Fish. 2012. "Indonesia: The benefits of civic engagement." *Journal of Democracy* 23 (1):70–84.

Mackie, James Austin Copland. 1976. "Anti-Chinese outbreaks in Indonesia, 1959–1968." In *The Chinese in Indonesia: Five Essays*, edited by James Austin Copland Mackie, 77–138. Honolulu: University of Hawaii Press.

Maerz, Seraphine F., Anna Lührmann, Sebastian Hellmeier, Sandra Grahn, and Staffan I. Lindberg. 2020. "State of the world 2019: Autocratization surges-resistance grows." *Democratization* 27 (6):909–927.

Magalhães, Pedro C. 2014. "Government effectiveness and support for democracy." *European Journal of Political Research* 53 (1):77–97.

2016. "Economic evaluations, procedural fairness, and satisfaction with democracy." *Political Research Quarterly* 69 (3):522–534.

Mainwaring, Scott, and Mariano Torcal. 2006. "Party system institutionalization and party system theory after the third wave of democratization." *Handbook of Party Politics* 11 (6):204–227.

Mair, Peter. 2007. "Left–right orientations." In *The Oxford Handbook of Political Behavior*, edited by Russell J. Dalton and Hans-Dieter Klingemann. Oxford: Oxford University Press.

Maksum, Ali. 2017. "Discourses on Islam and democracy in Indonesia: A study on the intellectual debate between Liberal Islam network (JIL) and Hizbut Tahrir Indonesia (HTI)." *Journal of Indonesian Islam* 11 (2):405–422.

Maksum, Ali, Priyono Tri Febrianto, and Esa Nur Wahyuni. 2019. "Interpretation of democracy, pluralism and tolerance among the young activists of Muhammadiyah and Nahdlatul Ulama." *Masyarakat, Kebudayaan dan Politik* 32 (3):275–289.

Masykuri, Romel, and Mohammad Fajar Shodiq Ramadlan. 2021. "Analisis Manifestasi Segregasi Politik Pelabelan dan Polarisasi di antara Kelompok Islam Sepanjang 2014–2019." *Politika: Jurnal Ilmu Politik* 12 (1):68–87.

Mattes, Robert, and Michael Bratton. 2007. "Learning about democracy in Africa: Awareness, performance, and experience." *American Journal of Political Science* 51 (1):192–217.

McCoy, Jennifer, Tahmina Rahman, and Murat Somer. 2018. "Polarization and the global crisis of democracy: Common patterns, dynamics, and pernicious consequences for democratic polities." *American Behavioral Scientist* 62 (1): 16–42.

Mechkova, Valeriya, Anna Lührmann, and Staffan I Lindberg. 2017. "How much democratic backsliding?" *Journal of Democracy* 28 (4):162–169.

Menchik, Jeremy. 2014. "Productive intolerance: Godly nationalism in Indonesia." *Comparative Studies in Society and History* 56 (3):591–621.

2016. *Islam and Democracy in Indonesia: Tolerance Without Liberalism.* New York: Cambridge University Press.

Mietzner, Marcus. 2006. "The politics of military reform in post-Suharto Indonesia: Elite conflict, nationalism, and institutional resistance." *Policy Studies* (23):I. https://www.eastwestcenter.org/publications/politics-military-reform-post-suharto-indonesia-elite-conflict-nationalism-and-institut

2008. "Comparing Indonesia's party systems of the 1950s and the post-Suharto era: From centrifugal to centripetal inter-party competition." *Journal of Southeast Asian Studies* 39 (3):431–453.

2013. *Money, Power, and Ideology: Political Parties in Post-authoritarian Indonesia.* Singapore: NUS Press.

2018. "Fighting illiberalism with illiberalism: Islamist populism and democratic deconsolidation in Indonesia." *Pacific Affairs* 91 (2):261–282.

Mietzner, Marcus, and Burhanuddin Muhtadi. 2018. "Explaining the 2016 Islamist mobilisation in Indonesia: Religious intolerance, militant groups and the politics of accommodation." *Asian Studies Review* 42 (3): 479–497.

2020. "The myth of pluralism: Nahdlatul Ulama and the politics of religious tolerance in Indonesia." *Contemporary Southeast Asia: A Journal of International and Strategic Affairs* 42 (1):58–84.

Mietzner, Marcus, Burhanuddin Muhtadi, and Rizka Halida. 2018. "Entrepreneurs of grievance: Drivers and effects of Indonesia's Islamist mobilization." *Bijdragen tot de taal-, land-en volkenkunde/Journal of the Humanities and Social Sciences of Southeast Asia* 174 (2–3):159–187.

Minardi, Anton. 2019. "The new movement of Islamic revivalist accommodationist and confrontationist (Prosperous Justice Party and Hizb ut-Tahrir)." *Journal of Indonesian Islam* 12 (2):247–264.

Morgenbesser, Lee. 2020. *The Rise of Sophisticated Authoritarianism in Southeast Asia.* New York: Cambridge University Press.

Mudde, Cas. 2004. "The populist zeitgeist." *Government and Opposition* 39 (4): 541–563.

Muharam, Moch Mubarok, Kacung Marijan, and Airlangga Pribadi Kusman. 2021. "Power relation of the 212 Islamic Group and the government in the 2019 presidential election." *Masyarakat, Kebudayaan dan Politik* 34 (3): 305–316.

Muhtadi, Burhanuddin. 2019. *Vote Buying in Indonesia: The Mechanics of Electoral Bribery.* Singapore: Springer.

Muhtadi, Burhanuddin, and Eve Warburton. 2020. "Inequality and democratic support in Indonesia." *Pacific Affairs* 93 (1):31–58.

References

Mujani, Saiful. 2003. "Religious democrats: Democratic culture and Muslim political participation in post-Suharto Indonesia." Doctoral dissertation, Political Science, The Ohio State University.

———. 2019. "Explaining religio-political tolerance among Muslims: Evidence from Indonesia." *Studia Islamika* 26 (2):319–351.

———. 2020. "Intolerant democrat syndrome: The problem of Indonesian democratic consolidation." *Jurnal Politik* 6 (1):7–38.

Mujani, Saiful, and R. William Liddle. 2015. "Indonesia's democratic performance: A popular assessment." *Japanese Journal of Political Science* 16 (2):210–226.

———. 2021. "Indonesia: Jokowi Sidelines Democracy." *Journal of Democracy* 32 (4): 72–86.

Mujani, Saiful, R. William Liddle, and Kuskridho Ambardi. 2018. *Voting Behaviour in Indonesia since Democratization: Critical Democrats.* Cambridge: Cambridge University Press.

Mujani, Saiful, and R. William Liddle. 2009. "Muslim Indonesia's secular democracy." *Asian Survey* 49 (4):575–590.

———. 2010. "Personalities, parties, and voters." *Journal of Democracy* 21 (2):35–49.

Munabari, Fahlesa, Nadia Utami Larasati, Rizky Ihsan, and Lucky Nurhadiyanto. 2020. "Islamic revivalism in Indonesia: The Caliphate, Sharia, NKRI, Democracy, and the Nation-State." *Jurnal Politik* 5 (2):281–312.

Nordholt, Henk Schulte. 2005. "Decentralisation in Indonesia: Less state, more democracy?" In *Politicising Democracy*, edited by John Harriss, Kristian Stokke and Olle Törnquist, 29–50. London: Palgrave Macmillan.

Norris, Pippa. 1997. "Representation and the democratic deficit." *European Journal of Political Research* 32 (2):273–282.

———. 1999. *Critical Citizens: Global Support for Democratic Government.* Oxford: Oxford University Press.

———. 2011. *Democratic Deficit: Critical Citizens Revisited.* New York: Cambridge University Press.

Nuraniyah, Nava. 2021. "The cost of repressing Islam." *New Mandala*, October 29.

Papke, Leslie E., and Jeffrey M. Wooldridge. 1996. "Econometric methods for fractional response variables with an application to 401 (k) plan participation rates." *Journal of Applied Econometrics* 11 (6):619–632.

Pauker, Guy J. 1958. "The Role of Political Organizations in Indonesia." *Far Eastern Survey* 27 (9):129–142.

Pauwels, Teun. 2014. *Populism in Western Europe: Comparing Belgium, Germany and the Netherlands.* London: Routledge.

Pepinsky, Thomas B. 2009. *Economic Crises and the Breakdown of Authoritarian Regimes: Indonesia and Malaysia in Comparative Perspective.* New York: Cambridge University Press.

Pepinsky, Thomas B., R. William Liddle, and Saiful Mujani. 2018. *Piety and Public Opinion: Understanding Indonesian Islam.* Oxford: Oxford University Press.

———. 2012. "Testing Islam's political advantage: Evidence from Indonesia." *American Journal of Political Science* 56 (3):584–600.

Pisani, Elizabeth, and Michael Buehler. 2017. "Why do Indonesian politicians promote shari'a laws? An analytic framework for Muslim-majority democracies." *Third World Quarterly* 38 (3):734–752.

Pitkin, Hanna F. 1967. *The concept of representation*. Berkeley: University of California Press.

Powell, G. Bingham Jr. 2004. "Political representation in comparative politics." *Annu. Rev. Polit. Sci.* 7:273–296.

Power, Thomas. 2018. "Jokowi's authoritarian turn and Indonesia's democratic decline." *Bulletin of Indonesian Economic Studies* 54 (3):307–338.

Power, Thomas P. 2020. "Assailing accountability: Law enforcement politicisation, partisan coercion and executive aggrandisement under the Jokowi administration." In *Democracy in Indonesia: From Stagnation to Regression?* edited by Thomas Power and Eve Warburton, 277–302. Singapore: ISEAS Publishing.

Priohutomo, Hardianto Widyo, Kamarudin Kamarudin, and Syahrul Hidayat. 2019. "The emergence of Gerakan Arah Baru Indonesia (Garbi) and factionalism in Partai Keadilan Sejahtera (PKS)." *Jurnal Politik* 5 (1):29–64.

Przeworski, Adam, Michael Alvarez, Jose Cheibub, and Fernando Limongi. 2000. *Democracy and Development: Political Institutions and Well-Being in the World, 1950–1990*. New York: Cambridge University Press.

Purdey, Jemma. 2005. "Anti-Chinese violence and transitions in Indonesia." In *Chinese Indonesians: Remembering, Distorting, Forgetting*, edited by Tim Lindsey and Helen Pausacker, 14–40. Singapore: ISEAS Press.

Reeskens, Tim, and Marc Hooghe. 2010. "Beyond the civic–ethnic dichotomy: Investigating the structure of citizenship concepts across thirty-three countries." *Nations and Nationalism* 16 (4):579–597.

Reher, Stefanie. 2014. "The effect of congruence in policy priorities on electoral participation." *Electoral Studies* 36:158–172.

2015. "Explaining cross-national variation in the relationship between priority congruence and satisfaction with democracy." *European Journal of Political Research* 54 (1):160–181.

2016. "The effects of congruence in policy priorities on satisfaction with democracy." *Journal of Elections, Public Opinion and Parties* 26 (1):40–57.

Rehfeld, Andrew. 2009. "Representation rethought: On trustees, delegates, and gyroscopes in the study of political representation and democracy." *American Political Science Review* 103 (2):214–230.

Robinson, Kathryn. 2008. *Gender, Islam and Democracy in Indonesia*. Vol. 6. New York: Routledge.

Robison, Joshua, and Rachel L. Moskowitz. 2019. "The group basis of partisan affective polarization." *The Journal of Politics* 81 (3):1075–1079.

Robison, Richard, and Vedi R. Hadiz. 2017. "Indonesia: A tale of misplaced expectations." *The Pacific Review* 30 (6):895–909.

Rocha, Rene R., Caroline J. Tolbert, Daniel C. Bowen, and Christopher J. Clark. 2010. "Race and turnout: Does descriptive representation in state legislatures increase minority voting?" *Political Research Quarterly* 63 (4):890–907.

Rohrschneider, Robert. 2002. "The democracy deficit and mass support for an EU-wide government." *American Journal of Political Science* 46 (2):463–475.

References

Rose, Richard, William Mishler, and Christian Haerpfer. 1998. *Democracy and Its Alternatives: Understanding Post-communist Societies.* Baltimore: The John Hopkins University Press.

Schäfer, Constantin, and Marc Debus. 2018. "No participation without representation: Policy distances and abstention in European Parliament elections." *Journal of European Public Policy* 25 (12):1835–1854.

Schraufnagel, Scot, Michael Buehler, and Maureen Lowry-Fritz. 2014. "Voter turnout in democratizing Southeast Asia: A comparative analysis of electoral participation in five countries." *Taiwan Journal of Democracy* 10 (1):1–22.

Sebastian, Leonard C., Syafiq Hasyim, and Alexander R. Arifianto. 2020. *Rising Islamic Conservatism in Indonesia: Islamic Groups and Identity Politics.* New York: Routledge.

Septiana, Elis Nugraha, Ridho Al-Hamdi, and Adibah Dhivani Gusmi. 2020. "Aksi 212 dan Kemenangan Anies-Sandi pada Pemilihan Gubernur Jakarta 2017." *JISPO Jurnal Ilmu Sosial dan Ilmu Politik* 10 (2):211–230.

Shefter, Martin. 1977. "Party and patronage: Germany, England, and Italy." *Politics and Society* 7 (4):403–451.

Shiraishi, Takashi. 1997. "Anti-sinicism in Java's new order." In *Essential Outsiders: Chinese and Jews in the Modern Transformation of Southeast Asia and Central Europe*, edited by Daniel Chirot and Anthony Reid, 187–207. Seattle, University of Washington Press.

Shulman, Stephen. 2002. "Challenging the civic/ethnic and West/East dichotomies in the study of nationalism." *Comparative Political Studies* 35 (5):554–585.

Sidel, John T. 2012. "The fate of nationalism in the new states: Southeast Asia in comparative historical perspective." *Comparative Studies in Society and History* 54 (1):114–144.

Sidel, John Thayer. 2006. *Riots, Pogroms, Jihad: Religious Violence in Indonesia.* Ithaca, NY: Cornell University Press.

2008. "Social origins of dictatorship and democracy revisited: Colonial state and Chinese immigrant in the making of modern Southeast Asia." *Comparative Politics* 40 (2):127–147.

Slater, Dan. 2018. "Party cartelization, Indonesian-style: Presidential power-sharing and the contingency of democratic opposition." *Journal of East Asian Studies* 18 (1):23–46.

2020. "Indonesia's tenuous democratic success and survival." In *Democracy in Indonesia: From Stagnation to Regression?* edited by Thomas Power and Eve Warburton, 45–62. Singapore: ISEAS.

Stecker, Christian, and Markus Tausendpfund. 2016. "Multidimensional government-citizen congruence and satisfaction with democracy." *European Journal of Political Research* 55 (3):492–511.

Sumaktoyo, Nathanael. 2019. "How "moderate" are Indonesian Muslims?" *New Mandala*, March 27.

Suryadinata, Leo. 2005. *Pribumi Indonesians, the Chinese Minority, and China: A Study of Perceptions and Policies*: Marshall Cavendish International.

Svolik, Milan W. 2018. "When polarization trumps civic virtue: Partisan conflict and the subversion of democracy by incumbents." *Available at SSRN 3243470*.

References

Svolik, Milan W. 2019. "Polarization versus Democracy." *Journal of Democracy* 30 (3):20–32.

Tan, Paige Johnson. 2012. "Reining in the reign of the parties: Political parties in contemporary Indonesia." *Asian Journal of Political Science* 20 (2):154–179.

Tanuwidjaja, Sunny. 2010. "Political Islam and Islamic parties in Indonesia: Critically assessing the evidence of Islam's political decline." *Contemporary Southeast Asia: A Journal of International and Strategic Affairs* 32 (1):29–49.

2012. "PKS in post-reformasi Indonesia: Catching the catch-all and moderation wave." *South East Asia Research* 20 (4):533–549.

Tessler, Mark, Amaney Jamal, and Michael Robbins. 2012. "New findings on Arabs and democracy." *Journal of Democracy* 23 (4):89–103.

Tomsa, Dirk. 2008. *Party Politics and Democratization in Indonesia: Golkar in the post-Suharto Era*. New York: Routledge.

Ufen, Andreas. 2008a. The evolution of cleavages in the Indonesian party system. In *GIGA Working Papers*. Hamburg, Germany.

2008b. "From "aliran" to dealignment: Political parties in post-Suharto Indonesia." *South East Asia Research* 16 (1):5–41.

Urbinati, Nadia. 2006. *Representative Democracy: Principles and Genealogy*. Chicago: University of Chicago Press.

Van Bruinessen, Martin. 2013. "Overview of Muslim organisations, associations, and movements in Indonesia." In *Contemporary Developments in Indonesian Islam: Explaining the "Conservative Turn"*, edited by Martin van Bruinessen, 21–59. Singapore: ISEAS Press *Singapore: ISEAS*:21-59.

Van der Kroef, Justus M. 1957. "Indonesia's first national election: A sociological analysis." *The American Journal of Economics and Sociology* 16 (3): 237–249.

Van Hauwaert, Steven M., and Stijn Van Kessel. 2018. "Beyond protest and discontent: A cross-national analysis of the effect of populist attitudes and issue positions on populist party support." *European Journal of Political Research* 57 (1):68–92.

Vickers, Adrian. 2013. *A History of Modern Indonesia*. New York: Cambridge University Press.

Waldner, David, and Ellen Lust. 2018. "Unwelcome change: Coming to terms with democratic backsliding." *Annual Review of Political Science* 21:93–113.

Wang, Ching-Hsing. 2014. "The effects of party fractionalization and party polarization on democracy." *Party Politics* 20 (5):687–699.

Wang, Gungwu. 1992. *Community and Nation: China, Southeast Asia, and Australia*: Asian Studies Association of Australia.

Wängnerud, Lena. 2009. "Women in parliaments: Descriptive and substantive representation." *Annual Review of Political Science* 12:51–69.

Warburton, Eve. 2019. "Polarisation and democratic decline in Indonesia." In *Democracies Divided: The Global Challenge of Political Polarization*, edited by Thomas Carothers and Andrew O'Donohue. Washington, DC: Brookings Institution Press.

Warburton, Eve, and Edward Aspinall. 2019. "Explaining Indonesia's democratic regression: Structure, agency and popular opinion." *Contemporary Southeast Asia: A Journal of International and Strategic Affairs* 41 (2):255–285.

References

Warburton, Eve, Burhanuddin Muhtadi, Edward Aspinall, and Diego Fossati. 2021. "When does class matter? Unequal representation in Indonesian legislatures." *Third World Quarterly* 42 (6):1252–1275.

Webb, Paul. 2013. "Who is willing to participate? Dissatisfied democrats, stealth democrats and populists in the United Kingdom." *European Journal of Political Research* 52 (6):747–772.

Welzel, Christian. 2007. "Are levels of democracy affected by mass attitudes? Testing attainment and sustainment effects on democracy." *International Political Science Review* 28 (4):397–424.

Welzel, Christian, and Ronald Inglehart. 2008. "The role of ordinary people in democratization." *Journal of Democracy* 19 (1):126–140.

Wertheim, Willem Frederik. 1964. "The trading minorities in Southeast Asia." In *East-West Parallels: Sociological Approaches to Modern Asia*, 39–82. The Hague, Netherlands: W. Van Hoeue.

Wessels, Bernhard. 1999. "System characteristics matter: Empirical evidence from ten representation studies." In *Policy Representation in Western Democracies*, edited by Warren E Miller, Roy Pierce, Jacques Thomassen, Richard Herrera, Sören Holmberg, Peter Esaisson and Bernhard Wessels. Oxford: Oxford University Press.

Winters, Jeffrey A. 2011. *Oligarchy*. New York: Cambridge University Press.

Young, Iris Marion. 2002. *Inclusion and Democracy*. Oxford: Oxford University Press.

Zechmeister, Elizabeth J., and Margarita Corral. 2013. "Individual and contextual constraints on ideological labels in Latin America." *Comparative Political Studies* 46 (6):675–701.

Zick, Andreas, Beate Küpper, and Andreas Hövermann. 2011. *Intolerance, Prejudice and Discrimination: A European Report*. Berlin: Friedrich Ebert Stiftung.

Index

abangan · 63
accountability · 6, 12, 20, 26, 28, 30, 134,
   195–199
Aceh · 19, 52–53, 109, 132
Africa · 169
Ahok · 87
anti-Sinicism · 86–89, 121
Asian Financial Crisis · 19, 187–188
Aspinall, Edward · 188

backsliding · *See* democratic backsliding
Bali · 34, 49–54, 63–64, 69–70
Benda, Harry · 19
Bermeo, Nancy · 24

catch-all parties · 61
centrism (measure of ideological
   congruence) · 150
Chinese Indonesians · 86–89
civil freedoms · 3, 166
   restrictions to · 194
civil Islam · 195
civil society · 39, 68, 82, 188, 194–195
clientelism · 11, 20, 33, 38, 44, 153–154,
   188, 195, 197
   and ideological representation · 153–154,
     196
   incidence in Indonesia · 153
colonialism · 34, 37–38, 86–87, 124, 132
conception of democracy · *See*
   understanding of democracy
congruence · *See* ideological congruence;
   representation, substantive

corruption · 3, 5, 8, 20, 22, 38, 64, 86, 129,
   188, 192
Crescent Star Party · *See* PBB
crime and security · 3, 5, 19, 25, 27, 129,
   189
critical democrats · 5
cultural backlash · 189

Darul Islam · 132
dealignment · 35, 44, 46, 55
   and electoral results · 71
   uneven development · 57–59
decentralization · 132–134, 156
   public support · 132–134
democracy
   and social norms · 4, 23
   backsliding · *See* democratic backsliding
   durability · *See* democratic durability
   erosion · *See* democratic backsliding
   positive record in Indonesia · 20, 199
   role of ordinary citizens · 23–24, 188,
     190–191
   satisfaction with · *See* satisfaction with
     democracy
   support for · *See* support for democracy
   understanding · *See* understanding of
     democracy
democratic backsliding · 1, 3, 11–12, 20–23,
   189–191
   and participation · 182
   and public opinion · 3, 12, 24, 190–191
   and social cleavages · 191
   and social norms · 4

democratic backsliding · (cont.)
  and understanding of democracy · 12, 24
  and voting behavior · 3, 12, 24
  perceptions · 3, 12
democratic durability · 10, 20, 27, 187–190
  and historical legacies · 189
democratic legitimacy · *See* legitimacy
Democratic Party · *See* PD
democratic performance · *See* government
    performance
democratic transition · *See* democratization
democratization · 1, 20, 23, 35, 78, 187
Demokrat · *See* PD
districts, administrative · 47
districts, electoral · 47

East Asia · 169
East Timor · 19
Eastern Europe · 46
Eastern Indonesia · 51–52
Easton, David · 5, 25
economic growth · 3, 5, 8, 22, 27, 86, 101,
    104, 128–129, 142, 196
economic redistribution · 74, 83–84, 97, 99,
    101, 130, 140, 142, 149, 180, 192, 201
  and meaning of left and right · 99
  and understanding of democracy · 180
education · 23, 176, 187
  and inequalities in representation ·
    144–145
  and participation · 41, 110, 145
  and partisanship · 59
  and political Islam · 77, 110
  and political knowledge · 112
  and representation · 139
  and understanding of democracy · 173, 179
elections of 1955 · 40, 45, 50
elections of 1999 · 35, 54–55, 57
electoral geography · 45, 50–54
electoral intimidation · 41
electoral reform of 2009 35, 59
electoral turnout · *See* participation, formal
elite · *See* political elite
elite survey · 75–77
ethnic violence · 19, 87, 187
ethnocentrism · 86–89, 119, 121
ethnolinguistic fractionalization
  and clientelism · 65
  and partisanship · 65–66
  and political behavior · 64
  subnational variation · 64

ethnonationalism · 117, 119, 179
Europe · 29, 32–33, 46, 169
executive aggrandizement · 21, 191
experiment · *See* survey experiment

factor analysis · 97, 118, 175
Feith, Herbert · 19
fiscal redistribution · *See* economic
    redistribution

Geertz, Clifford · 63
gender differences
  in descriptive representation · 77
  in political ideology · 108
Gerindra · 61–62, 114, 116, 148, 157, 159
Golkar · 61, 77, 94, 114, 116, 148, 189
government performance · 2, 128, 196
  and satisfaction with democracy · 3, 5, 22
  and support for democracy · 5
  in Indonesia · 3, 22
  inputs versus outputs · 6, 22, 27
Guided Democracy · 38, 93

Habibie, B. J. · 20
Hanura · 94, 102, 116
Hatta, Mohammad · 34, 87

identity politics · 200
ideological competition · 9, 16, 30, 44–45,
    73–75, 93–102, 138–163, 180, 189,
    193, 197
  and polarization · 198
ideological congruence, · *See also*
    representation , substantive
  and clientelism · 153–154
  and political party features · 150–152
  conceptualization · 136
  economic issues · 142, 146, 149
  inequalities in · 142–146
  measurement · 136–137
  political Islam · 138–140, 142,
    146–149
  political parties · 146–154
  variation across parties · 150–152
ideological differentiation · *See* ideological
    competition
ideological representation · *See* ideological
    congruence; representation,
    substantive
ideology-based voting · 197 see also voting
    behavior, and ideology

Index

income · 77
  and inequalities in representation · 144–145
  and political Islam · 110
  and representation · 139
income distribution · 91, 144
Indonesian Communist Party · *See* PKI
Indonesian Democratic Party-Struggle · *See* PDI-P
Indonesian National Revolution · 19, 38, 46
Indonesian Nationalist Party · *See* PNI
inequality · 3, 39, 49, 74, 77, 91, 113, 129, 142–146, 180, 191, 201
infrastructure · 27, 129, 175
institutional performance · *See* government performance
interest in politics · *See* political interest
Islamic bylaws · *See* perda agama
Islamic populism · *See* populism, and political Islam
Islamic world · 105, 108
Islamism · 4, 34, 37–39, 48, 55–60, 81, 105, 107, 116, 200, *See also* political Islam
  and economic redistribution · 201
  marginalization of · 12, 53, 91, 93, 104, 113, 133, 167, 194, 200
  repression of · 193, 197
Islamist resurgence · 4, 21, 39, 41, 44, 67–72, 105, 167, 189–190, 192, 200
  and accountability · 198
  and democratic backsliding · 11, 35
  and democratic consolidation · 199
  and participation · 67–72
  and representation · 12, 68
  and satisfaction with democracy · 5, 12
  positive implications · 5, 12, 68, 189
issue salience · *See* policy priorities

Japanese Occupation · 38
Java · 34, 48–54, 63–64, 67, 70, 76–77, 109, 132
Jokowi · 21, 151, 157, 159, 193

Kalimantan · 52, 64, 69
Kalla, Jusuf · 112
King, Dwight · 35, 44
knowledge about politics · *See* political knowledge
Kohn, Hans · 117

labor movement · 39
Latin America · 169

left and right · 73–74, 97, 137
left and right, meaning
  in Indonesia · 98–99
  in new democracies · 74
  in Western democracies · 73–74
legitimacy · 3–5, 26–27, 37, 42, 184, 189, 192, 194–196, 200, *See also* satisfaction with democracy
LGBT rights · 21, 39
Liberal Democracy · 19, 34, 38, 40, 46
liberal values · 2, 19, 23, 25, 91, 123, 167
  trade-off with representation, participation and accountability · 199, 201
Liddle, William R., 5, 104

mass organizations · 38, 82
Masyumi · 35, 38, 48, 50, 55–60, 63, 66, 132
  subnational variation in support · 52
meaning of democracy · *See* understanding of democracy
Megawati · 35
methodology · 13–15, 44–50, 75–77, 79–81, 97–98, 105–130, 136–137, 168–170
Mietzner, Marcus · 11
military · 10, 12, 20, 24, 35, 61, 78, 187–189
modernist Islam · *See* political Islam, modernist
Muhammadiyah · 34, 38–39, 78, 83
Mujani, Saiful · 5, 104
multi-level governance · *See* decentralization

Nahdlatul Ulama · *See* NU
NasDem · 61, 94–95, 116, 147
NasDem Party · *See* NasDem
National Awakening Party · *See* PKB
national identity · 117
  and understanding of democracy · 179
  attachment to · 121
  dimensions · 118–120
  ethnic versus civic · 117, 119
  measurement · 118
  structure · 118–120
National Mandate Party · *See* PAN
nationalist movement · 34, 37, 117, 188
Natsir, Mohammad · 34
New Order · 19, 35, 38, 40, 46, 74, 78, 93, 187–188

NU · 34, 38–39, 48, 50, 53, 55–60, 63, 66, 78, 82
    subnational variation in support · 51

oligarchy · 6, 20, 182, 192
opposition · *See* political opposition
organicism · 93

Paloh, Surya · 61
PAN · 48, 95
Pancasila · 97, 101
Papua · 19, 195
participation · 110–111, 182, 191–195
    and democratic backsliding · 182
    and democratic durability · 10, 39
    and legitimacy · 10
    and local politics · 69
    and representation · 191–195
    during Liberal Democracy · 38
    during the New Order · 38
    electoral · *See* participation, formal
    formal · 10, 40, 67–72, 194
    in Indonesia · 9, 37–42
    informal · 10, 40, 112, 194–195
    restrictions to · 194
    subnational variation · 69
    variation over time · 40, 67–72, 195
partisan affiliations · *See* partisanship
partisan dealignment · *See* dealignment
partisan erosion · *See* dealignment
partisan identities · *See* partisanship
partisan polarization · *See* polarization
partisan realignment · *See* partisanship, resurgence of
partisanship · 46, 191
    and electoral participation · 68
    and ideology · 159–161, 163
    intergenerational continuity · 46
    nonpartisan voters · 161
    partisan cues · 156, 159–163
    resurgence of · 59, 68
party families · 43, 48, 57, 70
party system · 11, 30–31, 33, 75, 134, 147, 153, 198
    in the 1950s · 53
    polarization · 99
    stabilization · 31, 199
patronage · *See* clientelism
PBB · 48
PD · 61, 94, 102, 116, 148, 150

PDI-P · 35, 48, 53, 55–60, 66, 71, 77, 94–95, 101, 114, 116, 148, 150–151, 157, 159
Pepinsky, Thomas · 11
perda agama (*perda* Islam) · 156
performance · *See* government performance
PII · *See* Political Islam Index
Pitkin, Hanna · 27
PKB · 48, 71, 94–95, 114, 148, 151
PKI · 34, 38, 46, 50, 63, 74
    subnational variation in support · 63
PKS · 48, 71, 94–95, 116, 148, 151
pluralism · 4, 34, 46, 48, 55–60, 65, 70–71, 81, 107, 188, 200–201
    and satisfaction with democracy · 201
    and secularism · 108
PNI · 34, 38, 46, 48, 50, 53, 55–61, 63, 66
    subnational variation in support · 51
polarization · 4, 11–12, 31, 41, 44, 163, 189, 191, 193, 195
    and accountability · 198
    and democratic backsliding · 31, 198
    and ideological competition · 198
    and participation · 195
    and perceptions of representation · 31
    and satisfaction with democracy · 4, 12
    in Indonesian public opinion · 11, 198
    positive implications · 12, 31
policy priorities · 85, 129
political culture · 2, 19, 23, 187, *See also* liberal values
political elite · 77–93, *See also* oligarchy
    assessment of party position · 96
    civic engagement · 78
    connection to the New Order · 78
    democratic attitudes · 89–93
    demographic profile · 77
    economic policy preferences · 83–85
    economic policy priorities · 85
    ethnocentrism · 86–89
    fragmentation · 188
    ideological groups · 81
    perceptions of political parties · 93–94
    perceptions of voting behavior · 95
    satisfaction with democracy · 90
    support for democracy · 90
    support for liberal values · 91
    views of Chinese Indonesians · 86–89
    views of political Islam · 80
    views of representation · 89
political interest · 111

Index

political Islam · 10, 74, 146–147, 189
  and anti-Sinicism · 88
  and attachment to nation · 121
  and clientelism · 71, *See also* clientelism,
    and ideological representation
  and conception of national identity · 120
  and decentralization · 132–134
  and democratic attitudes · 11, 122–123, 167
  and democratic durability · 14
  and economic evaluations · 128
  and economic policy preferences · 85,
    105, 128–132, 193
  and ethnocentrism · 11, 88
  and gender · 99, 108
  and identity politics · 200
  and legitimacy · 10–11
  and liberal values · 92, 168
  and meaning of left and right · 98–99
  and national identity · 11, 117–122
  and nationalist movement · 117
  and participation · 4, 10, 39, 67–72,
    110–113, 195
  and partisanship · 11, 159–161, 163
  and party choice · 113–117
  and perceptions of representation · 167
  and policy preferences · 11, 122–134
  and policy priorities · 129
  and political interest · 111
  and populism · 124–128
  and religious denomination · 81
  and religious fractionalization · 60
  and satisfaction with democracy · 9,
    90–91, 167
  and support for democracy · 90, 122
  and traditionalism · 98
  and understanding of democracy · 123,
    168, 176–181
  and voting behavior · 11, 37, 104,
    113–117
  as a social cleavage · 36
  concept · 9, 11
  during Liberal Democracy · 34
  during the nationalist movement · 34
  during the New Order · 35
  historical development in Indonesia · 9,
    34–35, 54
  ideological groups · 107
  measurement · 37, 79–81, 97, *See also*
    Political Islam Index
  modernist · 34–35, 48, 53, 55–60, 65–66,
    70

party positions · 43, 96–102
political parties · 146–149
public opinion · 105, 107–110, 117–134
sociodemographic profile · 108
substantive representation · 4, 11, 34, 37,
  138–140
traditional · *See* political Islam,
  traditionalist
traditionalist · 34–35, 48, 53, 55–60,
  65–66
political Islam cleavage · *See* political Islam
Political Islam Index · 79–81, 107
political knowledge · 111
political opposition · 198
political parties · 20, 43, 74, 77, 93,
  113–117, 146–154, 188, 194, 198
  candidates · 95, 116
  coalitions · 94
  cohesion · *See* political parties, ideological
    cohesion
  competence · 95
  core constituencies · 71
  drivers of party choice · 116
  electoral strategies · 94
  features · 150–151
  ideological cohesion · 101, 150
  ideology · 93–102, 150
  internal cohesion · *See* political parties,
    ideological cohesion
  leadership · 95–96, 116
  manifestoes · 96
  mobilization · *See* political parties,
    electoral strategies
  organization · 94, 150
  perceptions · 93–96
  policy-based appeals · 95, 116
  positions on economic issues · 99, 101
  positions on political Islam · 96–102
  religion-based appeals · 95, 116
  size · 150
political sophistication · *See* political
  knowledge
populism · 21, 32, 41, 124–128, 180, 200
  and democratic backsliding · 32
  and perceptions of representation · 32
  and political Islam · 124, 126
  and satisfaction with democracy · 126
  and understanding of democracy · 180
  concept · 124
  measurement · 125
  positive implications · 32

poverty alleviation · 22, 85, 129, 175
PPP · 48, 94–95, 101–102, 147, 150–151
Prabowo · 21, 61–62, 124, 157, 159, 199
pribumi · 88, 118–119
programmatic politics · 49, 154
progressivism · 39, 97, 99, 108, 176
  on fiscal issues · 142, 144, 149
Prosperous Justice Party · See PKS
public opinion · 22, 44, 190–191
Purnama, Basuki Tjahaja · See Ahok

radical Islam · See Islamism
realignment · See partisanship, resurgence of
regional autonomy · See decentralization
religious bylaws · See perda agama
religious fractionalization · 60
religious tolerance · 189
representation · 4, 6, 9, 27–33, 138–163,
    191–195
  and accountability · 28
  and clientelism · 29, 33
  and democratic durability · 8, 10
  and economic policy preferences · 145
  and government performance · 6
  and ideological divisions · 29
  and inequality · 142–146
  and legitimacy · 8, 28
  and modern democracy · 28
  and participation · 30–31, 145,
    191–195
  and polarization · 31–32
  and political party features · 150–152
  and populism · 32–33
  and satisfaction with democracy · 6, 8,
    29, 190
  and support for democracy · 8
  concept · 27
  descriptive · 28–30, 77, 140
  economic issues · 142–146, 149, 192
  functions · 28–29
  inequalities in · 142–146
  measurement · 136–137
  perceptions · 7, 167
  political Islam · 138–140, 142, 193
  political parties · 146–154
  substantive · 9, 28, 138–152, 191
  variation across parties · 150–152
  variation across policy areas · 138–152
  variation over time · 192
responsiveness · 192
retrospective voting · 6, 16, 196–197

santri · 63
Sarekat Islam · 37
satisfaction with democracy · 90, 165–166,
    184, See also legitimacy
  and democratic backsliding · 4
  and democratic durability · 26
  and electoral participation · 41
  and government performance · See
    government performance, and
    satisfaction with democracy
  and populism · 126
  and support for democracy · 25, 181
  and understanding of democracy · 26
  determinants · 24–27, 184
  over time in Indonesia · 1, 21
secularism · 34
Slater, Dan · 188
social class · 29, 110, 145
  and inequalities in representation · 144–145
social cleavages · 33, 36, 191
  and democratic consolidation · 34
  in Indonesia · 34
  Lipset & Rokkan · 33
  positive aspects for democracy · 200
social policy · See social security
social security · 74, 127–128, 141
sorting (into political parties) · 102,
    146–147, 153, 155, 163–164, 197–198
state capacity · 188
statism · 74, 83, 85, 97, 99, 101, 130, 140
  and meaning of left and right · 99
student movement · 39, 195
Subianto, Prabowo · See Prabowo
Suharto · 20, 39
Sukarno · 34, 87, 124
Sukarnoputri, Megawati · See Megawati
Sulawesi · 64, 69, 132
Sumatra · 34, 51–53, 63–64, 69, 76, 109,
    132
support for democracy · 90, 165, 184
  and satisfaction with democracy · 25
  concept · 25
  determinants · 24–27, 184
  in Indonesia · 5
survey experiment · 155–163

traditional Islam · See political Islam,
    traditionalist
traditionalism · 97
traditionalist Islam · See political Islam,
    traditionalist

Index

Tragedy of 1965–1966 · 35, 46
turnout · *See* participation, formal

understanding of democracy · 6, 26, 166
  and economic redistribution · 180
  and education · *See* education, and
    understanding of democracy
  and government performance · 6
  and legitimacy · 9
  and national identity · 179
  and other democratic attitudes · 181
  and participation · 9
  and populism · 180
  and satisfaction with democracy · 9, 182
  and sociodemographic factors · 177
  and support for democracy · 174, 184
  complexity · 169, 173, 190
  conceptualization · 169–170
  deliberative · 26, 166, 170, 175
  dimensions · 26, 166, 169–173, 190
  dualistic structure · 175–176, 180
  egalitarian · 27, 166, 170, 175, 179
  electoral · 26, 166, 170
  implications · 174, 181–184
  instrumental · 27
  intrinsic · 27
  liberal · 26, 166, 170, 175, 179

  measurement · 13, 169–170
  minimalist · 26
  participatory · 27, 166, 170, 175, 180
  procedural · 173
  social · *See* understanding of democracy,
    egalitarian
  structure · 174–176
  substantive · 173
United Development Party · *See* PPP
United States · 32, 163

voting behavior · 5–6, 11, 13, 24, 33, 44,
  46, 54, 61, 65, 68, 95–96, 104–105,
  129, 134, 154–155, 195, 197
  and ethnolinguistic fractionalization ·
    65–66
  and ideology · 43–44, 50, 196–197
  and religious fractionalization · 60
  complexity · 154, 195–199
  historical continuities · 53–60
  rationality · 200
  subnational heterogeneity · 50–54

Widodo, Joko · *See* Jokowi
women's rights · 39, 99, 156

Yudhoyono, Susilo Bambang · 61, 151